A F T E R

when someone

Y O U S A Y

you love

G O O D B Y E

dies of AIDS

AFTER

when someone

YOU SAY

you love

GOODBYE

dies of AIDS

PAUL KENT FROMAN, PH.D.

CHRONICLE BOOKS • SAN FRANCISCO

*A portion of the proceeds
from the sale of this
book is being donated
to AIDS organizations.*

Printed in the United States

Library of Congress Cataloging-in-Publication Data

Froman, Paul Kent.
    After you say goodbye : when someone you love dies of AIDS / by
Paul Kent Froman.
        p.   cm.
    Includes bibliographical references.
    ISBN 0-8118-0088-1 (paperback)
    1. AIDS (Disease)--Psychological aspects. 2. Bereavement.
    I. Title.
    RC607. A26F748   1992
    155.9--dc20
                                        91-34042
                                        CIP

Book and cover design:
Kathy Warinner
Back cover photograph:
Suze Lanier
Composition:
On Line Typography

Distributed in Canada by
Raincoast Books
8680 Cambie Street,
Vancouver, B.C. V6P 6M9

10 9 8 7 6 5 4 3 2

Chronicle Books
275 Fifth Street
San Francisco, CA 94103

for John,

*whose love is
unconditional,
whose patience is
limitless,
and whose support is
perfect.*

*Thank you and
I love you.*

contents

acknowledgments

I would like to acknowledge the heroes and heroines of the AIDS crisis, members of the lesbian and gay community as well as those in the heterosexual community. A list of your names and your many accomplishments would take a book of its own.

In the midst of so much dying, you have maintained your commitment to living. In the midst of so much suffering, you have never faltered in your efforts to ease suffering. In the midst of persecution and discrimination you have stood firm to the principles of liberty, justice, and compassion for all. In the midst of great fear, your courage is monumental.

I would like to specifically acknowledge those of you who are my friends and clients for allowing me to share your grief. You taught me the things I needed to know to write this book. You are with me as I experience my own grief.

My agent, Robert Drake, came to me with the idea to write this book, and then found a publisher. Thanks for your faith and support.

My editor, Jay Schaefer, and his assistant Karen Silver provided valuable support and insight throughout the entire publishing process. You have been a joy to work with.

And finally, thanks to Bumper, Jo Jo, Murphy, and Cooper for keeping me company while I was writing.

introduction

About fourteen years ago, I attended a party given by a friend of mine. Toward the end of the evening, I was standing outside on the deck, talking with a small group of men in their mid-to-late sixties. I was thirty-four.

After a while, the conversation turned to the topics of illness and dying as the men began to compare notes on who in their circle of friends had recently been hospitalized with a stroke or a heart attack, and who had died. It was clear that they were feeling their world shrinking around them, and each seemed to be wondering if he would be the next to go or the last to leave.

I was a little depressed as I returned home that night, thinking how sad it must be to find yourself near the end of your life and beginning to say goodbye to lifelong friends and companions. I comforted myself with the fact that I wouldn't have to face this situation for another thirty or forty years.

I couldn't have known then how wrong I was. Within three years, the dying had started. There was a difference, though. AIDS was taking young men at the peak of life, not in ones and twos, but by the thousands. My friends were dying just as their careers were beginning to take off, just as they were beginning to enjoy the fruits of their long years of education and training, just as some were establishing themselves in loving, stable relationships.

Today it's difficult to find anyone in the lesbian/gay community who hasn't lost someone he or she loves to AIDS. I know several who are the last of their circle of friends still alive, and they are only thirty years old!

The dying has gone on unabated now for over ten years. We have said goodbye to nearly 116,000 American citizens who have died of AIDS (as of June 1991). The dying will continue. The Centers for Disease Control in Atlanta estimates that 280,000 to 340,000 people will have died by 1993. Even though many of us are certain that AIDS is not going to succeed in killing everyone who is HIV-positive (has tested positive for the AIDS virus), it is inescapable that we will be grieving for many more deaths.

I am a gay man, a psychologist, who has spent the last eleven years working with gay men with AIDS, and with those who love them. *After You Say Goodbye* is based on that experience.

Several people have questioned me about the need for a book that deals specifically with AIDS deaths. There are lots of books about dying and death in general. "Aren't they adequate for someone who has lost a loved one to AIDS?"

I don't believe they are.

Death by any cause is never easy to face. The sadness and grief connected with death are as inevitable as they are painful. An AIDS death adds more elements to the grieving process. If these elements are not addressed, our grief cannot and will not be complete. We must also deal with the politics of AIDS: the fear, the ignorance, the bigotry, the guilt, the outrage, and the mushrooming numbers of those who are dying.

Please don't let this frighten you or overwhelm you now; I know how overwhelming it can seem. Part of learning how to deal with grief is learning how to confront the feeling of being overwhelmed. We'll do that in this book.

If you have just lost someone you love, don't worry about anything else right now if you're not ready. You have enough to do just coping with the loss and the loneliness and the pain. This book will help you to do that, too.

I know that the pain feels as if it may never go away. I know that it may seem as if you will never be able to fill the space left by your loss. But the pain *will* get smaller. While you may never be able to fill that space completely, you can learn how to fill the area around it with other nurturing relationships, possibly even another love, although that may seem impossible now.

This book was written out of front-line experience, not armchair theorizing. I, too, have had to say goodbye to people I love, and I will undoubtedly say goodbye to too many more. I have worked with people who were terrified of AIDS before it was called AIDS. I have accompanied friends and clients through their entire process from the discovery of being HIV-positive to the diagnosis of full-blown AIDS and, in too many of those cases, to their deaths. I have worked with lovers and spouses, family members and friends, as they have tried to cope with needless, senseless deaths.

I know the sadness, and I know the fear, the bigotry, and the outrage. I know how overwhelming they can seem. Yet I am firmly convinced that none of us can escape facing these issues. If we try, we will likely get stuck in our grief and become a victim of our losses.

The politics of AIDS is inextricably woven into the fabric of our grieving. Confronting the politics of AIDS, no matter how distasteful or disturbing it might seem, will be necessary. Whether we want to face it or not, the politics of AIDS has a devastating impact on those of us who are grieving. Examples of that devastation are painfully numerous.

I have a client whose lover died of AIDS in late October. They had had a wonderful relationship that had lasted over nine years. Because they owned and operated a business together, the death totally changed not only my client's personal life, but his career as well. He was grieving while trying to do both his lover's job and his own, or risk losing the business they had built together.

He dreaded the upcoming holidays, as that had been a special time for the two of them. He was terrified at the thought of spending it alone.

He was also long overdue for a visit to his family, and they were insisting that he spend this Christmas with them. Out of a desperate loneliness, he accepted their invitation.

Unfortunately, there was a complicating issue that made his decision a nearly lethal experience. Neither he nor his lover had "come out" to their families about being gay or about his lover having AIDS. He had told his family that his "roommate" had died of lung cancer. He was too afraid of their rejection to tell them the truth. He couldn't even tell them how much he was grieving for his "roommate," as he feared that they would think it odd.

He spent the Christmas holiday using every bit of self-control he possessed to hide his pain from his family. He did everything he could to appear to be having a swell time, and then quietly cried himself to sleep every night.

When he returned home to Los Angeles he was near emotional exhaustion and seriously contemplating suicide. Even though he still hasn't told his family the truth, he was willing to avail himself of a nurturing support group, and now is slowly putting his life back together.

I've heard stories like this one over and over during the last nine years. The fear of rejection, abandonment, persecution, and discrimination has forced many grieving people — heterosexual as well as lesbian or gay — to hide their grief, cutting themselves off from vital support and tender loving care. Some have not survived the alienation.

To complicate matters more, there are powerful religious and political forces who have shamelessly used the AIDS crisis to persecute the lesbian/gay community. The damage they have done is beyond comprehension. Not only have they frequently sabotaged the fight against AIDS, but they have loudly trumpeted the wicked lie that AIDS is God's punishment for a sinful lifestyle.

(Note: It may seem throughout this book that I am Christianbashing. I am not. I have the utmost respect for Christianity, and for those who practice it, so long as they do so in the ways Jesus taught, that is, with love and compassion and healing. I do intend to "bash" people who call themselves "Christians" while they practice Christianity in judgmental, hypocritical, and hateful ways that damage and destroy lives with homophobia, hatred, and persecution.)

In Chapter 1 we will look closely at the shameful distortion of both Christian values as well as "traditional American values" by those groups who continue to use AIDS as a political weapon. *Each one of us must learn how to confront their messages of shame and hate.*

For many individuals, especially those who haven't yet come to grips with their sexual orientation, the specious message of God's punishment is dreadfully damaging. Their guilt over who they are becomes entangled with their grief, with horribly traumatic results.

Another client, whom I saw in the early days of the crisis, blamed himself for years for his lover's death, even though he himself was and remains HIV-negative (that is, blood tests do not show that he has been exposed to the AIDS virus). Even though it is highly unlikely that he could have transmitted the virus to his lover, he still felt as if his lover's death was his fault, his punishment for being gay. He not only avoided anyone who could have supported him through his grief, but constantly punished himself for his supposed sin. He felt even more guilty that he had survived while his lover hadn't. He didn't feel "fit" to be with other people, gay or non-gay. He couldn't tolerate any type of support group. He is still surviving, but just barely.

Fear is another hugely complicating factor following an AIDS death, especially if the person who is grieving knows that he is HIV-positive. Any death will painfully remind him of his own mortality, of the possibility of his becoming ill and ultimately dying. An increasing number of women are now finding themselves in this same position. A person who is HIV-positive has most probably experienced many AIDS deaths, with his or her own fear increasing each time.

This fear can interact perniciously with one's grief. Another client of mine spent six months vacillating between grief and fear. When the grief would begin to subside, and his sadness become less painful, the fear would appear. As the fear subsided, the grief came back. He maintained this cycle until he finally began to see how he was allowing himself to become a victim of his grief as well as a victim of the virus. He eventually was willing to confront his fear of AIDS head-on.

Dealing with the fear of AIDS is a vital part of the grief process for anyone who is HIV-positive, as well as for many who are HIV-negative but still are ruled by the fear of AIDS. That fear can and must be defeated.

Along with a growing number of others, I am convinced that AIDS is not an automatic death sentence. If this statement shocks you, see my first book, *Pathways to Wellness: Strategies for Self-Empowerment in the Age of AIDS,* as well as Michael Callen's book

Surviving AIDS, both included in the Suggested Reading at the end of this book. There *are* long-term survivors of AIDS, and their number is steadily growing. As more and more effective treatments for AIDS-related conditions are found, that number will increase hugely.

Unchallenged fear of AIDS will complicate your grief process. It will also be most injurious to your own health.

Whether it is the fear, the guilt, or the outrage, the politics of AIDS will intensify the suffering and prolong the grieving and the dying. If you have just lost someone you love to AIDS, you may not be ready to deal with all this stuff right now. I understand that. But the time will come when you will want to understand how the politics of AIDS affects your grief. Doing so will be a necessary part of completing your process of grieving more quickly and with less pain.

Chapter 1 of this book will detail how the unique circumstances following an AIDS death can complicate the grieving process. Understanding these additional elements is necessary for you to complete your grieving without becoming a victim of grief.

Chapter 2 deals directly with victimhood and grieving. Although the circumstances around us are tragic, we must not allow ourselves to become victims of the disease, victims of homophobia, victims of our grief, or victims of the fear, the bigotry, and the outrage.

Becoming a victim of AIDS-related issues is all too easy, especially with the cooperation of the media and the people around us. It is always our choice to remain a victim in life, and we'll examine ways of making the choice to reject victimhood.

Chapter 3 looks at the individual grief process, doing it *your* way. *After You Say Goodbye* does not discuss the stages of grief, because I don't believe that the stages theory is a good model for an AIDS death. This chapter will pose an alternative model for the grief process that allows for individual differences and styles.

While there are no Right ways to grieve, there are certain principles about how to "grieve well" and suffer less in the process. We can't avoid the suffering; trying to do so only extends the grieving process.

The sadness is there, but eventually you will see that life *can and will go on.* No matter how sad you are now, you *can* learn how to rejoin life, how to rediscover joy and laughter, even how to play again—in time, in *your* time, when *you* are ready.

Chapters 4 through 8 examine the unique emotional factors involved in grieving for someone who has died of AIDS. Depression has its own distinct quality under these circumstances. Anger, which is almost always there with any death, can become outrage where AIDS is involved. Fear, too, is almost always part of the response to death, and AIDS can turn that fear into rank terror. I know that these may seem like unassailable emotions, but they can be defeated, as long as we are willing to keep defeating them over and over again. Doing it once will help for a while, but most likely won't last. We need to be vigilant and ready to challenge these powerful emotions whenever they occur.

Chapters 9 through 11 examine how you can best deal with AIDS deaths and take care of yourself at the same time, depending on your relationship to the one who has died. There are separate chapters for life partners/spouses, family members, and friends.

(Note: I use the terms *life partners* or just *partners* to refer to a committed relationship between two people, as opposed to *lovers, mates,* or *significant others.*)

Chapter 12 was written for those people who are in the role of caregiver while they are also grieving the death of someone they love. The caregiver role can be very difficult.

It is essential that we learn how to take care of ourselves and avoid "caregiver burnout." Even as we grieve, we must be paying attention to our own physical and mental health. If we don't take care of ourselves, we won't be able to continue to take care of those we love who are ill and who are depending on us.

I know most of us are tired, very tired. AIDS doesn't give us time to heal completely before we're faced with the next death, and the next one. Many people now plan their calendars around memorial services and funerals, or around the return of someone from the hospital who will need friends to take care of the simple household tasks he can no longer handle.

A breather would be nice—time to catch up, time to heal ourselves, time to rest. But we don't have that time. There is too much to do, and we are the only ones who can, or will, do it.

Chapter 13 makes suggestions for supporting someone you love who is grieving. Many well-intentioned people have caused unnecessary suffering with advice they have given to grieving friends. They are trying to help, but their advice lengthens if not thwarts the grieving process.

Each of us needs all the love and support we can get during this time. We don't need to get in each other's way.

Chapter 14 is about saying "goodbye," and then rejoining life when you are ready. When you finally are willing to say goodbye to the one who has died, it becomes easier to realize that life goes on. Then it becomes your choice as to whether and when you will go on with it.

Actually, it's not a difficult choice. Resisting the flow of life isn't really possible. The flow of life will take us along with or without our cooperation. The sensible choice is to relax and go with it to the very best of our ability. The only other choice is to wear ourselves out struggling against it, and that's one struggle that we will always lose.

I hope it will be your choice to grieve well and then rejoin the flow of life. I hope you will choose to avoid the paralysis of depression and reclaim your right to live fully, joyfully, and well, as soon as you are ready. You can learn to grieve while you are getting on with the rest of your life.

And you must know that joy and laughter are not a betrayal of the one who has died, but rather the ultimate way to honor his or her memory. Please don't fall into the trap that says you must trash your own life out of respect, or as evidence of how much you cared for him or her. That's nonsense.

Living your life now as well as you can, as joyously as you can, as successfully as you can is the most honorable way to express your love and your respect. Don't you really think that the one who has died would want you to do it that way?

As life goes on, we must realize the benefit of becoming involved in the fight against AIDS. *After You Say Goodbye* is based on the idea that when someone we love has died of AIDS, we must grieve, we must grieve well, and as soon as we are ready, we must get involved. If we allow our grief and loss to shove us back into the closet, back into hiding, we will suffer the more for it. (Please know that not only lesbians and gay men have closets. Parents and friends of lesbians, gays, and people with AIDS have closets too. They are just as well furnished and just as destructive.)

The solution to fear is not hiding. It is action. The solution to rage is not mindless temper tantrums. It is action that focuses on solving the problem. The resolution of our grief is not lapsing into victimhood. It is action, the willingness to be powerful in the face of crisis. If you have just lost someone you love to AIDS, you are probably not ready to hear about that. You are probably not ready to get involved. But there will come a time when you will be ready to take some kind of action, and you will have lots of choices for that action: social organizations, service organizations, political organizations, ACT UP, Queer Nation, and more. I don't care where you get involved. I just want to encourage you to do so. Your own health and welfare will be enhanced. Your own life will be enriched. Your grief will be easier to deal with.

I believe that the lesbian/gay community, and its friends, will keep on doing what we've been doing for the last eleven years. Whenever it looked as though we had run out of energy, we reached farther down and found new resources, new resolve, new strength, and new courage to continue the work. *The lesbian/gay community has been tested, and found magnificent.*

Grieving well following an AIDS death includes confronting extraordinary emotional issues, dealing with the impact of that death on our everyday lives, and beginning to get involved in the fight against AIDS. Please notice that grieving well is an ongoing process, not a finished product with a clear-cut end point. We can be in the process of grief for a very long time. That doesn't mean it will always hurt as much as it did immediately following the death.

If there is some kind of end point to grief, I don't know where it is. Frankly, I don't *want* to know where it is. I don't want not to feel sad when I think of someone I love who has died. *But neither do I want that sadness to control my life.*

It's my hope that *After You Say Goodbye* will help all of us be united in our grief and be united in our living. We are all in this together. And it's not that misery loves company, it is that we must stand united, for division will always intensify the suffering.

There are ways to minimize the ravages of our losses and the loneliness we feel without our loved ones. There are ways to discover that we are more powerful than our losses, and more power-ful than our grief. There are ways to begin to love again, and to allow ourselves to be loved again.

Look to this day, for yesterday is but a dream and tomorrow is only a vision, but today well lived makes every yesterday a dream of happiness and every tomorrow a vision of hope.

—Sanskrit wisdom

notes for reading this book

The most effective way to read this book is to start at Chapter 1 and work through it to the end, without skipping chapters or jumping ahead. Each chapter builds on the previous chapters.

The three chapters written specifically for life partners, family members, and friends assume that you have read the first eight chapters about dealing with the emotions of grief. Chapters 9 through 12 will be much more powerful for you if you already have some control of your feelings and understand some of the techniques for dealing with painful emotions.

If you would prefer to jump directly to the chapter that most clearly addresses your relationship with the one who has died, you may of course do that. Just be aware that those chapters may seem somewhat cold and unfeeling as they address practical issues. They do not address the emotions of grief.

AFTER

when someone

YOU SAY

you love

GOODBYE

dies of AIDS

PART ONE   **the emotions of grief**

when someone you love has died of AIDS

When someone dies of AIDS, his or her struggle is finished. For those left behind, the struggle continues, sometimes with an even greater urgency and ferocity. We can face and win that struggle. We can include grief in our lives without giving it control of our lives. We do not have to allow ourselves to become a victim of AIDS or of AIDS deaths.

The practice of grief counseling is a relatively new one. We're still learning how to do it. AIDS enormously increases the difficulty and complexity of grief, and in some cases changes the rules. We must appreciate the unique issues connected with an AIDS death if we are to be able to fully express our grief and, by so doing, to "grieve well."

I don't want to create a competition about what kind of death causes more pain. All death causes pain. As I was completing this manuscript, our good friend who lived next door to us in Cathedral City was diagnosed with cancer and died six months later. He was seventy-eight years old, and his wife was seventy-six.

I have spent many hours with her since his death. She has become my adopted "desert mom."

I know that there is no way that anyone who has lost his or her spouse or life partner to AIDS has grieved any harder or experienced more pain than she has. The person who shared the center of her world for so many years is gone, and she is alone.

Yet, in her grief, she is surrounded by a loving family and friends, all of whom are willing to do whatever they can to make her loss easier to bear.

A gay man who has lost his life partner to AIDS will hurt no more, *and no less,* than a heterosexual widow or widower. Yet, his grief process will be so much more complicated as he faces the discrimination, outrage, guilt, and fear that so often surround an AIDS death, not to mention the mushrooming numbers of those who are dying.

Without setting up a "pain competition," I would like to examine some of the aspects of an AIDS death that make grieving so complicated and difficult.

When someone you love dies of AIDS, you are frequently forced to deal with a lot more than death. Your support group is not guaranteed—in fact, it may have run screaming into the woods. Your job, your home, your insurance, your long-term security will be in possible jeopardy. You may become the brunt of discrimination if not persecution. This probably wasn't the first person you have lost to AIDS, and it probably won't be the last.

To grieve well will require that you make your way through a complex maze of emotions and interpersonal conflict. The more you understand about these issues, the more powerful you will be in the face of your grief.

AIDS *deaths don't come in ones or twos.* Grieving for one person is hard enough. Completing the grief process takes time. There are no shortcuts. Unfortunately, I don't know many people who have the "luxury" of grieving for only one AIDS death.

You know how overwhelming it seems when a lot of things go wrong all at the same time. You can imagine how you would feel if your car broke down, your roof started leaking, your boss threatened your job security, and you fell down a flight of stairs and broke your leg.

None of these events are remotely as severe as the death of someone you love. Any one of them would be troublesome and costly by itself, and would take time and energy to deal with.

All of them happening at once would make your job much more

difficult. Most people would be aghast at how many bad things were happening to you and wouldn't blame you if you seemed overwhelmed.

Those of us in the lesbian/gay community who are dealing with AIDS deaths are rarely dealing with one at a time. Most of us are dealing with dozens. Some of us are dealing with hundreds. Just as we are trying to cope with one loss, there is another, and another. And it's not likely that this situation will change in the near future. The dying is going to continue, and we will have more deaths to grieve.

The prospect is overwhelming. The emotions are intense. The result can be emotional chaos or the opposite, total shutdown.

We can't give in to the chaos, and we cannot afford to shut down. Our defenses will not hold under this kind of assault for very long. We must learn how to cope with our losses, as difficult as it may seem.

An AIDS death intensifies and multiplies our feelings. Powerful negative emotions are created by any death. Sadness, anger, guilt, and fear are almost always present in any number of combinations. AIDS can intensify and magnify each of those feelings.

An AIDS death can turn sadness into a lingering, grinding depression. This can be the direct result of the rising numbers of deaths that we are facing. Further, depression can be intensified if not caused by the repressed anger and fear that are unusually powerful following an AIDS death.

An AIDS death can turn anger into outrage. The more that comes to light about governmental inaction, incompetence, and indifference, the more rage enters the picture. People dying of AIDS are not only fighting for their lives and their health, they must also fight for their freedom.

An AIDS death can create guilt and shame. Guilt is frequently part of any grieving process. We didn't feel that we loved the one who died enough, we were angry at him for dying, or we didn't do enough before he or she died. This guilt is usually unwarranted, and always destructive.

AIDS brings up sexual guilt, which only makes things worse. This will be especially true for anyone who is still trying to deal with his sexual orientation. The guilt has been further magnified by the messages from religious leaders who have proclaimed AIDS God's punishment for a sinful lifestyle.

An AIDS death will frequently create terror. You don't have to be HIV-positive to experience that terror. I know a number of HIV-negative men who are still terrified by AIDS deaths even though they repeatedly test negative, and have done nothing that could lead to their becoming HIV-positive.

An AIDS death forces HIV-positive and frightened HIV-negative men to face their own mortality. For some, it may seem like a dire warning of what could be awaiting them in months or years to come.

The terror also can be there for people who are not in high-risk groups for AIDS. I hear many stories of people who avoid the memorial service for their gay sibling who died of AIDS because they are afraid they will somehow contract the virus and pass it along to their children. They tenaciously ignore information from public health officials about what does and does not transmit the virus.

Attending the memorial service of someone who has died of AIDS has never been attributed to be the cause of a single case of AIDS. Yet, people still stay away in droves.

Many intense emotions will be there for you following an AIDS death. This book is not about how to avoid them. That would not be wise or even possible. There are ways, however, to keep those emotions from controlling your life.

Expressing powerful negative emotions in any circumstance is difficult for many people. Expressing them in a context of AIDS grief can be even more difficult, *and even more necessary.* Chapters 4 through 8 will make practical suggestions for ways of dealing with these intense negative emotions and how you can avoid becoming their victim.

An AIDS death can cause you to hide your grief. The extraordinary circumstances surrounding an AIDS death can cause the grieving person to hide his or her grief. There aren't many other kinds of death that have this result.

A death is usually a call for uniting and joining together. It is no accident that so many different cultures have created their own version of the wake, where those who are grieving can come together in their sadness and loss to comfort one another and to help one another face the reality of the loss.

AIDS makes this impossible for many people. The fear of rejection, abandonment, persecution, and discrimination forces them to hide out, telling lies about how their loved one actually died. They have to live with the stress such lies will always cause, as well as the fear of being found out.

Spending too much time with others who loved the one who died will create too many opportunities for questions about the circumstances of his or her death. Consequently, other people are avoided as much as possible, and the cause of death is kept a secret.

I even know of men who have died quietly of AIDS whose families — estranged because of their disapproval of the gay lifestyle — are not even aware of the death.

It's been easy for some to criticize those people who have hidden their AIDS-related grief. While I encourage people to tell the truth in these circumstances, I do understand their wanting to hide out instead.

People whose life partners have died of AIDS have lost their jobs as well as their homes. People who might have been expected to comfort them run from them instead. In the face of those dire possibilities, many do choose to keep silent. *But it is important that they begin to realize that their silence can be deadly.*

Silence demands that you grieve alone, without support. It demands isolation and alienation at a time when love and understanding is needed. This silence and aloneness will be enormously damaging to anyone who is grieving.

It's also important to know that many families will not reject their gay son's partner and friends. While there may be some initial awkwardness, many families have been willing to join with the partner and friends in the mourning. They won't be able to do that if we don't tell them the truth in the first place.

AIDS can pit survivors against one another. Unfortunately, there will be cases where the family will not embrace their son's partner and friends. AIDS deaths are frequently experienced very differently by the survivors. Life partners, spouses, mothers, fathers, children, siblings, and friends each have their own unique needs and feelings as they face an AIDS death. Unfortunately, sometimes these needs pit the members of the different groups against one another.

A heterosexual widow whose husband has died in an automobile accident can generally expect support, respect, and assistance following that death, especially from the family of the one who has died. They can all grieve together, offering one another mutual caring and support. A whole community can come together in her support.

A family experiencing their grief when their son has died of AIDS may want to push their son's life partner and friends as far away as possible. Their presence is a reminder to them of their son's gay lifestyle, which they would like to forget. Consequently, the family ignores the partner's and friends' needs and their right to grieve for their loss. Instead of respect and support, there is antagonism and exclusion.

One of my clients was locked out of his own home by his partner's angry family, who immediately flew his partner's body back to the Midwest. He was not allowed to see the body or attend the funeral.

It's not only gay life partners who have to deal with this awful issue. Even the spouses of heterosexuals who have died of AIDS have experienced being pushed away by terrified family members who claim to be protecting their children from disease.

Such abandonment or rejection is clearly damaging to the life partner or spouse. In a much more subtle way, it is also damaging to the family. They will not be able to complete their own grieving process as long as they try to deny aspects of their son's life that they find offensive. *Complete grieving demands integrity, and that means wholeness, accepting all of what is or was.*

Complete grieving also demands compassion, understanding, and flexibility. Hatred and resentment will keep grief alive and painful.

It is my hope that this book will help minimize the adversarial roles that are played out following an AIDS death, as it helps members of the different groups understand and respect the different issues and needs of the members of the other groups. There is too much to do to allow our energy to be wasted battling with one another.

Sometimes a gay man can lose more than his life partner. A gay man who has lost his life partner will sometimes not only have to deal with the loss of the person with whom he shared his life, but, like the client I mentioned above, he may have to face the loss of his home and possessions to vindictive families supported by courts that won't recognize the legitimacy of gay and lesbian relationships.

I have heard an appalling number of stories about self-righteous family members descending on the home, dismantling it, and dividing it up among themselves, ignoring their son's life partner's rights and needs.

During such a time of grief, a number of men I know have made no attempt to recover their property. They just can't face going to court in what could be a lengthy battle, with no guarantee that justice will be done.

A gay man who has lost his life partner to AIDS may also have to deal with the abandonment by friends who aren't able to get past their own fear of AIDS. Other friends may have been too inundated with grief over their own losses, and just don't have the resources to help him out with his loss.

He must find ways to protect himself legally. He must form a new support network of people who are not freaked out by an AIDS death.

If your life partner has died of AIDS you will need to learn how to be assertive. You will need to insist on your rights. You may need to be willing to start over again from scratch. It may not be easy, but it will be better than remaining a victim of your losses.

This problem also points out the absolute necessity for each one of us to have a well-written will, detailing how we want things handled in the event of our death. A good attorney will know how to protect your life partner and friends. You don't have to be HIV-positive to need a will. You could get run over by a beer truck tomorrow, and your life partner and friends will still need your legal protection.

Family members of gay men have their own unique issues. Frequently you are not only dealing with the fact that your son, father, or brother has died, but that he was gay, and had a whole life you never knew about, populated with people you've never heard of.

I would like to suggest that you consider accepting the fact that your loved one was gay, and, further, would encourage you to enter into a partnership with his life partner and gay and lesbian friends. The mutual caring and support will be of great assistance as you go through your own process of grieving.

Many families buy a misconception that is trumpeted loudly by opponents of the lesbian/gay community. (Unfortunately, I have heard the same misconceptions from a number of gay men and lesbians.) That misconception is that gay men and lesbians cannot form close, meaningful, long-term relationships. These people, gay and non-gay, are wrong.

Gay men and lesbians form relationships as close as that of any married heterosexual couple. The loss of one's partner is no less painful than it is for any heterosexual.

For a family member to ignore this is to do a great disservice to the one who has died. He has the right to have the relationship he left behind respected and honored.

If you are a parent or a sibling and live in a small town in the Midwest, you may have your own discrimination to face. If your son had died in an automobile accident, you would likely have had an entire community to help support you, to be there for you. If you are alone in the Midwest with the knowledge that your son was gay and died of AIDS, that support will rarely be there. You will need to know how to go about finding a support group for yourself.

Suffering alone isn't necessary, and certainly not healthy for you. Chapter 10 will help you find a support group. There is a list of regional resources that are available to help you at the end of the book. (I don't mean to imply that the Midwest is the only place where you will find discrimination involving an AIDS death. It happens in the big cities as well. But at least in the large cities, there are support groups for grieving family members.)

Friends sometimes have to do it all. If you are a friend of someone who has died of AIDS, you will also have your own issues to deal with. If there was no life partner or family, you may have been the one responsible for taking care of the one who has died, as well as taking care of affairs after the death. You will have your own feelings and need to know how to deal with them in effective ways.

If you are HIV-positive, such a death will probably bring up some fear for you, as you watched your buddy deteriorate before your eyes, and as you wonder what might lie ahead for you. You need to know how to maximize your Wellness and take care of yourself physically, emotionally, and spiritually.

Remember that AIDS *is not an automatic death sentence.*

You may also need to know how to take some time off and heal, especially if you have gone through a number of deaths in a short period of time. You can't take care of your friends who are sick if you are neglecting yourself and your own health. There's a lot of work to be done, to be sure, but you won't last long if you're not paying attention to your own needs.

In Chapter 12, we'll deal specifically with what I call AIDS caregiver burnout, and why the solution might be joining a softball team or a bowling league instead of finding yet another support group.

AIDS, *Christianity, and traditional American values.* A consistent theme runs through most of the horrible uniqueness of AIDS deaths. That theme is the damage created by ignorance, hatred, and bigotry.

I have referred to this issue several times already in this book. It is critical that you understand it.

Too many lesbians, gay men, and their friends have bought into messages of shame and hate concerning the AIDS crisis. Their lives have been nearly destroyed by the fear and alienation engendered by such messages.

Much of this suffering has been caused by people *claiming* to be Christians and *claiming* to represent traditional American values. I cannot estimate the number of people who are dead as a direct result of these groups' sabotage of the fight against AIDS.

Every person who is grieving an AIDS death must know how to challenge those forces and effectively reject their messages wherever they rear their ugly heads.

You see, we are not just fighting a disease on a medical front. Our war has many fronts: social, political, economic, and sexual. We dare not ignore those other fronts while we try to take care of ourselves and our loved ones who are ill.

People with AIDS have to fight not only for their health, but for their freedom and for their human rights. They have to fight not just the virus, but also those forces in our society who use AIDS as a weapon, as justification for discrimination and bigotry against lesbian and gay citizens as well as against people with AIDS.

In addition to dealing with the grief that accompanies our loss, we have been subjected to the terror, shame, and rage created by societal prejudice against anyone with AIDS, and even against those who love someone with AIDS. Our grief process has become steadily more complex and complicated. We will not be able to complete our grieving if we allow the shame and guilt to go unchallenged.

That shame and guilt has been largely caused by the intrusion of right-wing politicians and radical "born-again" preachers. They have entered the fight against AIDS, not to cure the disease, but to use the disease to pursue their own political agendas, including long-standing vendettas against the lesbian/gay community.

These people lay loud claim to traditional American values and the principles of Christianity. They then distort those values and principles to suit their own ends, and wield them as weapons against us. Any means seem to justify the ends as they seek to gain more and more political power, and ever-larger financial contributions, by spreading fear and hatred.

They tell a person fighting for his life that God is taking his life as punishment for his sexual sins. They tell a mother who has just buried her son that her gay son deserved to die. They condemn an entire community for the actions of a virus.

They tell their constituents and congregations that a child with AIDS represents a grave threat to the health of their own children, and create needless hysteria that has torn apart whole communities. In spite of overwhelming medical evidence and the testimonies of public health experts, they persist in stoking the fires of AIDS terror, as long as it serves their purpose.

Their intrusion has made our battle with the disease and its aftermath much more difficult. Their intrusion has added unnecessary pain and suffering to those who are grieving.

It is time to take a firm stand against the efforts of these homophobic politicians and radical preachers. The only weapon we need is the truth. We are not battling against the "American way," or against the principles of Christianity.

Our community stands in full support of the *real* traditional American values. Our battle against AIDS is founded on those values. I'm talking about the values of liberty and justice for all. I am talking about courage. I am talking about truth.

People are dying, and we have a president who has spent more time worrying about flag burning than he has about AIDS. What a travesty! The flag represents our nation. What is our nation if not its people? How can one honor the flag without honoring the sanctity of every human life that makes up that nation? How can empty patriotism that masks bigotry be a traditional American value?

We dare not allow those politicians to continue to misrepresent and then condemn us. We must not allow them to wrap themselves in the flag while they pervert the Constitution and ignore the Bill of Rights. We cannot allow them to claim to represent traditional American values while they support practices of hatred, persecution, exclusion, and discrimination.

We are in a war, with thousands of young men and women dying. If they were dying in a war against another nation, they would be called heroes, and rightly so.

Those fighting for their lives against a dreaded disease haven't been given hero status. They are treated like lepers and excluded from fellowship, frequently in the name of "traditional American values." A more shameful mockery of fairness would be hard to find. The impact on the grieving process is unimaginable.

Those homophobic politicians and preachers are the kind of people our forefathers and foremothers were running away from when they founded this nation. It was because of their experience of the widespread religious persecution in Europe that the framers of our Constitution included freedom of religion in the Bill of Rights. The right-wing preachers and politicians persist in ignoring that fact, even though any child's American history book attests to its truth.

Neither are we battling Christianity and Christian values. We are battling certain radical "born-again" preachers and intrusive Catholic archbishops who have continually sought to sabotage the fight against AIDS. They have blocked funding for research and for taking care of people with AIDS, stopped AIDS education programs, and given tacit permission to hate and persecute people living with AIDS. That they do this in the name of Jesus and Christian values is the true abomination.

As a community we have no quarrel with Christianity and its message of love, compassion, and healing. Our fight is with those who subvert Christianity's values for their own political, financial, and power-grabbing agendas.

As a boy, I was brought up in an evangelical fundamentalist Protestant church. Our behavior was always held up to the yard-stick of "What do you think Jesus would do if He were alive in the world today?" This was usually followed by, "You don't think He would be drinking and smoking, do you? You don't think that He would go to dances or to sin-filled movies, do you?"

I think it is time that someone asked the question, "What would Jesus do, if He were alive on the planet today and facing the AIDS crisis?" Anyone who has read the Bible knows the answer to that question.

In His time, Jesus didn't hand out moral inventories or ask for religious affiliation or theological correctness before He healed the sick. He just made them well, offering them unconditional love and compassion and hope. This is the central message of Christianity. How can Christians today do any less?

Our fight is not with Christianity, but the way certain preachers are preaching it. Hopefully, there may come a time when the Christian community wakes up and joins us in our fight against suffering and death and hate.

The political community needs to wake up as well, and begin to recognize that it is no longer just gay men who are angry about AIDS. The loss and the sadness is not limited to the gay community. For every gay man who has died, there are parents, siblings, friends, coworkers, and neighbors who are grieving. There are also growing numbers of people in the heterosexual community who have also battled the AIDS virus and the prejudice that goes with it.

Soon there will be millions of heterosexuals who love someone who has AIDS or who has died of AIDS. That group has not yet reached a critical mass, but when it does, changes will be made.

Until then, we must resist victimhood. We must vigorously challenge messages of shame and hate. Grieving is hard enough without being subjected to persecution from hypocrites and hate-mongers.

Grieving when someone we love dies of AIDS is no simple matter. The issues are tough. The pain is intense. The challenge is formidable. Yet we can triumph in our fight against AIDS, and against those who obstruct our efforts.

It would be nice if we had the liberty to grieve simply and quietly, but we don't. Yet with all that is before us, I am convinced that we can transcend the issues, move through our pain, and triumph over this challenge.

grieving without becoming a victim

Whether we are alone or have a support network, an AIDS death is tough to deal with. We will feel pain. We will feel loss. Our life will be changed in ways that we could not have imagined. We will suffer, but that doesn't mean that we have to become a victim of AIDS and AIDS deaths.

Victim is a harsh word with lots of negative values attached to it. Most of us are loath to admit that we have become a victim. There is no reason for anyone to feel guilty for allowing him- or herself to become a victim.

It's easy to slip into a victim role without realizing it. We just need to be ready and willing to get out of that role at the earliest opportunity. Feeling guilty will only keep you in the victim role longer, and increase your suffering immeasurably.

In my first book, *Pathways to Wellness*, there are several chapters about the victim triangle. I have only recently discovered whom to acknowledge for the wisdom of this model. The victim triangle was first written about by Stephen Karpman in his article "Fairy-tales and Script Drama Analysis."[1] Karpman called it the drama triangle.

It is important to understand how the victim triangle is related to the experience of grief. Here is a brief summary of the dynamics

[1] *Transactional Analysis Bulletin* (no. 26, April 1968): 39–43.

of the victim triangle, with attention to its role in the grief process.

THE VICTIM TRIANGLE

PERSECUTOR

VICTIM   RESCUER

Whenever we are feeling powerful negative emotions such as fear, anger, depression, helplessness, or hopelessness, it is likely that we are on the victim triangle. Being aware that you are on it provides you with the opportunity to get off it.

There are always three roles to be played on the victim triangle. If there is a victim, there has to be a persecutor, and there almost always is a rescuer, or at least the search for one.

The victim is the one in pain, the one who is feeling helpless and hopeless. A victim almost always feels powerless to do anything about his or her plight. A victim is at the mercy of the powerful forces in his or her environment, which are usually embodied in the persecutor.

The persecutor is whoever or whatever is doing "it" to the victim. Another person can be the persecutor. A virus can be the persecutor. An event, an emotion, or something someone has said can be the persecutor.

Things can get really interesting when a victim has become his or her own persecutor. If you've ever been mad at yourself, or beat yourself up for making a mistake, you've become a victim of your own persecutor.

The rescuer is also someone or something that is thought to be more powerful than the victim. A minister or a therapist can be a rescuer. A good friend whom you depend on to drag you out of a mess can be a rescuer. Mom or Dad and their checkbook can be a rescuer. Scotch or dope can be very dangerous rescuers. Alcoholics Anonymous has names for another kind of rescuer: enablers or co-dependents.

An old Chinese proverb says: "If you give a man a fish, you feed him for a day. If you teach him how to fish, you feed him for a lifetime." Rescuers give away a lot of fish, as well as chicken soup. They'll take the responsibility and do it for you.

Whether they mean to or not, they will likely be taking away your power. Fortunately they really can't take away your power, unless you choose to give it to them.

There is one other very important aspect of the victim triangle: *The roles always shift.*

Victims have a strange way of becoming persecutors. They can get angry and launch a counterattack. That can turn their persecutors into victims. Victims can also get angry at their rescuers and turn on them. Thus, rescuers become victims.

If victims don't get well or better, their rescuers can get angry at them, which means that the rescuers become persecutors. Rescuers can also start to persecute the persecutors. On and on it goes, and it doesn't stop as long as you're on the victim triangle.

I suspect that the roles shift because victimhood is not a natural condition for human beings. We resist victimhood almost as much as we resist being rescued. We don't like the powerlessness of being a victim, any more than we like the powerlessness of being rescued. We'll get even with the persecutor, and we'll make our rescuer pay, too, for thinking we can't handle our life. Maybe we can't, but how dare they assume that.

Have you ever tried to help someone out and had them get angry at you? "Mother, I'll do it myself!" You were just trying to help and now they're persecuting you and you have become a victim.

Or have you ever gotten angry at someone who was honestly trying to help you because you resented the intrusion? Have you ever tried to help someone out, and they refused to take your advice so you got angry and frustrated with them? It's far too easy to play on the victim triangle.

Not only will the roles shift, but you can play all three roles all by yourself. An example is when you get angry at yourself for making a mistake and then slug down a shot of scotch or smoke a joint to make yourself feel better. In your anger you became the persecutor, and having the drink of scotch or the joint is the rescuer. In such a scenario, you are generally a victim before, during, and after.

Riding the victim triangle is never dull. In fact, all good drama and comedy must be based on the victim triangle. The tension between these three elements must be present or there isn't much excitement or interest.

"I Love Lucy" would have been very dull if Lucy had not been a class-act victim, a class-act rescuer, and a class-act persecutor, sometimes in the same episode.

"Dallas" would have been dreadfully uninteresting — and in fact *has* been dreadfully uninteresting — if the writers forgot about the tension of the victim triangle. If J.R., the villain, is never victimized, it stops being exciting. It's not fun watching someone just be mean and never have to pay for his meanness.

If a victim on a soap always stays a victim (remember Crystal on "Dynasty"?), he or she stops being a sympathetic character, because we don't care anymore how badly he or she gets treated. Victims must rise up and get the bad guy, or they are just pathetic.

Clint Eastwood and Sylvester Stallone have made successful careers out of movies that are based on the classic victim triangle. The worse they are treated at the beginning of the movie, the more butt they are going to kick by the end. You can bank on that, and they do.

Being a victim is very dramatic and interesting in a movie script, but in real life it always results in pain. Relationships that exist on the victim triangle won't work, either. They can last a long time, and do a lot of damage in the process, but they will never work.

Some people make their real life more exciting by playing on the victim triangle. They aren't necessarily aware that that's what they're doing, but they are on it. For them, life is about attack, defend, and suffer. A life on the victim triangle will certainly be dramatic, but it won't be as satisfying or fulfilling, and it won't be as fun or energetic, as life off the triangle.

AIDS, GRIEF, AND THE VICTIM TRIANGLE

If your grief has placed you on the victim triangle, you will suffer. Working through your grief successfully will require that you get off the victim triangle.

However, if you *have* become a victim of AIDS or a victim of your AIDS grief, don't waste time feeling guilty. It's not something to feel guilty about. In fact, guilt always will put you on and keep you on the damn triangle.

Most of us find ourselves on the victim triangle a lot, and we always have help getting and staying there. A large group of people seem to have a major investment in keeping us on the triangle. In the AIDS community, I call these people "the doom-and-gloom sisters." As far as they're concerned we're all dead, so we might as well just shut up and give up. Far too many people listen to them, but the rest of us dare not shut up — silence *does* equal death.

So if you find that you're on the victim triangle, don't waste time feeling guilty. Just be committed to doing whatever it takes to get off it, as soon as possible.

The choices for victimhood are numerous where AIDS is concerned. We can be a victim of HIV, a victim of AIDS, a victim of the fear of AIDS, a victim of people like William Dannemeyer, Lou Sheldon, or Jesse Helms, or even a victim of our rage about AIDS. We can be a victim of any aspect of AIDS that makes us feel helpless and hopeless.

It was an incredibly important step when people with AIDS started insisting that they be called that, instead of victims of AIDS.

There is no question that politicians like Helms and Dannemeyer want to victimize us, but they can't do that without our cooperation. No one can make us a victim just because they decide to act like a persecutor, or because they do something that hurts us. No matter what they do, we don't *have* to become their victim. Being a victim is *always* a matter of choice.

That idea angers some people. No one likes to be called a victim, and no one really likes the idea that being a victim is a matter of his or her choice.

But our power over victimhood rests on our knowing that it *is* our choice to become a victim. *If we can choose to become a victim, then we can also choose not to remain a victim.*

So don't divert your energy by feeling guilty about discovering that you have allowed yourself to become a victim. Instead, just take responsibility for the problem. Oops — talking about AIDS and responsibility usually brings up even more anger for some people.

I suspect that this has something to do with the widespread confusion between guilt and responsibility. They are not the same thing. They are not synonymous with each other.

If we feel guilty about our choices it will only increase our victimhood. Taking responsibility for our choices is the way to get off the victim triangle.

Responsibility says, "I did it." Then it says, "Here's what I am going to do to fix it." There is no time for guilt. All of your energy goes into fixing the problem as best you can.

Guilt says, "I did it and I am bad and wrong for having done it. I deserve to suffer or be punished for my mistake."

Blame says, "I did it, but it's your fault I did it and you deserve to suffer and be punished."

The only approach that actually results in doing something about the problem is taking responsibility. Guilt and blame not only waste time, and don't result in cleaning up the problem, but they also tend to perpetuate the problem, all but guaranteeing that the mistake will happen over and over again.

The issue of responsibility and AIDS produces intense emotions. Some people get outraged at the suggestion that anyone is responsible for having AIDS.

Yet there are those who are convinced that the solution to the AIDS problem starts with the belief that we create our own health. These people believe that a person with AIDS has somehow chosen to have that condition.

This idea works only if you believe in the metaphysical concept of reincarnation. If you do, you will believe that your eternal soul made a choice, before you were born into this body, that this body would have AIDS because there is a lesson for you to learn as part of your spiritual evolution.

If you don't believe in reincarnation, that idea of responsibility sounds silly or infuriating. Some even think it is a cruel idea.

The important point is that you don't have to believe in reincarnation in order to deal with AIDS, or your grief about AIDS. If a person has AIDS, I don't really care if he takes responsibility for having created AIDS, or for having chosen it before he was even born. If that concept works for him, great. If it doesn't, that's OK too. It's up to him, and he gets to do it his way.

What I do care about is the level of responsibility he is willing to take for his life and his health, right now, given his diagnosis. He may not have had a choice about having AIDS, but he definitely has some choice about what he's going to do about it.

If someone you love has died of AIDS, you don't have a choice about his or her having died. You do have a choice about how you are going to grieve, and how much you are going to let it affect your life.

Let's look at a less dire example of all this. When I was about eight years old, I was climbing a tree, playing Tarzan. The girl playing Jane pushed me out of the tree and I fell on the back of my neck and cracked my left wrist. Since that time, I have had chronic neck pain. (My wrist healed just fine, thank you.) A lot of my stress seems to zero in on my neck and upper spine.

Now, did I choose to come into a body that was going to live with chronic neck pain? Frankly, I don't know. Frankly, it doesn't matter.

What I do know is that I have a body that experiences chronic neck pain, and that I am the only one who is responsible for dealing with it.

It is up to me to take care of it, to see that I receive appropriate treatment. It's up to me to choose to do relaxation and guided imagery to help relax it and heal it. It's up to me to buy that ergonomically designed desk chair to reduce the neck and back strain that I get by spending countless hours sitting in front of my computer screen.

If a person sustains an injury to his spinal chord and finds himself paralyzed and in a wheelchair, it doesn't matter to me if he thinks he chose to come into a body that was going to be paralyzed. It does matter that he exercises his choice about what he's going to do about being in a wheelchair.

Is he going to hide out at home, feeling like a freak, rarely going out in public?

Hopefully, he will choose to make the best he can out of his life. He will become involved in the Wheelchair Olympics or organize his own wheelchair basketball or tennis team.

If a person has AIDS, is he going to remain a victim of AIDS for the rest of his life? Is he going to give up and get ready to die?

Hopefully, he will choose to make the best he can out of his life. He will live life to the fullest extent he is capable of. He will maximize his Wellness—physical and mental well-being—in spite of his disease. He will learn how to live with his disease, not be controlled by it.

If you have lost someone you love to AIDS, are you going to become a victim of your grief for the rest of your life? Are you going to decide that life isn't worth living?

Hopefully, you will decide to grieve well, and get on with the rest of your life, sadder, but still able to find joy and satisfaction.

Frankly, where AIDS is concerned, I think that it is inevitable for all of us to go through periods of time where we feel like victims. When I see someone I love hooked up on a respirator, with numerous tubes coming out of his body, feeding him, draining him, and medicating him, I don't know how to tell him not to feel like a victim. Yet I know some people who have not allowed such a condition to victimize them, and I admire them.

The important thing is not to feel blame for someone who has become a victim, or to feel guilty if you are the one who has allowed yourself to become a victim. Guilt and blame are not necessary, they are not kind, and they are not helpful.

They are damaging. They are deadly. They need to be confronted and let go of. They can be replaced with responsibility.

Taking responsibility for your choices, especially where your victimhood is concerned, is a powerful act. It is a liberating and empowering act.

I believe that we always have a choice. We may or may not choose some of the circumstances of our lives, but we can choose how we are going to react to those circumstances. Hopefully, we will choose to renounce quickly all forms of victimhood.

GETTING OFF THE VICTIM TRIANGLE

Whenever you notice your grief has put you on the victim triangle, you can get off by doing three things:
1. Take responsibility for your feelings and your grief.
2. Tell the truth about how you are feeling.
3. Take action.

Taking responsibility means that you acknowledge that you are the one responsible for your choices about what to do with your life now that someone you love has died of AIDS. Blaming someone else won't work. Feeling guilty won't work. Only taking charge of your responses to what happens in your life will work.

In Chapter 4, we will discuss telling the truth about your feelings and your grief, as opposed to denying your feelings or getting stuck in them. If you are afraid, be afraid, but be willing to push past your fear and live life with dignity and vitality and passion, regardless of your fear.

If you are angry, be angry, but be committed to expressing that anger in a way that works, in a way that will make a difference, in a way that will produce positive results for you, for the lesbian/gay community, and for people with AIDS.

In Chapters 4 through 8, we will look at depression, anger, guilt, and fear and at what you can do about them if you think you have allowed yourself to become a victim of your emotions. Experiencing these emotions is inevitable, but you don't have to become their victim, to stop living, to stop loving, to start hiding while you get ready to die. I want to do everything I can to convince you not to make this choice.

Once you tell the truth about how you are feeling, get ready to do something about it. If you're not willing to take action, you'll keep experiencing the same emotions and falling back onto the victim triangle.

The solution to fear and the solution to anger are the same. Do something about the problem. Get involved in the fight, and please don't try to pretend that it isn't a fight. It is a battle of monumental proportions, and the stakes are life or death. Commit yourself to something that is bigger than yourself, that is bigger than your grief, that is bigger than your illness.

Commit yourself to making a difference in a world that is in desperate need of changing, almost at the cellular level. There is no one who is too old, too poor, or too sick to be able to make a difference. Some of you will be on the front lines committing civil disobedience with ACT UP. Others of you will be behind the lines answering telephones or doing "lick, stick, and stuffs" (that is, stamping and addressing envelopes), taking people with AIDS to their doctor appointments, or raising money.

Where you do it doesn't matter. It only matters that you do

something, that you get involved in whatever way works for you.

You can't wait until you are no longer afraid before you start to act. You can't wait until you are no longer angry before you start to act. None of us has the luxury of time to do that. We must be prepared to act while we are afraid, while we are angry, while we are filled with sorrow, while we mourn the loss of someone we love to an AIDS death.

Regardless of your choices about victimhood, or your experience of being a victim, life must go on. Actually, it will go on anyway. Your choice is to go with it or resist it. Your own life is not over until it's over and you hear the fat lady singing. In the meantime, you deserve to enjoy life and live it to the fullest.

The credit belongs to the man who is actually in the arena, whose face is marred by dust and sweat and blood; who strives valiantly; who errs and comes short again and again; who knows the great enthusiasms, the great devotions, and spends himself in a worthy cause; who at the best, knows the triumph of high achievement; and who at the worst, if he fails, at least fails while daring greatly, so that his place shall never be with those cold and timid souls who know neither victory nor defeat.

—Theodore Roosevelt

grieving well

" feel like I'm going crazy." "I don't feel anything at all." I hear
these two sentences over and over as I work with people who are
grieving.

People who feel as if they are going crazy are experiencing too
many unfamiliar emotions at an intensity that they aren't used to.
That doesn't mean that they are going crazy. In fact, if they weren't
having those emotions they would be in a lot more trouble.

People who don't feel anything are firmly covering up those
"crazy" emotions, usually without being aware of doing so. They
will pay a heavy price for the cover-up, and the feelings will never
go away.

Grieving well requires learning how to deal with each of these
conditions. It means learning how to experience and express "crazy"
feelings without becoming overwhelmed by them.

"Crazy" feelings are a normal part of the grief process. Sadness,
depression, anger, guilt, fear, and any other negative emotions can
be there in diabolical combinations. But having "crazy" feelings
does not mean that you are crazy. It just means that you are normal.

It's important to have a thorough understanding of the emotions
connected with grief. Lack of understanding can make the process
a lot more difficult.

Grief is what we experience whenever we lose something or

someone that we love. Sadness and depression are the emotions most often associated with grief. Many people use these three words— *sadness, grief,* and *depression*—interchangeably, as though they mean the same thing, as though they were synonymous.

In fact, they are far from synonymous. If we are to effectively deal with our loss, we need to understand the important distinctions between sadness, grief, and depression. *That understanding will help us keep sadness or grief from plummeting us into a serious depression.*

Sadness is a feeling, an emotion, but it is rarely a permanent emotion. It exists in response to a loss or a disappointment. In time, it will almost always go away, as long as we are willing to have the feeling of sadness instead of trying to cover it up or pretend it isn't there. Such a cover-up will guarantee that we are stuck with the sadness.

Grief is a complex of several different emotions, one of which is sadness. The others are usually anger, guilt, and fear. Any unpleasant emotion (such as frustration, bitterness, or resentment) can be part of the grieving process, as we struggle to come to grips with our loss. If sadness is the only emotion that we experience, our grief will be incomplete, unfinished. The other unexpressed emotions will still be with us and working on us.

Depression can be the direct result of our unwillingness to experience sadness or the other emotions of grief. In our attempt to avoid pain, we close the door to our feelings. Our experience of the pain may be lessened, but it will rarely go away completely, no matter how well we repress it.

Unfortunately, as we dampen the impact of our negative emotions, it seems that we also dampen the experience of our positive emotions. We don't experience the full brunt of the pain, but we also don't get to experience much joy. This is a high price to pay for the momentary dulling of our pain.

In order to "grieve well," we must be willing to experience all the emotions connected with grief, no matter how painful they may seem. Your feelings don't have to make sense. They don't even have to be fair, kind, or comfortable, but they must be expressed. You can't release emotions that you aren't willing to have.

"Grieving well" may sound strange to some of you, like an

oxymoron. "Sweet sorrow" may be an oxymoron, but "grieving well" is not.

You see, grief is not automatically a "bad" experience. I know that it's not pleasant, and can even be agonizing, but grief is necessary and therefore healthy to experience. *Grief is normal.* Grief is a vital part of the healing process. Without it, life would not return to normal following the loss of someone we love. Without grief we would be emotionally constipated and spiritually stunted.

"Grieving well" simply means allowing ourselves to experience our grief, and all its attendant emotions, fully and completely: If we are sad, we allow ourselves to cry; if we are angry, we allow ourselves to be angry. Whatever feeling is there, we are willing to experience it, and to express it fully in ways that are not self-defeating or self-destructive, or carelessly damaging to others. Only then can we let go of it, and be free of it.

There are four elements of grieving well.

1. Be willing to experience your feelings, as opposed to repressing or stuffing them, or getting stuck in them.
2. Realize that you are still in control of your life.
3. Grieve in your own way.
4. Be willing to take action.

EXPERIENCE AND EXPRESS YOUR FEELINGS

The idea of all these feelings is frightening to many people. It seems as if the flood of feelings will overwhelm and suffocate them. Consequently, it seems logical to "stuff" away the feelings, to just deny that they are there.

Unfortunately, that will never work. Any emotion that we are unwilling to acknowledge and experience will always stay with us. It will have a profound effect on our lives. That effect may be sometimes quite subtle; at other times it will be screamingly blatant.

If I refuse to acknowledge my anger over a death, the anger will still be there, I just won't be aware of it. I will still experience the anger, but in other, less direct ways. I can become the driver from hell, and terrorize the freeways with my angry driving. I can displace the anger to my partner, or to our pets, or to my friends. I can become a constantly surly person. The choices are myriad. If I don't express the anger about the death, I am stuck with it, and with its effect on my life.

It is essential that you realize that just because you are not conscious of an emotion, that doesn't mean it isn't there. Over the period of our lifetime we develop various strategies for dealing with unpleasant emotions, the ones that we feel are too painful for us to experience. Psychologists call these strategies *defense mechanisms.*

Their purpose is to keep us from hurting. Occasionally they are helpful, but most of the time all they accomplish is a fragile, momentary reduction in our pain, while keeping the source of our pain hidden. The hidden emotion will do a lot of damage in the meantime.

The only solution is to be willing to experience your "crazy" feelings. I know it can be scary when the feelings of anger, guilt, and fear begin to come up. It's important not to be surprised by these emotions. It's even more important that we don't start to repress our emotions again.

Also, remember that feelings of grief become even more complicated and intense when we're dealing with an AIDS death. We're grieving for many, not just a few. An AIDS death is frequently the cause of terror and shame. The people left behind following an AIDS death are not always united in their grief; sometimes they are pitted against one another. Because of likely discrimination, many AIDS deaths are kept hidden, and those affected must hide their grief as well, while they suffer quietly alone — in thunderous silence. These differences can make grieving well very difficult, but far from impossible.

In the following chapters we will look at how to let those feelings come up without allowing ourselves to be overwhelmed by them, and without "going crazy."

YOU ARE STILL IN CONTROL OF YOUR LIFE

A death, its impact on our lives, and our consequent powerful negative emotions can make it seem as if we have lost control of our lives. In some respects we have, but in others we have not, and we need to understand the difference.

Many who are grieving a death for the first time are terrified of the unknown, the unpredictable, the helplessness, and the certain loneliness. We grasp at anything that looks solid, that promises stability and sureness in the midst of the chaos we are feeling. We look for comforting truths and try to react sensibly.

We are bound to be disappointed. The only truths about death are that it happens, and, when it does, it creates emotional chaos. It's as if the placid river of life has suddenly turned into turbulent rapids with danger lurking behind each rock.

Anyone who has ever gone river-rafting knows that there's only one way to get through a set of rapids. You hang on tight, and do your best to steer clear of the big rocks. You can't escape the facts that it's a bumpy and scary ride and you're going to get wet.

In the raft on the rapids, you *could* say that you are out of control. The river will take you downstream whether you want to go there or not. You can't go back upstream, and often you can't even make it to one of the banks. To the extent that you are in a raft that is being swept along by the river, you *are* out of control. That terrifies some people so much that they won't consider going river-rafting.

Yet, even in the river, you are not totally out of control. You can still steer the raft. You can guide it surely around the hazards, while you are flowing with the river. In this respect, you are very much *in* control.

After a death, things will happen in your life that you may have little or no control over. Unfortunately, you can't opt out of life the same way you could opt out of a river-rafting expedition. You are in life, and you will encounter death, and you will consequently lose control over certain parts of your life.

It is critical that you know that you are not *totally* out of control of your life following a death. You are still in charge, still able to set a course and steer your life in the direction in which you want to go, hopefully avoiding the big hazards along the way.

I could beat this metaphor to a pulp by talking about periodic capsizing, but I think you get the picture. The important thing is that we learn to accept the facts that there will always be those things in life that are beyond our ability to control, and that we must accept those things as graciously as possible. This wise acceptance will empower us to control what we can.

GRIEVE YOUR OWN WAY,
INSTEAD OF THE "RIGHT" WAY

As we learn how to express and experience our emotions without being overwhelmed by them, we must face the question of how to do that in the most effective way. There will be lots of people telling you about the way you *should* do it. Don't listen to them.

If there is a truth about the Right way to grieve, it's that there is no Right way. You must find the way that works for you, not the way that works for someone else, including the author of any book about grief, even this one.

The stages of grief. In *After You Say Goodbye* I will challenge some of the notions that some people have about the stages of grieving. For them, grief is something like a baseball game, with the players traveling to first base, then second, then third, and finally home. You go through one stage at a time: Now you're in denial, then you're in anger, and so on. You don't get to skip steps or try to stop early, but once you're done, you're done. I don't know many professionals who feel this way, but there seems to be this gross misunderstanding of the grief process on the streets.

In my experience, I have not found the idea of the stages of grief to be very helpful. It is too simplistic to be relevant to AIDS deaths, partly because there are so many of them. The stages of grieving over one death soon bang up against the stages of another one, and another one, and so on. The result is a chaos of emotion.

The idea of dividing the grief process into stages can be the basis for a rigid interpretaion of the grief process. It can put too much emphasis on people grieving the Right way, as opposed to grieving well.

"You mean you're still angry? You should have been through that stage a long time ago." "You mean you're still crying? You should be past that stage by now, don't you think?"

No, I don't. This isn't a kind or helpful thing to say to anybody. Yet I have had many grieving clients who have heard similar accusations and worse.

It seems to me that grief is really more like a pinball game, and you're the little ball randomly bouncing around between the different emotions. It's pretty unpredictable. You can bang back and forth between a couple of emotions for a long time, while you completely avoid others. You can be sad and tearful one minute and angry the next, then numb again. There is no rationality or order to your feelings. Trying to figure out what stage of grief you are in is not very useful or frankly very interesting.

(Please know that in this game, you are also the game player, not just the pinball. You are the one who decides how to play the game.)

You are unique and so is your grief. Your experience of grief is unique because you are a unique person. There is not another one of you anywhere in the universe. You are the sum total of your genetic inheritance and your life experiences, and more.

As a child, you observed the world around you and made certain decisions about love and safety. You are very likely still influenced by those decisions. As you were growing up, you developed certain belief systems about life, about death, and about the meaning of both. You learned to experience and express your feelings in your own unique way, as you watched your parents and others, and experienced their reactions to you.

This uniqueness will strongly influence your experience of grieving when someone you love has died of AIDS. What works for your best friend may work for you, *and it may not.*

About the only truth about death is that it will bring up a lot of emotions for those left behind. What emotions are brought up, how they are experienced, and for how long, will be a very individual process.

Your emotions depend on your unique needs. Experiencing the death of someone you love hurts. There is no way to avoid that, short of total emotional shutdown, and that is not healthy. For most people, it's not even possible. Grieving well generally begins with the need for you to be willing to recognize your feelings, all of them. Your feelings likely will be mixed up: rational and irrational, helpful and unhelpful, loud and quiet, blatant and subtle.

Some people's feelings take to the recliner in front of the TV. Others' feelings find the steepest roller coaster around, and away they go, sky high one minute and in the pits the next.

We've talked about the most common emotions that follow an AIDS death: sadness and depression, anger, guilt, and fear. This is a list of possibilities, not a list of certainties. Even with these feelings, there will still be exceptions.

For example, a person who is a devout Christian may be certain that the one who has died is going to heaven. Any sadness or anger that this person feels about the death will probably be short-lived, and tempered by the belief that the loved one has gone on to a better place. Yet, even with devout Christians, there will be dramatic differences. There will be some who, in spite of their belief in heaven, will still grieve horribly following a death.

Staunch advocates of reincarnation believe that their loved one has simply undergone a transformation to another plane of existence as part of his or her spiritual evolution. Anger or sadness may be there, but not in significant quantities, or for very long. Some even consider this to be a time of celebration.

Yet there will be differences here too. There will be those who believe in reincarnation but who will still find themselves overwhelmed by depression and anger following the death of someone they love.

Some people are certain that they did everything they could possibly do for the one who has died. They will probably not experience any guilt following the death. And there are those who did everything possible and still feel guilty, because they have learned to feel guilty whenever anything goes wrong around them.

A gay man who has come to grips with his relationship to the AIDS virus likely will not experience much fear following an AIDS death. If he does, he will simply deal with it again. Yet there may be some deaths that are harder to take than others, and that bring up fear in new and terrible ways.

There may be other differences, depending on how many deaths you've experienced. Some people will grieve just as deeply for each death, while others may notice that they somehow just get used to the awful process.

When you first learned that someone you loved was HIV-positive, you reacted in ways that were unique to you. Your reaction was probably consistent with how you dealt with strong negative emotions before you learned that your loved one was HIV-positive. It was undoubtedly influenced by your knowledge of your own HIV status. As your loved one battled with the disease and approached death, again your emotions were your own.

Some people become overwhelmed with sadness and are essentially paralyzed. Others become full of manic energy and wear themselves out doing good work. Some use enormous powers of denial, and somehow get through the whole process without it disrupting their lives too much, at least as far as the eye can tell. Others become chronically angry. Others are overcome with guilt.

People will have vastly different ways of reacting to their grief, some completely contradictory to the ways others use. I have known some men who have lost their partners to AIDS who then went into self-imposed seclusion for many months. Some were still being celibate years after the death. I have known others who were dating and having sex in a matter of weeks.

Unfortunately, a lot of people think that secluded celibacy is the Right way to do it. It's supposed to show how much you loved the one who has died. *There is no connection between how long you grieve and how much you loved.*

Different people will have different needs, and those needs will usually dictate how they handle their grief. Those who date quickly obviously have a need to be close to someone else, perhaps even to make love to someone else. That need has nothing to do with how much they did or did not love their partner.

The person who is being celibate probably needs seclusion and time by himself or herself. That's fine, too, but it is not more noble. It is just a different strategy based on different needs.

Some people will want to surround themselves with friends who will spend a lot of time talking about the "good old days" they had with the one who has died. Others will not want to do that, at least for a while, if ever.

Some people who are grieving will express their grief loudly and vigorously. Others will choose silence. The only important thing is to be sure that those who express their grief loudly aren't getting stuck in their emotions and to be sure that those who are silent are not stifling their feelings. Both groups will need to come around in their own time, however. *You cannot drag people kicking and scream-*

ing through their grief process. They have to do what works for them.

Do what works. What does "works" mean? If something "works" for you, it means that your life is enriched. It means that you aren't stuck with strong negative emotions. It means that you get to be fully involved with life as opposed to just getting by or just surviving.

What if the way you dealt with your feelings prior to the death doesn't work very well? Does that mean you are stuck with grieving badly now? No.

We are always more powerful than our feelings. Since we are the ones who create our feelings, we are also the ones who can change our feelings. Chapters 4 through 8 will explore this idea and give you powerful and practical ways to change your feelings. If the way you experienced your feelings before the death didn't really work too well, and got you into a lot of trouble, you do not have to follow that same course. You *will* follow that course, though, unless you take some aggressive action to confront the old ways that aren't working. Even so, you must still do it your way.

Strategies for dealing with grief will vary as much as strategies for living day-to-day life. Trying to fit into someone else's picture won't work as you live life, and it won't work as you grieve. Grieving well means grieving your own way.

Grieving well vs. grieving the Right way. I can hear some of you muttering, "What's the difference between grieving well and grieving the Right way?" Sometimes it is a tricky distinction to make.

The Right way is always supposed to work for everyone, and your job is to fit into it. If you can't do it the Right way, you get to feel guilty, bad, and wrong. This isn't helpful.

Grieving well follows the same rules as living well: You take responsibility for your own life. You have the integrity to tell the truth about how you are feeling. You are willing to do whatever has to be done. Within these ideas there is enormous latitude for you to do things your own way, a way that will work for your needs and for your life.

If you are trying to support someone who is grieving you need to recognize this. Does this mean that if you are watching a friend be consumed by grief that you can't intervene, or make suggestions? Of course not.

I am a psychotherapist, and when people come to me because they are grieving too painfully, I don't just sit there and tell them to do it their way, period. I'll make suggestions, but I won't give directions.

My advice and suggestions to them must honor who they are and how they function in general. I can point out ways that might work better than the way they are doing it, but I have to be willing for them to ignore my suggestions.

Sometimes, as in other areas of life, learning to grieve well is a trial-and-error process. We'll try it this way, and if it doesn't work, we'll try another way. There just isn't any Right way to do it.

TAKE ACTION

As you are willing to experience all of your feelings, to reclaim control in your life, and as you work out your own way to grieve, it is time for the next step: Take action. Do something about the problem.

Taking action can mean doing something as insignificant as balancing the checkbook for the first time since your loved one went to the hospital, or reorganizing a closet.

It can mean looking at your emotions and deciding what you need to do in order to feel as if you are in control of them again, not at their mercy. You may have to learn to challenge certain unworkable beliefs and attitudes.

It can also mean that you need to get involved in the fight against AIDS, and against bigotry and prejudice. Whether you are taking care of someone who is ill, participating in an ACT UP demonstration, or working on a hotline, your life will be enriched and your grief process eased as you concentrate your attention on making a contribution to something outside yourself.

If you're not ready to do any of that yet, don't worry about it. The time will come when you will be ready, even though that may seem impossible right now. Just know that the possibilities are there.

Regardless of what action you take, the most productive approach involves learning to focus your attention on today and on living it well, in spite of your loss, as best you can, with whatever energy you have available.

"Today well lived" may look difficult. Where AIDS is involved it perhaps looks impossible. Yet regardless of our circumstances, "today well lived" is our best offense, our best defense, our best chance at living a rich and full life.

Living today well does not require that life be perfect. Nor does it require that you live it perfectly. It simply requires that you live it the best way you can, giving it whatever you have to give and knowing that sometimes you'll have a lot more to give than others.

Today is all you have. Yesterday is gone, and tomorrow isn't here yet. Be willing to make today the best it can be, for you.

If that looks like staying inside your home and being quiet and still, then that is what you should do. If it looks like going out and partying, then do that. If it looks like throwing yourself into the things you need to do for your career, go for it.

Whatever you do, do it as passionately as you can, with 100 percent of the energy that you have available. If there is not a lot of energy today, that's O.K. Tomorrow there may be more. Deal with it tomorrow.

"Today well lived" can include illness, even death. It can include grieving, and the emotions that go along with it. As you will see in future chapters, it requires only that you acknowledge that you are more powerful than your circumstances, no matter how horrible they may seem, no matter how powerless you may feel.

After You Say Goodbye is based on the belief that "today well lived" can nurture and empower you as you make your way through the process of grieving, even when it is complicated by the fact that the person died of AIDS.

"Today well lived" is the ultimate way to take care of yourself and to honor the one whom you've lost.

So, be willing to take action. Choose your course wisely. Don't waste energy trying to change things you can't do anything about. Go for what works.

The Serenity Prayer used by Alcoholics Anonymous summarizes it beautifully.

God, grant me the serenity to accept the things I cannot change, the courage to change the things I can, and the wisdom to know the difference.
—Reinhold Niebuhr

There is no better advice to apply to the process of grieving.

depression and grief

Several years ago, a physician friend of mine referred one of his patients to me. Matt's life partner had died about six months before. Matt had dealt with all of the necessary tasks rather efficiently, and had returned to work several days after the funeral. His life went on, and he did the best he could to keep it on track.

About two months after his partner died, Matt noticed that he was becoming easily fatigued. He seemed tired all the time. Fear set in, as this was the way his partner had first discovered that he was ill.

Matt finally scheduled an appointment with his physician for a checkup and blood studies. He knew he was HIV-positive, although at the time of his last checkup, all of his blood studies had been normal.

Matt fully expected that the tests would be bad, indicating that the virus was now actively destroying his immune system. However, his physician discovered no alarming symptoms, and the blood studies came back still well within the normal range. As far as his physician could tell, Matt was in fine health.

Yet Matt knew that something was wrong, and even though he had been going to this physician for many years, and had always trusted him, he couldn't accept the findings, so he scheduled an appointment with another physician, who repeated the tests and did a thorough medical workup. Again, no abnormalities were found.

Matt returned to his original physician somewhat sheepishly, but frantic to find out what was wrong. His work was suffering. He could barely get through his day, and would go home exhausted. He was sleeping ten to twelve hours per night and still waking up fatigued. His appetite had disappeared, and he was losing weight slowly but steadily.

He was more than a little offended when his physician suggested that he consult a clinical psychologist. He wasn't crazy, and it wasn't all in his head. What good would seeing a shrink do?

He reluctantly made his first appointment with me. It didn't take long to figure out what was going on.

Matt was clinically depressed. Every one of his symptoms was a classic symptom of depression. In the absence of any medical findings that would indicate a physical disease process, the diagnosis was clear.

He greeted my suggestion with mixed feelings. He was relieved to finally have a diagnosis for what was going on with him, but he couldn't believe it was depression. He didn't feel particularly depressed; he didn't feel much of anything. What could depression have to do with all those physical symptoms?

As we talked more about depression, he began to understand that depression was more than just feeling sad. The reason he wasn't feeling much of anything was because he had been repressing a lot of his feelings. He was refusing to acknowledge his intense rage over his partner's death and some of the circumstances that surrounded it. He had never been one to express anger, much less rage. It seemed too uncool, too out of control. Consequently, he kept his rage locked away.

He was stuffing away a fair amount of guilt over the fact that he had survived and his partner hadn't. He was feeling a lot of guilt that he hadn't been as good a partner as he could have been.

He was also avoiding his fear. Matt had been so intensely involved with taking care of his partner that he had been able to avoid thinking about his fear regarding his own HIV status.

He could not express any of these emotions. To do so would have meant giving up his carefully constructed lifelong strategy of always staying in control of his feelings. He was just trying to get through each day. Unfortunately, his strategy had resulted in a serious depression. As he recognized this, he entered psychotherapy with a vengeance.

He responded well to treatment, although he had a very hard time learning that it really was OK to have all of these messy emotions. Within several months, many of his symptoms had disappeared, and the rest were much more manageable.

Matt wasn't "crazy," and his symptoms were not all in his head. His symptoms were very real and were physically debilitating to him, but they were caused by repressed emotions, not by a physical agent like a virus.

(*Please note:* If you notice symptoms of tiredness, fatigue, loss of appetite, and loss of weight, your first trip needs to be to your personal physician for a checkup. If he or she comes up empty-handed, the next logical step would be to consult a psychologist to investigate the possibility of depression.)

Contrast Matt's experience with Adam's. Adam was a client of mine who came to me following a suicide attempt. His life partner of many years had been dying for several months and was nearing the final stages of life. He was so overwhelmed with his grief over the impending loss of the man with whom he shared his life that one night in despair he tried to kill himself.

Fortunately, he survived the attempt, and his physician referred him to me for psychotherapy. He was mortified that he had attempted suicide. He knew his partner still needed him, and he was feeling immense guilt over the fact that he had nearly abandoned his partner.

Still, he could not imagine what life would be like with his partner gone. He wasn't sure that he could survive the loneliness. He was barely able to make it to work each day. His performance there was so poor that he was on probation. He was also dealing with guilt over his angry feelings that his partner was putting him through so much pain.

His partner died several weeks later, and Adam was devastated. We were able to arrange for a medical leave for him, since it was now impossible for him to get to work. He spent his days crying, not even wanting to get out of bed. If it weren't for a good friend, he wouldn't have made it to his psychotherapy sessions.

He felt helpless to make any changes or even take care of the details of everyday living. He felt hopeless as he contemplated a powerless life without his partner. He hated himself for his weakness. His guilt grew steadily.

There was nothing that he could imagine enjoying. Even food had lost its taste and required too much energy to prepare and eat.

It took a long time for him to begin to climb out of his depression. Once we started to see a little progress, the rest came more easily, though very slowly.

He was eventually able to return to work, but was still moderately depressed. It took many months for him to deal with all of the feelings that he was having. It took even longer for him to begin to socialize once again and include his friends back in his life.

Even though their experiences were vastly different, both Matt and Adam were going through a depression. They represent two extremes on the depression continuum. There are innumerable possibilities between the two extremes, and some people can swing wildly between the two extremes.

WHAT IS DEPRESSION?

We need to understand that depression and sadness are not the same thing. As we discussed in the last chapter, sadness is a single emotion. Depression, like grief, is a complex pattern of many emotions, with sadness only one of the possibilities.

Depression itself can cover a wide range of intensities. It can be so painful that suicide seems preferable. It can be a kind of numbed-out feeling where you aren't feeling much of anything. You can stay at one intensity, or somewhere in the middle, or swing back and forth between the pain and the numbness.

The emotions of anger, guilt, and fear will be there in varying intensities, sometimes very clear, at other times well disguised.

If someone you love has died, you may feel devastated, or you may just feel numb. Either reaction is completely understandable.

It is important to know that feeling devastated won't last, even though at the time it may seem as if it will never end or diminish in its intensity. It will. The horribly painful feelings will begin to subside, given time and some effort on your part.

Feeling numb can also start to fade as you feel more and more capable of facing the awful truth of what has happened. You will be able to feel again, and not fear being overwhelmed.

Unfortunately, both the devastation and the numbness can slide into a depression. That is what we want to avoid if at all possible.

Sadness and depression. This chapter on depression is not going to tell you how never to be depressed. Most of us will feel depressed from time to time in our lives.

Neither can I tell you how not to feel sad. If you have experienced the death of someone you love, you are going to feel sad. There is nothing that can or should be done to prevent that sadness.

You can live your life with sadness. *Sadness is a healthy, normal emotion that means you are in touch with your needs and in touch with reality.* While unpleasant, it can be tolerated without making a major impact on your life. You can still work, play, and relate to other people. You can feel sad and still be in charge of your life.

I wish there were a way not to hurt so much. I wish I could tell you how to keep from waking up in the middle of the night, praying that this is all a dream, that the one you love is still here, but I can't do that. It will probably take a while for that to stop happening to you, but it will stop.

I wish I could tell you how to avoid that empty, sinking feeling when you find yourself reaching for the telephone before remembering that he's not there to answer it. I can't tell you that either. I'm still reaching for the telephone.

What I can tell you is how to avoid being a victim of those feelings, and consequently how to suffer less. The willingness to suffer a little can prevent our suffering a lot. Getting in touch with your sadness will be the first step in preventing a more serious depression from setting in.

Remember, depression is more than just looking and feeling sad. In fact, like Matt, some people don't even consciously feel very sad.

Depression can be a tricky concept, as it is experienced in many different ways by different people. Some people will experience a few of the classic symptoms. Others will experience them all, and perhaps add a few of their own.

Depression will almost always result in a loss of energy and a loss of motivation. The depressed person has little or no ambition, and has a reduced drive to accomplish things. Just getting through the day can seem draining. "I just don't care anymore" is frequently expressed.

Self-esteem usually suffers in a depression. It's hard or impossible to feel very good about yourself. You don't feel worthwhile or valuable to anyone. In more serious depressions, there can even be self-hatred.

Depression can result in the loss of joy from your life. Things that used to be enjoyed no longer seem like fun. In fact, nothing looks like fun. Having a good time seems irrelevant, if not impossible.

Even though depression is about repressing one's feelings, that rarely happens perfectly. Consequently, there are usually feelings of anger, guilt, and fear present for many depressed people.

Some depressed people develop a surly, antagonistic, critical manner. They annoy and are annoyed by their friends. Social events seem like enormous intrusions.

For some, sexual energy all but disappears. There is no interest in sex, either with another person or with oneself. For others, sex can become an obsession that offers little satisfaction. This is particularly true in the case of masturbation.

Food doesn't taste good or seem necessary to some people. They will begin to lose weight. Others will begin to eat compulsively and gain huge amounts of weight.

Sleep patterns can change. Some, like Matt, will spend unusual amounts of time sleeping. Others will not want to sleep. Or even if they want to, they may have trouble getting to sleep, or they will wake frequently in the middle of the night.

Drinking or using drugs may seem necessary to get by. For some this can develop into a serious dependency problem that can also include prescription medication, especially sleeping pills and tranquilizers.

Unfortunately, sleeping pills and tranquilizers, as well as street drugs and alcohol, can cause you to become depressed much more easily, or make an existing depression worse. Remember, sleeping pills, tranquilizers, and alcohol are all depressants.

Some people will begin watching television many more hours

a day than they ordinarily would. At some extremes they can become more involved in the soap opera lives of Erica Kane and her many lovers, or with the trials of Rosie O'Neill, than they are with "real" people. Other people won't even have the energy to watch TV.

All of these symptoms can be mixed with a powerful sense of helplessness and resultant hopelessness. There is so much to be done, and no interest or energy for doing it, and no belief that you are capable of doing it anyway. Why bother?

A depressed person is truly a victim in his or her own life. Living life with depression is extremely difficult. At its worst stages, suicide begins to look like the only way out.

The more of these symptoms you are experiencing, the higher the likelihood that you are depressed. The depression can be the direct result of a tragic event in your life. If this is the case, the depression usually isn't too hard to work out of.

There is a growing number of people for whom depression has become a lifestyle in the absence of any specific event. The longer you have been depressed, the harder it will be for you to work out of—harder, but not impossible. No matter how long you have been depressed, you can still make your way out of it. All you need is the willingness to do so.

If you aren't able to do that by yourself or with a support group, please don't hesitate to seek professional help. Psychotherapy can be very effective in treating depression.

THE CAUSES OF DEPRESSION

Entire books, large books, have been written on this topic. Psychologists have debated the causes of depression for years, with no one winning viewpoint at this time.

I am going to cover the topic in a few pages, by focusing on what I think is a practical model that is most helpful for coming to grips with depression and grief.

Depression and genetics. There are some who think that depression is a genetic condition; that is, we inherit the tendency to be depressed from our parents. I suspect that this may be true, if we are talking about inherited tendencies as opposed to inherited certainties.

Yet there are many people with depressed parents and grand-parents who don't experience significant depression themselves. There also are depressed people who have no other family members with a history of depression.

While genetics may have a part to play, I doubt that genetics will ever supply a complete explanation for the phenomenon of depression. The human mind is far too complex for such a simplis-tic solution.

Depression and biochemical imbalances in the blood. There are others who feel that depression is caused by biochemical imbalances in the blood. Researchers have indeed discovered biochemical dif-ferences in the blood of depressed people. However, it is not clear if the biochemical differences *caused* the depression, or if the depres-sion *caused* the biochemical differences.

Again, there may be involvement of biochemical elements in the formation of a depression, but I don't think that such an imbal-ance, by itself, is sufficient to explain depression.

People who hold to the genetic and biochemical imbalance the-ories will frequently look to drugs for the solution. Antidepressant medication is widely used. We'll talk more about that later.

Depression is caused by a variety of emotional problems. As you can probably tell, I am not satisfied with either the genetic approach or the biochemical approach. Both may have an effect, but neither are sufficient to explain the phenomenon of depression to my satisfaction.

I believe that we create our depression. We may not mean to, but we do. Don't feel guilty about this. This realization is actually a cause for celebration. If we create our own depression, that means that we can learn to "uncreate" it.

One of the ways we create depression is by our unwillingness to experience painful emotions.

People who are depressed have generally refused to experience some of the inevitable feelings about death and about loss. These denied feelings are frequently sadness, anger, fear, and guilt.

Grieving is a painful experience, yet there is no way to avoid it when we have lost someone that we love. We will hurt. Some of us are so afraid of that hurt, or so unwilling to experience it, that we repress our painful feelings. We just won't feel them. They aren't there. We try to go through life as though nothing has happened. We may get some momentary respite, but we won't get true peace of mind, and we will become depressed.

Refusing to acknowledge your feelings may help you avoid feeling pain in the short run. In the long run, however, it won't work, because you can't release what you are not willing to express. You will truly be a victim of your unexpressed feelings.

Feelings are not to be feared. Feelings are part of the human experience. Some even say that we would lose our very humanity without them. Feelings are not a sign of weakness. Rigidly controlling our feelings is not a sign of strength. Actually, the reverse is true.

Having our feelings, experiencing them, and expressing them fully is an act of strength, and results in a powerful, dynamic life. Refusing to recognize feelings is an act of fear and causes a desperate clinging to the status quo that is tenuous at best.

Feelings can be covered up and ignored, but that won't make them go away; *they just go underground, where they can wreak havoc.*

Feelings that are experienced fully tend to subside more quickly, leaving less damage in their wake and allowing us to get on with our life. In this way, emotions flow easily, unrestricted by barriers, defenses, and feeling log-jams. People who respond to pain this way will be emotionally healthy, with a full and rich experience of the broad range of feelings that are available to human beings. These people will usually grieve without getting stuck in awful, painful emotions.

Damming up emotions takes a whole lot of energy that is then unavailable for living life fully or well. You will generally be physically exhausted and easily depressed.

Damming our emotions is much like damming a river. It is expensive to build a dam. It takes a lot of energy to stop the flow of the river. But it takes virtually no energy to just let the river flow where it will.

Stifled feelings cause you to feel numb, insulated. You may feel as if there is an emotional distance between you and the people around you. It is hard for other people to reach you through this barrier of numbness.

Some people aren't aware of how inaccessible they become to others when they are in the process of stifling their feelings. This can result in their feeling abandoned and deserted in their hour of need.

In fact, they haven't been abandoned. Their friends are just honoring their apparent need for distance. This whole scenario adds loneliness, confusion, and unhappiness that they don't need in their life.

In addition, if we refuse to experience our painful negative emotions we will not be able to experience the wonderful positive emotions. It's sort of like Mother saying that if we don't eat the spinach we don't get dessert either. If we put a lid on our feelings, we will miss out on the good ones as well as the bad ones. Life becomes a little less painful perhaps, but with little chance for enjoyment and satisfaction.

Is it always wrong to dam up your feelings? No.

There may be times when your emotions become so intense that you will want to put a damper on them. This frequently is true in the period right after a loved one's death. It is also true for those special dates or occasions following a death, such as the first holiday alone or the next anniversary.

At times like these, it is perfectly sensible to put a lid on some of your feelings. Try to do this consciously, so that you know you are doing it. Then you will be aware of the need to slowly let go of your emotions as soon as you feel strong enough to do so.

If you refuse to undam your feelings, you will eventually experience depression again.

Depression will cause you to suffer. It will prolong the grieving process, sometimes indefinitely. Depression is one of the ultimate expressions of victimhood, as you are no longer in charge of your own life. Most of your relationships will be on the victim-persecutor-rescuer triangle.

Depression is created whenever our thoughts, attitudes, and beliefs about death create such dire emotions that they must then be dammed up and unexpressed.

Depression can be caused by catastrophic thinking. This idea involves the realization that every emotion you ever had, you created. That means that you can also change it or release it. This is a powerful realization.

Unfortunately, for some people this is a difficult concept. For them, emotions come from outside themselves, descend on them, and take over their lives. They feel at the mercy of these powerful emotional forces. This looks like victimhood.

Dealing with any powerful negative emotion will be much easier if you realize that it does not originate from outside yourself. Every feeling you have ever had, you created with your thoughts, attitudes, and belief systems.

For example, some people get depressed whenever they get rejected. They think that rejection is what causes feelings of depression. Rejection does not do that. It cannot do that. It is simply an event.

Our response to rejection is completely dependent on our thoughts, attitudes, and beliefs about rejection. If you believe that rejection is a serious invalidation of who you are, that it means you are no good and have no worth to other people, your consequent emotions about being rejected will be serious, painful, and awful.

These thoughts about rejection are examples of catastrophic thinking. You experience strong negative emotions whenever you are rejected and, consequently, try to avoid the possibility of being rejected by hiding out.

If your attitude about rejection is less catastrophic, your emotional response will be less negative. If you know that rejection is just a "so what," your emotions will not be so painful.

No one escapes being rejected. It just means that the other person doesn't want to play with you right now, and you may never understand why. It probably has very little to do with you, anyway. It usually has to do with the other person's needs and their personal preferences. *Rejection is not some kind of cosmic judgment.*

If you think of rejection in this way, you may be annoyed, but not outraged. You may be disappointed, but not seriously depressed. Who has time to worry about something so inconsequential? Your actions will not be influenced by your fear of invalidation by rejection.

By changing your thoughts, attitudes, and beliefs about any event—even a death—you can gain tremendous power over your feelings. You can change your feelings from catastrophic levels to levels that are much easier to deal with, that don't hurt as much, and that won't disrupt your life as much.

This idea was first proposed by a psychologist, Dr. Albert Ellis, in his book *The New Guide to Rational Living.* Dr. Ellis is the founder of a school of psychotherapy referred to as Rational Emotive Therapy.

I should point out that many gay and lesbian psychologists feel strongly that Dr. Ellis is somewhat homophobic, based on his earlier writings. I personally find his categorical rejection of any concept of spirituality somewhat offensive as well. However, his model of the relationship between emotions and thoughts is brilliant. I have used it extensively in my work as a psychotherapist, with excellent results. I believe I have achieved the same excellent results in my own personal growth using this model.

Ellis's model can be a very useful tool in dealing with your grief. When you are in the midst of your grief, your painful feelings can seem overwhelming and insurmountable. You may not be able to imagine being strong enough to do anything about them.

Your feelings can be so strong that they seem to create your reality. They do not. If you believe that feelings create reality, you will always be a victim of your feelings and emotions. Not only do feelings not create reality, they frequently have nothing at all to do with reality.

Feelings are something that we make up. There is freedom and personal power in that statement.

Feelings are like daydreams. You can get lost in them, just as you can get lost in a good book or in a TV show.

Your power over your emotions comes from the knowledge that it is always your choice to pull out of your feelings whenever you want to, the same way you would stop a daydream, put a book down, or turn off the TV.

If you are still feeling overwhelmed by your feelings following a death, this may seem like an impossible idea. It might even seem cruel of me to suggest it.

I know it may seem impossible now, but I promise you that as time goes on, and as you continue to grieve, controlling your emotions in this way will begin to look possible, and even desirable. If you're not ready to challenge those feelings just now, don't worry about it. Whenever you are ready will be soon enough.

You will become truly powerful when you realize that you create your emotions with your thoughts, attitudes, and belief systems. Then you will be ready to take the next step.

Our feelings determine our actions.

THOUGHTS ··········> FEELINGS ··········> ACTIONS

Our thoughts create our emotions, which in turn result in action. If our thoughts are powerfully and unnecessarily negative, if they are catastrophic in nature, then our feelings will be painful and our actions will be limited or ineffective or overly stressful.

If we challenge negative thoughts and replace them with less catastrophic thoughts, our feelings will not be as dire or as painful, and our actions will be more effective and appropriate. By changing our thinking, we can change our feelings, and consequently our actions. (Remember: Your feelings won't be gone, they'll just be much more manageable.)

Please notice that I did not say replace your catastrophic thoughts with *positive* thoughts. How can you have sincere positive thoughts following the death of someone you love? I don't know how to do that.

If positive thoughts are honest, they can replace catastrophic thoughts. But if you are only pretending to have positive thoughts, you will just be playing a mind game, and it won't work.

If you are lying about your feelings, then all the positive thinking in the world will be useless at best. Instead of "positive thinking," learn to tell the truth, without catastrophizing, and then take action to do something about the situation.

If our feelings are the result of our belief systems, then our grieving is the result of our belief system about death.

If you believe that the death has taken away your reason to live, if you believe that life is no longer worth living, if you believe that you will not be able to survive this death, and if you feel that no one else will ever love you, your feelings will be catastrophic, hurtful, painful, and destructive, and could even lead to suicide.

I don't want to encourage anyone to feel guilty if their grief feels this strong. I have felt that way. I may feel that way again, but if I do, I don't want to stay stuck in that much pain. As soon as I can, I will start to challenge the beliefs that are behind the intense pain.

When we are ready, we can start to replace catastrophic beliefs with more workable, realistic ones. The more workable beliefs will create less dire emotions.

We need to realize that the death of people we love is a fact of life, something none of us can avoid, and something each of us can survive. Experiencing a death will indeed hurt, maybe a lot, but that hurt will eventually go away. Your grief will ultimately not be as severe. Life will go on, and one day you will be able to rejoin it. You will survive.

If these are your beliefs about death, your emotions will still be negative, but not catastrophic or debilitating. You can feel sad, you can feel lonely, you can miss the person, you may even be angry that they are gone. However, your life will not be destroyed by your overwhelming emotions.

Our beliefs about death and loss will determine the shape and texture of our grief. It is important to remember that our beliefs are a matter of our choice; they are not Truths, unassailable and immutable. If they don't work, they can be changed.

Emotions based on workable beliefs will be tolerable. They will result in effective action that may one day even produce some joy. I will discuss workable beliefs in further detail at the end of the chapter.

Depression and self-esteem. Self-esteem is a concept that runs through the entire process of grieving. It plays a significant role in depression.

Self-esteem is your appreciation of your own worth and value. It encompasses your willingness to be responsible for your own life, and your willingness to behave in socially responsible ways. Self-esteem determines your perception of your personal power in your own life.

(Note: This definition of self-esteem is based on the definition proposed by the California State Task Force to Promote Self-Esteem and Personal and Social Responsibility, of which I was a member.)

People with self-esteem problems generally feel that their self-esteem is dependent on external factors. They believe that self-esteem is the result of always being successful and never making a mistake. To these people, any mistake or failure will be an indictment of their worth, an occasion for guilt and self-punishment. No performance will ever be perfect enough to convince them that they deserve high self-esteem.

Others feel that self-esteem comes from the approval of other people. If people approve of them and like them, they can feel good about themselves. If people don't approve of them or like them, their self-esteem plummets, and their sense of their own value evaporates.

These people are sitting ducks for rejection or disapproval by others. No one will ever be able to approve of them or like them *enough* to convince them that they deserve self-esteem.

Still others are sure that self-esteem comes from what they have. The more successful they are, the more money they have, the bigger their house, the higher up on the hill they live, the fancier their car, and the more fancy toys or furnishings they have, the better they get to feel about themselves.

The trouble is that there will always be someone else with a bigger house and a fancier car. People who believe this way tend to feel somewhat superior to the people who have less than they have, but that doesn't keep them from feeling inferior to those who have more. They will never have enough to feel as if they deserve self-esteem.

Self-esteem that is externally based is fragile at best, causing people to become victims of mistakes, losses, rejection, and disapproval.

Depression and self-esteem have a complicated relationship. Low self-esteem can be the result of depression, as well as a significant cause of depression. As self-esteem drops, depression can become more severe. This lowers self-esteem even further, and depression consequently deepens, in a vicious downward spiral.

Happily, as self-esteem begins to improve, depression can start to lift, which can clear the way for self-esteem to improve further, in a positive upward spiral.

Low self-esteem brings with it a sense of helplessness and consequent hopelessness. If you do not like yourself, and don't feel good about your own capabilities to deal with the problems of everyday life, what hope can you have of surviving? Something like the death of a loved one can cause that sense of helplessness to mushroom.

The only self-esteem that counts, that is worth anything, that works, is self-esteem that comes from within. It is our ability to love and value ourselves unconditionally, regardless of what we have done or what we have.

This is not the same thing as arrogance or self-centeredness, which are just strategies to cover up a lack of real self-esteem. True self-esteem, by definition, involves being responsible for your behavior and being responsible for your relationships with other people.

You deserve to have self-esteem just because you exist. You don't have to earn the right. You can learn to love yourself unconditionally. You can learn that mistakes are not indictments, just opportunities to learn and grow. You can learn that rejection or disapproval by someone else has nothing to do with you and your ability to have self-esteem. You can learn that nice things and success are fun to have, but not necessary for you to feel good about yourself and your capabilities.

Many of the circumstances that surround an AIDS death will be a severe challenge to your self-esteem. If you are blaming yourself because you are gay, or because you are HIV-positive, or because you love someone who has died of AIDS, your self-esteem will suffer, if not be obliterated.

You don't have to feel any guilt for being gay, for being HIV-positive, or for loving someone who has died of AIDS. Remind yourself frequently that AIDS is a disease caused by a virus. It has nothing to do with self-esteem.

If improving your self-esteem is an issue for you, I'd encourage you to read my first book, *Pathways to Wellness,* which contains a chapter about learning to love yourself unconditionally.

Depression and fear. Fear will bring about its own contribution to depression. Fear will definitely increase our feelings of helplessness and hopelessness. The more afraid we feel, the more helpless we become in the face of the object of that fear.

We can be afraid of the future. We can be afraid of our inability to deal with necessary things. We can be afraid of AIDS and our own HIV status. We can be afraid that we don't have what it takes to deal with life.

As fear grows, depression can worsen. As fear is released, depression can lift.

We can never be totally rid of fear, especially where AIDS is concerned. I would be suspicious of anyone in a high-risk group who claimed never to be afraid. I would think there was a lot of denial going on.

The point is not to never feel fear, but to be willing to feel fear without becoming its victim. As the book title says, *Feel the Fear and Do It Anyway.*

We'll discuss fear in a lot more detail in Chapter 8.

Depression and loneliness. This is another case of a vicious dynamic interaction. Loneliness can help cause depression. Depression in turn can result in loneliness.

Loneliness is a frequent visitor where AIDS is concerned. There are far too many people who have chosen to isolate themselves rather than face the rejection that they fear from someone knowing that they are HIV-positive, or that they are with someone who has AIDS, or loved someone who has died of AIDS.

Unfortunately, there are those who will run away if they know that you are HIV-involved in any way. Frankly, that is their problem. Don't make it yours.

There are increasing numbers of people who are not afraid of being with people with AIDS, or with the people who love them. Spend your energy finding those people, not mourning the lost friendships of those who have run away.

I don't believe that human beings do well in isolation. We are basically social creatures. We need to be with one another. We need to touch one another. We need to love and be loved.

Isolating yourself will only make your grief worse. It will deprive you of needed support and nurturing.

That doesn't mean that it's wrong to want to spend time alone. Being alone is not the same thing as loneliness.

You are the only one who can do anything about your loneliness. It is up to you to reach out to other people. If you encounter rejection, don't waste time feeling bad about it, just keep reaching out.

Check where you are reaching out. Be sure the type of people you are seeking are there. A lot of us tend to look for prime rib at McDonald's, then get angry and discouraged when we don't find it.

Look in the appropriate places, and be willing to risk possible rejection as you seek out people who will want to spend time with you. They do exist. Don't let your experience with a few rejecting people cause you to turn off to the possibility of having other relationships.

If you are deeply depressed, this will be tough. It will take a lot of energy. If you don't have enough energy, find a good support group or a good therapist to help you. As you work through the following suggestions, you will find it easier to begin to reach out to other people, to have them be there for you, and for you to be there for them. Just be sure you are not finding rescuers. That will keep you a victim.

GETTING RID OF DEPRESSION

First of all, none of us can ever get rid of depression once and for all, forever. Each of us will be depressed from time to time. This section is about how to be sure that you are the one *having* the depression, not the one being controlled by the depression.

Medication as a solution. One of the ways many people use to deal with depression is with antidepressant medication. There are some people for whom that seems to work. Frankly, I haven't worked with very many of them.

A number of people have become my clients while already on antidepressant medication. They frequently hate the side effects. They feel numb and insulated from all of their feelings and don't like that, either.

Some, strangely, have continued taking the medication, even though they don't think it does much good. They take it so the depression doesn't get worse, I guess.

If you are on antidepressant medication and it is working for you, I am not suggesting that you stop taking it. That is a decision that you should make only in consultation with your physician, hopefully a psychiatrist.

In fact, I don't think anyone should take psychiatric medication unless he or she is consulting with a psychiatrist. Psychiatric medication is a very inexact science. There is no way for anyone to know just exactly how a person will respond to any specific dosage of any medication. We may know how most people are supposed to respond, but there is no guarantee that everyone will respond the same way.

If you are taking psychiatric medication, a psychiatrist should be monitoring your use of that medication, discussing its effects with you, and adjusting the dosage as necessary. If you are not doing this, you may be taking more than you need to, or you may not be taking enough.

It's not uncommon to see people on such small doses that the actual effect is minimal. Taking an aspirin would produce about the same effect. If people improve on this level of medication, it is due to the placebo effect.

Others have been on the medication for so long that its current effect may only be minimal. If that works for them, why should it be a problem? I think the issue is one of personal power.

If someone is responding to a placebo, or a too-small dose of medication, he or she will still credit the medication for any improvement. I would much rather that people realize they are the ones who should take the credit, not the medication. If people are no longer depressed, it should be because of something that *they* have changed, something that *they* are doing, not the result of a pill they are taking.

If taking medication following the death of someone you love is absolutely necessary for you to get your job done, then by all means take it. But take it only as long as you absolutely need it. Don't come to rely on it as a permanent crutch.

Also, don't rely on the medication to do the job all by itself. Medication is not magic. You'll get through the whole process much more quickly if you are helping by learning how to deal more effectively with your grief.

I also believe that if you are on psychiatric medication, you should also be involved in psychotherapy. You need to be dealing with the cause of your depression, not just covering up the symptoms. Your goal should be to get off the medication as soon as possible, if that is feasible for you.

If you are taking psychiatric medication, ask yourself the following questions:

"Do I ever feel really great, really joyful?"

"What is the impact on my day-to-day functioning? Am I as productive and as energetic as I could be? Am I as clear mentally?

"Is there something I could do that might get at the root of the problem without just covering it up with drugs?"

After answering these questions, I would recommend that you discuss the subject with your therapist. If your medication or your therapy isn't getting you the results you want, you should tell your therapist. If you are frustrated, your therapist may be frustrated too and be waiting for you to bring it up.

If you still don't get the results you want, you may need to think about changing therapists. You deserve to be getting results.

Dealing with depression by being willing to experience your painful emotions. Unfortunately, grieving well means that we must be willing to experience pain. Most medical experts who treat chronic physical pain will tell you that the more you resist the pain, the more it will control your life. Pain clinics all over the country are based on the principle that you can feel pain and still get the job of living life done. Somehow, the pain assumes less awesome proportions, or even disappears, when you are willing to experience it and get on with life anyway.

The same is true for emotional pain. It will diminish, if not disappear, whenever we are willing to fully experience it and express it.

You need to experience your feelings, fully and completely, no matter how uncomfortable or painful that might be. If the feelings come back, just be willing to experience them again, challenge them again, and let go of them again. As you continue to do that, they will come back less frequently, with less intensity, and with a less disruptive effect on your life.

This process is about learning how to allow your feelings to flow through you without damming them up. Damming them up will always ensure that you are stuck with them and that you will continue to be influenced by them.

You must begin telling yourself the whole truth about how you are feeling. This is especially true for any socially unacceptable feelings that you may be having, such as being very angry at the one who has died. If you are willing to express even those socially unacceptable feelings in ways that are not self-defeating or damaging to others, your depression will start to lift.

Chapters 6 through 8 will go into very practical detail about how to express the different feelings that come up as the result of our experience of a death of someone we love. Once you express them, you can learn how to challenge them and keep from creating them again.

Dealing with depression by changing your thinking. If depression is created by our unwillingness to experience certain painful feelings, then the solution is to learn to change the feelings, not repress them. We can change our feelings whenever we are willing to challenge the thoughts, attitudes, and beliefs that created them in the first place.

Dr. Albert Ellis uses the following model:

A x B = C

A is the actual event,

B is the belief system about the event, and

C is the consequent emotion.

It is the actual event (a death), *multiplied* by our belief system about death (and this death in particular), that produces our emotions.

If our beliefs are reasonable and reality based, then the emotion that is produced will likely not be intolerable, overwhelming, and catastrophic.

If our beliefs are dire and catastrophic, so will be the emotion.

Ellis's school of Rational Emotive Therapy teaches that we can change our feelings by challenging the unworkable beliefs that we have about the events in our lives. In my experience, this always produces good results.

This does not mean that we won't experience emotions at all. That isn't healthy or possible. It does mean that with practice and diligence we can continually challenge our unworkable beliefs, and, by so doing, we can avoid becoming a victim of catastrophic emotions that can ruin our lives and our health.

If you are suffering from low self-esteem, I guarantee that this view of yourself is based on unworkable beliefs such as caring too much about what others think, or needing to be perfect all the time. These aren't Truths, they are merely learned beliefs that you can unlearn, let go of, and replace with more workable thoughts.

Your fear will also be subject to your unworkable beliefs. One such belief might be that worrying about your HIV status makes sense. Worrying will not help your HIV status; in fact, it could worsen it with the stress such worrying causes.

Fear is a major stressor that is harmful to both your health and your quality of life. Be willing to confront the beliefs that create your fear.

Where grief is concerned, a lot of people suffer extensively from the unworkable belief that they can't survive their loss. In many cases, they have been saying that for many months, even years. Through all of those months, their lives have been devastated by their grief and their depression.

The belief that they won't survive is a chief culprit. They even have evidence of the unworkability of that belief. They have, in fact, survived. Their belief that they wouldn't survive didn't keep them from surviving, but it did destroy the quality of their life.

I know that it may really seem as if you can't survive. But you must know that you can, and that you will, especially if you are willing to replace your unworkable beliefs with more workable ones that will lead to hope and a return to a full life.

If all you can do right now is just hang on, then do that. The time will come when you will feel ready to move on. *After You Say Goodbye* will help you hang on, and then you can move on whenever you are ready.

No matter how bad it may seem, you always have a choice about the thoughts and the feelings that you want to nurture. You always have a choice about the actions you will take based on your feelings. Your choice will give you the power to resist becoming a victim of your grief. Your choice will help you avoid becoming a victim of your depression.

regaining emotional power

In the last chapter we looked at the ways to work out of depression. There are two strategies for doing so. The first is learning to experience all of our feelings fully and completely. The second is learning to change our catastrophic thinking, which creates the feelings in the first place, and makes them so powerfully painful that they must be repressed.

One of the key elements of my book *Pathways to Wellness* was the Victim-ectomy Formula. This formula is about how not to be a victim of your emotions. It was designed to help people regain their power over their feelings. This formula works for depression as well as any other emotion that may be troubling you, even those that are grief based.

We'll cover the basic idea here and expand on it in the chapters that follow, which deal specifically with anger, guilt, and fear.

There are five steps to the Victim-ectomy Formula:

1. Acknowledge how you are feeling.
2. Experience and express the emotion.
3. Clean it up.
4. Learn from your experience.
5. Let it go and get on with life.

STEP 1:
ACKNOWLEDGE HOW YOU ARE FEELING

Step 1 is to simply acknowledge how you are feeling. This step requires making a simple statement about the emotions that you are experiencing: "I am feeling sad." "I am furious." "I am terrified."

That's all there is to Step 1. You don't have to do any more at this step. Most of us will have no trouble here. Unfortunately, some people have learned that the best way to deal with unpleasant feelings is to not even be aware of them.

If this is your strategy for dealing with painful feelings, just acknowledging the feeling will be a difficult task. You will be full of reasons why it isn't necessary for you to surface your emotions. "What good will that do?" "It'll just make me feel worse than I already do." "I don't know how to feel anger." "People will think I'm nuts."

Regardless of your beliefs about the necessity for keeping your emotions dammed up, it is essential that you challenge those beliefs, and undam your feelings. If you don't, you will suffer more in the long run.

If refusing to acknowledge our feelings is so damaging, and expressing our feelings is so liberating and healthy, then why does anyone bother to stifle his or her feelings? This is one of the most frequent problems I encounter as a psychotherapist.

There are lots of reasons for this stifling. Most of them aren't very good ones. At best, they can only promise less discomfort for the moment, while they put off what is inevitable. Those feelings will have to be experienced at some time. The longer you wait to do it, the more you will suffer in the meantime.

Reasons for not acknowledging our feelings.
A. *We were trained to do so as we were growing up.* Most feeling-stiflers learned this behavior as they were growing up. Their parents didn't openly express emotions, so they just never learned how. Some people were punished for expressing their feelings, particularly anger or rage, so they learned to keep them hidden.

If this is so for you, you need to learn that you can now do things differently. You are an adult, and able to determine what works best for you. *You are not stuck with your historical way of expressing, or not expressing, your feelings.*

B. *We fear that our feelings may overwhelm us with their intensity.* Where grief is concerned this can be a major fear. The magnitude of our loss can look potentially devastating if we stop and think about it.

As a result, some of us keep very busy. We keep on the move, making sure our lives are full and cluttered. We'll do anything to avoid having those few minutes of quiet time when our feelings might find the crack to slip through into our consciousness.

Others of us just clamp down on the feelings, and refuse to recognize that they are even there. We also get very depressed in the process.

We're afraid that if we start crying we may never stop, that if we start to experience the depth of our feelings we will be crushed beneath them.

I know it may look like that, because I used to be one of the all-time-great feeling-stiflers. I know how sensible it seems to just not feel anything that hurts so much. I also know how self-defeating it was for me to try to deny that hurt.

Pain that is denied will never go away. If we deny it, we are stuck with it.

If you are terrified of being overwhelmed by your feelings, you need to seek professional help as soon as possible. Let someone else be with you as you work through that fear, and then through your grief.

In most major cities, there are now support groups for people who are grieving AIDS deaths. They can be enriching and wonderfully comforting, as long as they encourage you to acknowledge and express your feelings and then move on. If they only help you stay stuck in your denial, or stuck in your feelings, run screaming for the woods. Look for another group, or start your own.

C. *We don't think our feelings are socially acceptable, because we don't want to appear weak or crazy, or because we think people won't like us if we are too open.* This is especially true for feelings of rage or terror. Strangely enough, guilt is about the only emotion that seems socially acceptable, and, of all the emotions, guilt is the most useless and by far the most dangerous.

Some men buy the strong, silent John Wayne image of stability or masculinity. Strong men don't cry, and all that other bull. According to this myth, it is OK for men to be angry, as long as they keep it under control, unless of course someone really asks for it.

While women still generally have more societal permission to express their feelings, there are limitations put on that freedom. It's OK for a woman to cry, but it's not nearly as OK for her to express her anger or rage. If she does that she's frequently called a bitch.

We also stifle our feelings because we don't want to appear weak or crazy. We don't want people to be angry back at us, or to think we are cowards.

As we have already discussed, the expression of feelings is a result of honesty and courage, not weakness and fear. The refusal to experience feelings is truly coming from weakness and fear.

We stifle our feelings because we think people won't like us if we are too open about our feelings. If someone would withdraw his or her affection from you because you are being emotional and telling the truth about how you are feeling, I would seriously question the value of that relationship. A true friend will encourage you to tell the truth about your feelings, even if it makes him or her uncomfortable.

This doesn't mean that people who want to help you stifle your feelings are bad people. It probably means that they have trouble with their own, and that they have their own unworkable beliefs about feelings. Don't let their problems become yours.

Feelings must be acknowledged whether they are socially acceptable or not. We need to find those people who are wise and strong enough to allow us to tell the truth about how we are feeling.

As you will see later as we continue with the discussion of the Victim-ectomy Formula, the first stages of our expression of our feelings is best done in private. You don't have to worry about what anyone else would think or do. You can tell the truth without fearing reprisal. Then at the next step you can decide what effective action you want to take.

D. *We believe that if we keep our feelings hidden, maybe they will just go away.* This is a variation of the belief that time heals all wounds.

Actually, time does not heal all wounds, especially emotional ones. In time the pain can fade for some people, but it can stay fresh and painful for others. Time alone won't help us grieve well if we are refusing to experience our feelings.

Refusing to acknowledge your feelings will drag out the time it will take you to get over your loss and to complete your grief. In that time you'll also be minimizing your opportunity to experience joy, vitality, and passion in your life. Those emotions are just not compatible with the repression of other, less enjoyable feelings.

E. *We believe that it won't do any good to express our feelings.* "But what good will it do to acknowledge my feelings?" If it does nothing else, it will at least mean that you aren't carrying those feelings around with you. What is more important, it sets you up for the next step, for regaining power over your feelings. You can't let go of something you aren't willing to admit exists.

F. *We believe that acknowledging our feelings will just make us feel worse.* It's true that you may feel worse as you start to allow your feelings to surface. Unfortunately, there is no way around that. But it is necessary, and it will be worth it.

The pain won't last if you're willing to go on to the following steps. The result will be that you have experienced pain in the process of ridding yourself of it. This is not unlike going through the discomfort of having a tooth pulled in order to be rid of the day-to-day grinding toothache.

G. *The "Enlightenment Syndrome" folks stifle their feelings because they think negative feelings are not enlightened.* There is one last group of feeling-stiflers that I would like to address. I call this group "the Enlightenment Syndrome" folks.

People who fit into this group generally are involved in various New Age, Science of Mind, or other metaphysical philosophies. They read *The Course in Miracles* or listen to Louise Hay tapes, or take consciousness-raising workshops.

And they *misunderstand* the lessons about emotions.

They think that negative emotions are unenlightened and always unacceptable, to be avoided at all costs. Unfortunately, this usually leads to the repression of emotions, and that means that personal integrity suffers. They may be thinking good, positive thoughts, but unfortunately they are not telling the whole truth.

The Course in Miracles does not encourage you to feel guilty about having any emotion, even anger. It does not encourage you to lie about it. It *does* encourage you to deal with it. Louise Hay also states clearly that if you are angry, you must express that anger before you can go farther. Just don't get stuck in it.

Unfortunately, there are still too many people who misunderstand the need for integrity in the expression of feelings. They believe that acknowledging any negative emotion will draw more of that emotion to them. They think that if they are afraid of AIDS and say so, it will attract AIDS to them. Or that if they are angry, they are guilty of judging another person, and that is not acceptable.

These people are acting on the understanding that New Age philosophy is based only on the principles of love and forgiveness, and that anything else is inappropriate.

If you are a part of this group, I urge you to consider that, along with love and forgiveness, truth is also a cornerstone of New Age thought. If you are lying about the way you are feeling in an attempt to appear enlightened, you will suffer, your effort won't work, and you won't grieve well.

I am in total agreement that holding onto anger toward another person will have a negative impact on your life. I agree that forgiveness is a vastly liberating experience. However, if you are angry at someone, it won't work to try to deny it, or to keep that feeling hidden behind a loving facade. That person will sense that you are lying and stop trusting you. You will be stuck with the lie.

There is a significant difference between the open acknowledgment of a negative emotion and wallowing in that emotion. Acknowledging your anger does not damage you or the other person. Acknowledging that you are afraid of AIDS does not attract AIDS to you.

Grieving well means telling the truth, the whole truth, and nothing but the truth, in an attitude of gentle respect and love. This is especially true where your feelings are concerned. It means acknowledging the feelings that you have, even if they seem "wrong," unpleasant, irrational, or inappropriate.

STEP 2:
EXPERIENCE AND EXPRESS
THE EMOTION

Step 2 comes after the acknowledgment of your feelings. In this step, you must get the feeling out into the open by experiencing and expressing it. That means having a complete experience of the emotion by expressing it out loud. If you have stated that you are angry, it's now time to feel the anger, to express it fully and sincerely.

This is not a dainty, thoughtful step. It is for the loud expression, the raw regurgitation of feelings. It doesn't matter if your feelings are socially acceptable or not, whether they make sense or not, or whether they are comfortable or not.

In fact, if you're dealing with a death your feelings most likely aren't socially acceptable, sensible, or comfortable. But they still must be experienced and expressed in a way that is not self-defeating or self-destructive, or carelessly damaging to another person.

It's vital to know that just thinking about your feelings will not be enough. *You've got to speak or write them.*

You can think a whole lot faster than you can talk, or write. At the thought level it is difficult if not impossible to identify the unworkable beliefs that are creating a painful feeling.

At the thought level, all of your problems look of equal, dire value. The very real ones will be mixed up with inconsequential ones. The ones you can actually do something about will get mixed up with ones that you cannot do anything about. At the thought level it is much easier to become overwhelmed with the problems that confront you.

As you slow down your thought processes, you will have a much easier time sorting out your problems. You will be able to pick out the ones that need your attention now, and ignore those that you can't do anything about right now.

You will also have a much better chance of discovering the unworkable beliefs that are creating the feeling. Step 3, "Clean it up," will be much easier. You can't clean up an emotion that you haven't experienced and expressed!

Your success in dealing with your grief will demand that you do not skip this step even though it may not be your "style." The avoidance of this step can begin the slide into depression.

The complete expression of our feelings is wonderfully cleansing and healing. It may be uncomfortable while we are actually doing it, but we will feel much better once we've done it.

Unfortunately, there is a lot of resistance to this step also.

Reasons for not wanting to express our feelings. Reasons for not wanting to express our feelings are similar to the reasons for not wanting to acknowledge our feelings in Step 1.

A. *We were trained to fear the expression of our feelings as we were growing up.* This can be selective. Some families can tolerate sadness, but not anger. Other families won't tolerate any kind of emotional display, as in "Don't you cry, or I'll really give you something to cry about." Unfortunately, most families *can* tolerate guilt.

Some of us learn to not express emotions because we were exposed to people expressing violent emotions all during our childhood, and we decided never to do that ourselves. Those of us brought up in rage-filled homes frequently have the hardest time expressing anger. We never want to act like that. (There are others who were brought up in rage-filled homes who will choose to express their anger in violent ways, just as they saw it done at home.)

The good news is that you are not stuck with the way you learned to express or not express your feelings. You can change that anytime you want to.

B. *We fear the expression of our feelings may overwhelm us with their intensity.* You may have started to cry and wonder if you will ever be able to stop. You may be afraid that if you start to let go of your anger, you will seriously hurt someone, maybe yourself.

You *will* stop crying, and you won't destroy anything that you don't want to. In fact, if you do Steps 1 and 2 in private, you won't have to worry about that. You will be in control of your anger.

If you try to skip experiencing and expressing your anger, it will be lying in wait for the right cue to burst out onto the scene at the most inopportune times. And it will frequently then be much worse than it would have been if you had expressed it right away.

If you are worried about being overwhelmed by your emotions, you may want to get professional assistance to help you learn how to do it safely.

C. *Expressing our feelings out loud may not be socially acceptable, and we're afraid that we will look weak or crazy and that people won't like us.* If the feelings you express are socially acceptable, you probably aren't expressing all that you need to.

Some people are afraid to express their feelings because they think it will make them look weak or crazy. Like acknowledging your feelings, expressing your feelings, appropriately, will be coming from strength, not weakness or craziness. Your refusal to express your feelings will make you pay a heavy price for your sane appearance.

We may be afraid that if we express our feelings, other people won't like us. Unfortunately, this will be true for some people. There are a lot of people who won't understand your need to express your feelings, particularly anger. That's because they likely have their own problems with anger, and your anger will make them uncomfortably aware of theirs.

Others will be uncomfortable with your expressing your sadness because they are trying to suppress theirs, and yours will make that much more difficult. They won't see your need to release the emotion. They will only see their need to avoid it. They don't mean to be mean, but they aren't being at all helpful.

You'll get a lot of support for "keeping a stiff upper lip" (whatever that means). "Don't cry, it'll be OK." (What will be OK, and when, and what am I supposed to do in the meantime?) "Calm down, you're just upsetting yourself." (I've never understood this one. Of course I'm upsetting myself. I am upset, you nitwit.) And, "How can you be angry at someone you love? That's disrespectful." (Ignorant bullshit, in the very kindest assessment.)

You can always be sure that a lot of people will enthusiastically support your lack of emotional expression. We live in an emotionally constipated society. But we're cool, don't you know?

Let your emotions out in private, and you won't have to worry about whether or not the emotions you are expressing are socially acceptable, or whether someone will think you are weak or crazy, or won't like you.

In fact, you should expect that the emotions you need to express are probably going to be socially unacceptable, and give yourself permission to have them anyway. You are, after all, only human, and you deserve to have some strong feelings when bad things happen.

D. *We believe that if we don't express our feelings, maybe they will just go away.* Unexpressed feelings will never go away. They will be expressed, if not directly, then indirectly.

Some of us will experience unexpressed feelings in our bodies, in the form of headaches or stomach problems. What we really need to do is express our anger, not create a headache.

Some of us can experience our feelings, but we tend to displace them onto a less fearful object, such as traffic or slow checkout clerks in the grocery store, the dog, or even a friend. This doesn't make a lot of sense, but it may feel safer than telling the truth about our "crazy feelings" following the death of someone we love.

For example, I had two clients who didn't know how to get in touch with and release their anger over the deaths of their loved ones. They displaced their feelings following the deaths and became the commuters from hell. Their friends claimed that driving with them was like driving with Rambo.

They eventually saw that they were releasing the anger that they felt over the deaths whenever they got behind the wheels of their cars. It's better than not having the anger come out anywhere, but it won't help them grieve well, and it creates secondary danger when they complicate their lives with freeway temper tantrums and resultant mishaps.

The point is, express your feelings safely and they will be ready to be let go of.

E. *We think that it won't do any good to express our feelings.* I often hear, "Why bother? It won't bring him back. It won't make me feel any better."

No, it won't bring him back, but it will help you feel better. You may be uncomfortable during the expression, but you will feel much better afterward. Remember the toothache?

You can never clear up what you are unwilling to express. This means just telling the truth about how you are feeling.

F. *We believe that expressing our feelings will just make us feel worse.* Expressing your feelings *will* probably make you feel worse, for the short time that you are expressing them. However, that will fade. Any emotion that you experience fully and completely will start to fade almost immediately, if you let it. It will open the way for you to start feeling better.

G. *The "Enlightenment Syndrome" folks think that expressing their feelings could be unloving or judgmental, or could attract more of the feeling to themselves.*

The "Enlightenment Syndrome" folks have a real tough time with this one. Acknowledging the emotion was hard enough. Now they actually have to feel it?

Yes. Dealing with emotions is all about integrity. If the feeling is there, you must express it truthfully. Remember, you're doing this in private. No one is going to be damaged. You're just emptying yourself out.

How can you forgive what you've not expressed in the first place? Many people try, and wonder why it doesn't work as they discover that they are still harboring ill will toward the other person.

Telling the truth about your feelings is very enlightened and enlightening. Don't skip this step.

Your feelings will probably not surface in neat, well-organized little stages. They will come up in interesting combinations. They will surface repetitively, frequently out of sequence, sometimes randomly, sometimes in response to specific events or circumstances in the environment.

Unpleasant feelings may reoccur months or even years after the death. Even though we thought we were through the grieving process, we find ourselves becoming saddened or angry all over again. This is not pathological or abnormal. It is simply part of the grieving process. It's messy, it's complicated, it's unpleasant, and it's unavoidable.

Each time the feelings reoccur, and they most likely will reoccur, they must be experienced again and then confronted again and then let go of again. It doesn't have to take more than a few minutes. It only requires persistence and a willingness to keep doing it as often as you need to.

Doing this once or even a dozen times may not be enough, so be patient and keep at it. It will get easier as you feel more and more powerful in relation to your feelings. It will also get easier if you understand what is going to happen at the clean-it-up step, Step 3.

Getting stuck in your feelings. There is another group of people who have trouble with Step 2. They have no trouble expressing their feelings. Their problem is that they are stuck in their feelings. They *can't stop* expressing their feelings.

You may be stuck in anger and find yourself becoming angry, easily, in lots of different situations, some justified and others not. You'll notice that you are getting angry at things that didn't used to make you angry. You'll notice that your anger is frequently all out of proportion to the incident that you are angry about.

You may be walking or driving around entertaining various "grudge fantasies" about how you would like to get even with someone you feel has wronged you, such as some bigot at work, or a class-act homophobic bigot such as Jesse Helms or Lou Sheldon.

Don't feel guilty if you fall into this category. There is too much agreement in the world that the strong and silent types — the feeling-stiflers — are the ones to be admired and emulated.

In fact, your choice is generally the healthier choice. Your feelings are more accessible and therefore more available for changing. It's just that there are so many of them, and they last so long and they can be so destructive. You don't want to stay stuck in them.

You can be stuck in just about any feeling that it is possible to have. Anger and fear are probably the most common to get stuck in, but guilt is also widespread.

How can you know if you are just telling the truth about how you are feeling — miserable — or if you are wallowing in your feelings? This is a tricky question, and there is no foolproof way to know the answer. Sometimes, it just comes down to trial and error.

Frankly, if you're still going at it after fifteen or twenty minutes, I suspect you may be stuck. Express it one last time and get on with Step 3. You will then be able to discover what you are doing that keeps recreating the feelings.

When in doubt, express your feelings. Whenever possible, express them thoughtfully so that you don't create a bigger mess to clean up. For example, it doesn't usually work to express your rage to your boss. He or she may understand, but he or she may not, and you will be looking for a job at a time when you aren't really in the best shape to do that.

Always remember that you are more powerful than your emotions, because you are the one who has created every emotion you have ever had, with your thoughts, attitudes, and belief systems. Not only did you create them in the first place but you always have a lot of choice about when and where to express them. It's also your choice to begin to tell yourself when it is time to get over them.

How long is too long to be expressing your strong negative emotions following the death of someone you love?

That's virtually impossible to determine. There are so many individual factors involved that a simple rule of thumb wouldn't be too useful. Individual differences and individual needs will determine your timetable for grieving.

Some people need to go into a total seclusion for several weeks or longer, to allow themselves to be inundated with emotion. When they've cried themselves out they will emerge and rejoin the flow of life. If this works for you, and if you can afford the time, go for it.

I belong to another group. Being secluded and isolated and inundated with emotion doesn't feel good to me. I need to get back to work as soon as possible. After the first few days, I need to release my grief in short bursts, and then get on with business.

You are the only one who can determine if you are stuck in your emotions. The only way to do that is to see how much of your life is being disrupted by your expression of emotion, and then ask yourself if you are willing to have it be that way.

Is your expression of emotion keeping love and support away from you? I know several people who are so angry so much of the time, that their support group has run screaming into the woods. If this has happened to you, you need to decide: Is expressing your anger more important than having your friends around?

Are your constant needs for support and "rescuing" driving your friends screaming into the same woods? Remember, even the best rescuers get tired eventually, and then they leave or turn into persecutors. Again, you have a choice.

If you can't seem to get unstuck, you probably need to seek professional assistance. Be cautious about whatever support group or therapist you choose. Either should be able to support your telling the truth about your feelings, and then help you to get beyond them.

If it's been more than six months after the death and you still feel totally stuck in your emotions and your life is being disrupted, you would probably be doing yourself a favor by seeking professional assistance.

Grief is a difficult thing to go through, but it doesn't have to control your whole life. Be willing to challenge your victimhood.

Remember, grief is a process, not a finished product. You'll move in and out of it. You'll think you're through it, and then it will reappear again. Months later, you may still need to have a temper tantrum, even though you thought you were through with that kind of thing.

Finally, please don't get stuck with your grief out of some kind of idea that by doing so you are honoring the one who has died. It's an unfortunate and erroneous idea that the extent of our grief reflects the extent to which we loved the person who has died.

I suspect this goes back to the days when it was socially correct to mourn for at least a year, wearing black and eschewing fun of any kind, out of respect for the one who had died. This was a custom, but it isn't Truth. I think that we have lots of other options.

If I were to die, the last thing I would want my partner John to do would be to trash his life out of some kind of respect for my death. I would want him to have as full and rich a life as possible, as quickly as he was ready to do that.

Many people I talk with seem to feel that if the death hasn't destroyed their life, then they must not have loved the one who has died. Having fun and enjoying life looks and feels like a betrayal. It is not! The way to truly honor a loved one who has died is to live life fully and compassionately, to live today well.

Above all else, don't assume that the way you are feeling right now will be the way you will feel tomorrow, or next week, or next month, or certainly next year. Many of us can be so immersed in an emotion that we're certain that we will always feel that way. We can't imagine feeling any other way. But we *will* feel differently eventually, maybe even sooner than later.

No matter how intense your pain is, it will pass. It probably will come back, and then pass again, and on and on. It would be nice if we could be done with it and get it over with once and for all, but it doesn't work that way.

Grieving well means being willing to experience the pain, without getting stuck in it, while we continue with life. This takes us to the next step.

STEP 3:
CLEAN IT UP

Step 3 is about cleaning up your situation. Once you have told the truth about how you are feeling, you are ready to get on with the process by springing into action. Here is where you do whatever is necessary to deal with your situation.

Acknowledge that there's nothing more you can do. *Clean it up* can mean that you simply recognize that there is nothing further you can do about the problem. What's done is done. There is no way to fix things, no matter how badly you may want to. You just have to be willing to get over it and move on. If that looks tough to do, you probably have more experiencing and expressing to do.

Take action to fix what can be fixed. *Clean it up* can also mean taking some kind of action to deal with whatever is bothering you. In some situations that can mean calling an attorney to protect yourself. More frequently it will mean calling another person to discuss your differences.

You've already dumped out your anger, and now you want to do something to heal the relationship. The other person will likely respond well to your saying, "What you did made me really angry, but I value our friendship too much to let it get in our way. What can we do to fix this?"

You should realize that the other person may not have had the chance to express his or her feelings yet. You may need to give the other person that opportunity without getting defensive and going on the counterattack. After the other person has spoken up, the two of you can begin to negotiate.

Forgiveness. *Clean it up* usually requires forgiveness. You may have to forgive other people, and, most probably, you will need to forgive yourself.

Forgiveness is not about condoning someone's bad behavior, or approving of it, or saying that it was OK that someone hurt you. It simply means giving up resentment and your desire to punish the other person.

You will be imprisoned by your unwillingness to forgive. You will be liberated by your willingness to forgive.

Challenge your unworkable beliefs. To deal completely with your emotions, you will need to examine your feelings and then discover the unworkable beliefs that produced them. Then you will be in a position to challenge them and replace them. Remember that your thoughts create your feelings, and your feelings determine your actions.

Any changes that we try to make at the action level will be hard. It is always easier to challenge the feelings that produce the action, and far easier to challenge the thoughts that are behind the feelings.

When I was a boy growing up in Kansas, one of the banes of my existence was dandelions. These are pretty little plants that grow flat against the ground and send up long stems with yellow flowers. One or two in a yard would look nice. A yard that has been taken over by dandelions is not nice. They seed easily and spread vigorously, and can kill a lawn. It was my job to see that they didn't do that.

Now, you can control dandelions by just going out and picking off the flowers. You'd have to do it several times a day, day after day throughout the entire summer. Miss a day, and those little devils will seed and you'll have thousands more plants starting. This is what trying to change your actions at the action level is like: continually picking off dandelion flowers, being constantly vigilant, and probably being doomed to ultimate failure.

The only effective and ecologically sound way to get rid of dandelions is to dig them up by the roots—which seem to reach to the other side of the planet. Once that is done, you can relax, and wait for the next batch of seeds to blow over from the neighbor's yard.

Dealing with your problem behavior at the root by challenging the feelings and the thoughts that produced them is like digging up dandelions. It will truly rid you of unwanted behaviors.

If you can identify your unworkable beliefs and then repeatedly challenge them, you will notice a significant decrease in unpleasant emotions.

The following list of unworkable beliefs is taken from *Pathways to Wellness:*

1. When you make a mistake, you should feel guilty.
2. It's terrible if someone doesn't love you, or rejects you.
3. If you're smart enough, and "good" enough, you can avoid pain and disappointment.
4. You should be able to have relationships without conflict.
5. Intimacy is dangerous and will result in pain, eventually.
6. If you hide your anger, it will go away.
7. It makes sense to blame another person for your feelings.
8. Your best is never good enough.
9. You mustn't tell the truth if it hurts someone's feelings.
10. If someone does something bad, they must be punished.
11. If you forgive someone, you are the loser and they get off scot-free.
12. Your emotions are more powerful than you are.
13. If you don't worry constantly, something bad will happen to you. Worry protects you from nasty surprises.
14. If you feel fear you should stop what you're doing.
15. Love must be earned and deserved, and is therefore conditional.
16. Blaming other people for your problems keeps you safer.
17. People can't really change themselves in any significant way.
18. Loneliness is preferable to vulnerability.
19. Change is threatening and to be avoided.
20. You should hate someone who has wronged you, or who is different from you.
21. If you get sick, only a doctor can cure you.
22. While being gay may not be such a bad thing, it isn't as good as being a heterosexual.
23. Being gay (or black, female, Latino, physically challenged, or whatever) automatically makes you a second-class citizen.

You can add the following unworkable grief-based beliefs to the above list, and probably come up with a number of your own as well:

· I can't survive without him or her.
· Life isn't worth living without him or her.
· I'll never be happy again.
· I'll never love again.
· Love only happens once in a lifetime.
· No one will ever love me the way he or she did.
· You can't find a new lover in the time of AIDS.
· If I am HIV-positive, no one will want me.
· Relationships can't last, so why bother?

These beliefs are seductive. To a lot of us, they look very sensible and rational. Yet each of them can be challenged and replaced with a more workable belief, by following these steps:

1. Review the above lists of unworkable beliefs.
2. Select those beliefs that you thought were true, and that now cause you trouble.
3. Examine their impact on your life. Do you like that impact? Do you want to keep getting this result or find a better one?
4. Challenge each unworkable belief. Call it the lie that it is.
5. Replace it with a more workable one.

Let's try an example: "When you make a mistake you should feel guilty."

This belief creates guilt and probably some depression. It creates fear as you try to do new things, worrying that you might fail or make a mistake. Doing new things gets to be very stressful.

Do you want to keep getting this result? Hopefully not.

How can you challenge this belief? Say out loud, or write down if you have to: *Mistakes are never an occasion for guilt.* Mistakes are a normal occurrence. You have never learned to do anything without making a mistake; in fact, making mistakes is a powerful way to learn.

The only thing you have to do when you make a mistake is clean up the mess, fix it, do something about it, and above all, learn from the experience. Do the very best you can, and if you make a mistake, forgive yourself, see what you can learn, and then get on with it.

Be willing to remind yourself of your new belief as frequently as you can. After all, how many times have you reminded yourself that a mistake is an occasion for guilt?

Another belief is "Life isn't worth living without him or her." Obviously, this is a tougher one to challenge. If you have just lost someone you love very much, you may indeed feel this way, quite sincerely.

I know that it feels that way, *right now.* Challenge the idea that it will *always* feel that way. It won't. It will get better, especially if you are challenging your other unworkable beliefs regularly. Let tomorrow bring what it will. Your experience today is only that, your experience today.

It will be possible, eventually, to enjoy life once again. If that doesn't seem possible right now, don't worry about it. Your outlook will change as time goes along.

Also, watch for the "self-talk" that comes from these unworkable beliefs. If you're constantly saying, "I'll never be happy again," you can make that come true.

Instead, remind yourself to say, "I know that right now it feels like I'll never be happy, but I'm going to wait and see if I feel the same way next week, or next month, or next year. I'm not going to make today worse by assuming that tomorrow will be just more of the same."

This technique will work for any emotion and the belief system that causes it. If you have trouble challenging any particular belief, ask for help, and see if someone else can be more objective about it. Don't be surprised if someone else thinks that the unworkable belief is true. We have all learned these unfortunate lessons well, because they are taught pervasively in our society. That doesn't mean they can't be changed.

Finally, don't expect perfect or instant results. You've probably held on to your unworkable beliefs for a long time. They won't just vanish because you want them to. Be prepared to challenge them each time they come up. Be willing to do it over and over again. You will get results.

Your belief system about death will determine the emotions that you experience and how long they last, and how your behavior is affected. Your belief system about death will determine how your grieving process goes.

STEP 4:
LEARN FROM YOUR EXPERIENCE

Step 4 is learning what you can from each experience. This way you won't have to keep acknowledging and expressing the same emotions over and over again. Learning as you clean up your unworkable beliefs will definitely make your job easier as you go along.

This is basically Monday-morning quarterbacking. See how you could have responded to a given situation differently and suffered less in the process. If you're feeling guilty about what already has happened, stop that now. You can't learn much when you're wasting time feeling guilty.

STEP 5:
LET IT GO AND GET ON WITH LIFE

Step 5 is recognizing that you have done all that you can, and that now it is time to get on with life. This step only takes a few seconds or possibly minutes. If it takes longer, you probably have more expressing or cleaning up to do.

Start at the beginning and see if you've left anything out. Be sure you have expressed all there is to express fully and completely. Be sure you have taken action to clean it up. Sometimes we know what we need to do, but neglect to take the required action. Don't forget to forgive.

When you have successfully completed each step, it will be impossible for you to remain a victim of your feelings. Your depression should be well on its way out.

This is the Victim-ectomy Formula. It has been developed over my twenty years of working with people as a psychotherapist. It works. It works even with the really tough stuff that you never thought you could change. Just give it a chance. Allow time for practice, and don't forget to do each step in sequence. If you leave any out, you will just have to go back and do them later.

get mad

Today the lesbian/gay community is a community filled with rage. Not everyone acknowledges that. But the rage is there, either simmering just below the surface or sometimes boiling out into the open.

I suspect that some of you would be more comfortable if I didn't talk a lot about rage, especially if you were expecting this to be a comforting book about grief. I wish it were possible to honor that notion.

Frankly, several editors turned down the proposal for *After You Say Goodbye* because they didn't want to deal with anger. They were looking for a gentle little book about coping with AIDS grief. But a gentle, comforting book about AIDS grief would be as woefully inadequate as it would be irrelevant.

It is impossible to be in the midst of the AIDS crisis, in the midst of losing tens of thousands of young men and women — soon to be hundreds of thousands — and not be angry.

Our grief process will not be complete if we do not deal with the anger that is connected to an AIDS death and with the circumstances that surround it. We cannot complete our grieving if we refuse to experience our anger.

Some of you may not feel anger yet. If that is true for you, don't be surprised or start to feel guilty, but start looking for your anger.

See if you're blocking it for the reasons we looked at in Chapter 5.

Most of us have been very well trained to suppress feelings of anger, and to obliterate any feeling as strong as rage. The fact that we're not right now aware of rage doesn't mean that it isn't there. It just means that we need to find it and uncover it, so that we can release it.

If dealing with anger is something that you don't feel ready to do right now, that's OK. But you should know that your life will be easier if you're not hanging onto it. Do it as soon as you are ready. Don't hesitate to seek professional assistance if you are too afraid of your anger. If you don't release it, you will become its victim.

Unfortunately, dealing with anger has never been easy in our society. When anger is connected to an experience of death, it is frequently even more formidable.

Some of us choose to repress our anger because we think it is a sign of mental weakness, a lack of control, a lack of love or compassion, or a sign of being unenlightened. Others of us choose to over-express our anger, and wind up wallowing in it full time, becoming its victim.

As the crisis grows, it gets harder and harder to deny or to repress rage. It gets easier and easier to wallow in rage. Neither strategy will work. Anger must be first confronted and then released so that it doesn't keep getting in our way.

Like sadness, anger is a normal, healthy emotion to have. It's an OK place to visit, but you don't want to live there.

Anger is not a crazy emotion, and you are not crazy for being angry. It is not a weak emotion. Hiding from your anger is not coming from strength. Anger is not even an unloving emotion, though many feel that it is.

Being angry at someone you love is quite normal, common, and frankly healthy. It means that the relationship is based on integrity and telling the truth about how you are feeling.

It's impossible to be alive and living with other human beings and not be angry from time to time. The closer you are to someone, the more opportunity there is for anger. Feeling angry is not being disloyal to the relationship.

The only way two people can have a workable relationship is if they trust one another enough to tell the truth about how they are feeling. This is especially true where anger is involved.

Don't confuse telling the truth about your anger with fighting. They are two very different things. Telling the truth about your anger works. Fighting is about wallowing in being Right.

You should be concerned if you never experience anger, because that means you're probably repressing it. You will pay a price for your momentary comfort. That price could be depression. In addition, relationships are hard to maintain if you aren't telling the truth about how you are feeling, especially where anger is concerned.

In this chapter we will discuss ways for you to get in touch with your anger, and then look at strategies for releasing anger in safe, nondestructive ways that won't complicate your life, and that will lead to productive action.

If getting in touch with your anger bothers you or frightens you, please don't stop reading. It will probably not be as difficult or as scary as you might think. It is so important that you realize that the only way for you not to be a victim of your anger or your AIDS rage is for you to be willing to feel the anger. Only then will you be able to deal with it in effective ways.

Even though the constant theme of this book is that there is no Right way to grieve, there are certain principles that will hold true for almost everybody. The need to express anger as part of your grief is one of those principles. There is no Right way to express it. You must do it your way.

As with the Victim-ectomy Formula, uncovering and then expressing your anger is best done in private or with a trusted confidant. Recognizing your anger will not require you to go around having public temper tantrums. That would complicate your grieving process and perhaps push away the very people you need to have around you at this time.

Avoiding public temper tantrums doesn't mean that you can't get outrageously angry. Remember: You can't release what you don't express. Also remember that telling yourself the truth about your feelings is an essential part of your grieving.

If you have started having public temper tantrums, don't waste time feeling guilty. Just know that there are other, more effective, ways for you to deal with your anger that won't complicate your life nearly as much as temper tantrums.

After you experience and express your anger, you can decide what you need to do about the situation that has angered you. Just as action is the solution to sadness, action is also the solution to anger. Doing something to change the situation will be the most effective way to deal with your anger and with your grief.

WHAT IS ANGER AND WHAT CAUSES IT?

As with depression, it is helpful to understand just what anger is and how we create it. That way we can better understand how to release it and get it out of our way.

Anger is a normal, healthy emotion. We feel anger whenever something happens that displeases us, or disappoints us, or means that we don't get to have it our way.

We can be angry at ourselves as easily as we can be angry at other people. We can be angry at something we or someone else has said or done. We can be angry at friends as well as strangers. We can be angry at circumstances, even though they may be beyond our control. We can be angry at a mind-set, such as bigotry or lack of compassion. We can be angry at a government, or even at God.

Our anger can be rational or irrational. Either way, we must still be committed to dealing with it, because hanging on to it will always be irrational.

Anger that we hold on to becomes like an emotional cancer. Every minute we are angry is a minute we can't use for other, more productive activities, such as taking action against the source of the anger. Hanging on to anger will introduce an adversarial element to most, if not all, of our relationships.

Albert Ellis and anger. Turning once again to the work of Dr. Albert Ellis, we can find a very useful model for anger. Ellis believes that anger is the result of a combination of a "sane" statement and an "insane" statement. I prefer to use the terms *workable statement* and *unworkable statement.*

The workable statement is "I don't like what you did." This is a simple statement of preference. Just saying it doesn't produce much anger, or even irritation.

The unworkable statement is ". . . and you shouldn't have done that; you don't have the right to do that. How *dare* you do that. It's wrong for you to do that, and you should be punished." Anger starts to build even thinking those words.

If we understand this simple formula, we can see more clearly what we must do to challenge anger. The workable statement is fine. We don't need to change anything there. We are just noticing that we don't like the way something is. We are just stating a preference.

The most effective way to deal with our anger is to challenge the unworkable belief it is based on. If we are angry, an unworkable belief will always be present.

"I don't like what you did, and *how dare you do it!*" is based on an unworkable belief that is guaranteed to create anger. Unfortunately, our objection does not change the situation. Our objection cannot undo what was done, no matter how bad it is. We just get to feel Right, and we get to feel anger, and little is accomplished.

In fact, holding onto our Rightness and our anger will make any solution or repair of the problem highly unlikely. It is hard to inspire cooperation when we are being intensely Right and righteously angry. It is hard to take effective action when we are at the mercy of our angry feelings.

"But how about when the other person is clearly, undeniably Wrong? Don't we have a right to be angry then?" Of course we do.

However, holding onto that anger—nourishing it, feeding it, even enjoying it—won't do anything to correct the problem. It will decrease our personal effectiveness.

Does that mean that we just have to roll over and take it when someone has done something bad to us? No, it doesn't. We can learn to effectively release our anger and then spring into very effective action to do whatever is necessary to protect ourselves.

For example, it is Wrong for Jesse Helms to continually sabotage the fight against AIDS. It is a hateful, heinous, and shameful thing for him to do.

However, if we merely stand back proclaiming that we don't like what he is doing and that he shouldn't be doing it, where are we? We are stuck in our rage, period.

Now, this is better than just watching what he is doing in silence, but it still won't solve the problem of Jesse Helms. The only way we can solve that problem is to recognize our anger, and then move immediately to what we can do about it.

In 1990, some of us tried by supporting Harvey Gantt, the man who was running against Helms for the Senate. That didn't work. Now, we must be sure that we are giving maximum support to those congressmen and congresswomen who are willing to fight Helms every step of the way.

We can still be angry, but we are not stuck in our anger as long as we are doing something about the problem. That way, anger will not be controlling our lives.

Looking at a less dire problem, if your partner or roommate continually leaves his dirty underwear in the middle of the bathroom floor, you can get angry. You can find dozens of other people who will agree with you that this is untidy and unhygienic. You can then get even angrier and start to snipe or nag. You will have become a victim of your anger, and the problem will still be there. The underwear will probably still be in the middle of the bathroom floor, while you stew in your own juices.

There are only two sensible choices for effective action. You've either got to have a serious conversation with him and explain how important it is to you for him to pick up his dirty underwear, or decide to pick them up yourself. After all, in the scope of the universe, how important are the few seconds that it will take for you to pick them up?

If it's so easy, why doesn't *he* just pick them up? Clearly, he doesn't pick them up because it's not important to him to remember to do that.

"If he loved or respected me he would pick them up." Watch out. The words *If he or she loved me* are deadly. *They assure that you eventually will feel unloved.* They practically guarantee that you will be continually disappointed in the other person, as you expect him or her to read your mind.

What is more important, you are the one linking his or her behavior to loving you. He or she isn't doing that. One thing has nothing to do with the other.

Take action. Discuss the problem, or pick up the damn underwear yourself. Just don't stay angry.

Anger can be rational or irrational. In many cases, your anger can make perfect sense: you can go out and find thousands of other people who will agree that you have a right to feel angry. And anger can be completely nonsensical, with no one agreeing or even understanding why you are angry.

It doesn't matter. If you are angry, it is your anger, and you must feel it regardless of what consensus you find out in the world.

Whether it is rational or irrational, anger is still real. It is not wrong to feel anger. It isn't wise, however, to want to hang on to it. Remember, anger can never solve a problem by itself. In fact, it can create new and bigger problems.

Anger is not a productive emotion unless it results in action that will take care of the problem. It helps a little just to get the anger out of your system. It heals a lot if you can turn your anger into positive action.

We must be willing to recognize our anger, eager to challenge the unworkable beliefs that caused it, and committed to taking action, doing something about it. Otherwise, we remain a victim of our anger.

AIDS rage.   AIDS offers lots of opportunities for anger. AIDS rage can be directed at many different targets.

You can be angry at yourself. You can be angry at the disease. You can be angry at the alienation and discrimination that accompanies the disease.

You can be angry at the government for the unbelievable lack of concern in responding to the AIDS crisis. Seventy-six thousand people had died by the time President Bush gave a speech about AIDS, fourteen months after he came into office. His lips still aren't moving on this one, and we continue to wait for honest action.

AIDS rage is also fueled by politicians like Senator Jesse Helms, Congressman William Dannemeyer, and radical born-again preachers like Jerry Falwell and Lou Sheldon who have made careers or personal fortunes by pouring gasoline on the fire of AIDS fear.

These hate-filled men have tried for years to suppress and eliminate the lesbian/gay community from American life. They were failing miserably until AIDS gave them the weapon they had long been looking for, and now they wield it with a vengeance. How one can witness this travesty of justice, this fraudulence and hypocrisy, and not be outraged is beyond my comprehension.

There is no end to the sources of AIDS rage. One of the most difficult types of anger to face is anger at a loved one who has died of AIDS. You need to give yourself permission to feel this anger without feeling guilt. This kind of anger is perfectly understandable, even though it seems unkind. Trying to ignore it won't work. You'll be stuck with your anger, and probably with a lot of guilt as well.

Just as we all live in different ways and experience grief and other emotions differently, we also experience dying differently. The person who died may have at times behaved very badly, rudely, and insensitively to you or to others during his illness. You may have felt hurt and embarrassed, then angry, then guilty. "After all, he is dying, how could I feel angry at him?" This doesn't work.

Your loved one deserved to be sick in his own way. If that meant bad behavior, that was his right. It is your right to have found it offensive, and to have been angry about it. *Your anger doesn't mean you didn't love him. It just means that you loved him, and that he behaved like a jerk.*

Many of my clients who have lost their partners have reluctantly admitted that they are angry because they are left with all the work, with a huge mess to clean up. The death may mean that they can no longer afford to live in their home, with just a single income. The death may mean that they are now subject to discrimination and alienation. More than one has told me that a new "friend's" response to the knowledge that their partner had died of AIDS was to run screaming into the woods.

I think they are better off if such a person runs for the woods. I hear a lot more stories about people who are wise enough not to care if someone's partner died of AIDS.

A gay man whose life partner has died of AIDS may experience anger at friends and family who have pulled away from him, just when he needed them most, because of their fear of the disease, or their unwillingness to face their own mortality. He may be angry at a society that refuses to acknowledge the depth of his love for his partner, or a legal system that refuses to recognize the legitimacy of his relationship.

We can be angry at the members of our own community who are blithely trying to ignore the presence and the devastation of

AIDS, who somehow manage to struggle through life in blissful ignorance, who have never lifted a finger to help. They may deserve our anger, but it will not do much to educate them or motivate them to change.

If you see yourself as a member of the group that is trying to ignore AIDS, don't waste time feeling guilty about it. Forgive yourself. Get over it. And get to work. It's never too late to be involved.

We can be angry at the members of the media, members of the medical profession, and even members of our own community who seem so vigorously driven to convince everyone who is HIV-positive that they are as good as dead. They seem so concerned about the heinousness of what they call "false hope."

I am HIV-positive. I would rather live every day of my life with "false hope" than to live the rest of my life with no hope. I don't believe that the hope is false, but even if it turns out to be so, at the end it's just "oops." In the meantime, the quality of my life is vastly superior to what it would be if I were living without hope.

Family members of someone who has died of AIDS will each be dealing with their own anger. They may not have known that their son or brother or father was gay, and now they are having to make that adjustment at the same time that they are working through their grief over his death. They are angry at having been kept in the dark. They are angry over the possible persecution that they will experience because their relative died of AIDS.

Some families blame their son's partner for being responsible for their son having AIDS. Until such time as they realize the pointlessness, inappropriateness, and uselessness of that idea, the partner will have to learn to deal with their anger.

I have spoken with a number of people—partners, family members, and friends—who have experienced a form of anger that puzzled and concerned them. They began to notice that they were angry at others who were surviving. This included HIV-negative individuals as well as healthy HIV-positive individuals. It was as though they resented the fact that their loved one was dead and these other people were still alive and apparently healthy.

Some of the people understood the cause of their anger, and while it surprised them, once they admitted it to themselves they were able to drop it immediately. It caused only momentary discomfort.

Others were like my client, Clint. Clint's best friend had recently died of AIDS after a long series of illnesses. Clint seemed to be dealing with his grief pretty well, but he was somehow managing to alienate most of his friends, even his coworkers.

That was why he entered psychotherapy, not to deal with his grief over his friend's death. He told me about frequent angry outbursts at people for doing relatively innocuous things that would not have bothered him previously. In other cases, he talked about anger for which he could find no reason at all. He was just angry.

As we continued to talk, it became clear that the real reason behind his omnipresent anger was his resentment that his friend had suffered and died while other people were still going about their everyday business as though nothing had happened. He discovered that he even resented his HIV-positive friends who were still healthy.

He quickly realized that this kind of anger made little sense. He welcomed the chance to let go of it.

There is no reason for guilt over this kind of irrational anger. While it may be irrational, it is certainly understandable. We just need to take responsibility for our feelings, challenge our unworkable beliefs, and then let go of the anger.

Caregiver anger is also vitally important to understand. I know of few other kinds of anger that can produce such unnecessary guilt.

A client of mine, Kevin, worked long hours in a high-stress career. When one of his best friends with AIDS took a turn for the worse, Kevin's life became consumed by his efforts to take care of his friend.

Even after the friend was hospitalized, Kevin would leave work, grab a hamburger on his way to the hospital, and spend the evening with his friend, sometimes far into the night. With three or four hours of sleep he would return to work the next morning.

Kevin's friend survived far longer than anyone had expected. He was in respiratory ICU for over two months. In that time, Kevin's work performance suffered so badly that he was almost fired. His home became a disaster area. His new boyfriend ran off to greener pastures, as Kevin just didn't have the time or the energy to spend with him.

In the final two weeks of his friend's life, Kevin and other friends formed an around-the-clock watch. The hospital made a compassionate exception to the "relatives only" rule. Kevin took a brief leave of absence from work in order to be with his friend when he died.

The friend did die. Kevin was exhausted. Unfortunately, he was also consumed with guilt because he was so angry at his friend. Once he had even caught himself wishing that his friend would just die and get it over with. Kevin couldn't see how he could have cared for his friend if he was capable of thinking such a contemptible thought.

I have heard countless stories very similar to this one, as so many of us are involved in taking care of our friends and loved ones. *Caregiver anger is no occasion for guilt.*

Kevin did love his friend. There can be no question about that. He was also aware that his friend's illness and death nearly cost him his job, it cost him a relationship, and it didn't do his own health any good either.

His anger is understandable and appropriate. It is not contemptible. The important thing is that he didn't let his anger get in the way of his being there for his friend. He didn't act out of his anger.

It is easy to feel guilt for being angry at someone who is dying. Yet we don't have to feel guilty. The anger is understandable, and not heinous. The anger has nothing to do with how much we love the one with whom we are angry.

Even if you've acted out of that anger and avoided someone or hurt their feelings, you don't need to get stuck in guilt about it. That will only make the problem worse. If there is something you can do to make up for the damage you did, do it. If there isn't, forgive yourself and do what you can to see that it doesn't happen again.

If you do hang onto your guilt about the anger, you will probably keep on being angry. That won't help you or anyone else.

I have worked with many people in caregiver positions, both formally and informally. Caregiver anger and caregiver guilt are rampant. While anger is appropriate, guilt is not. Its presence will only serve to further disrupt your life and damage your own health.

Causes for anger are rampant where AIDS is concerned. I don't want you not to be angry. I do want you do be willing to deal with it, and then do something about the problem.

GETTING RID OF ANGER

We'll use the Victim-ectomy approach here as well.
1. Acknowledge your anger.
2. Experience, express, and ventilate your anger.
3. Clean it up, forgive, and challenge your unworkable beliefs.
4. Learn from it.
5. Get on with your life.

DEALING WITH ANGER BY BEING WILLING TO EXPERIENCE IT

This is a combination of Steps 1 and 2. It means simply to acknowledge that you are angry and then be willing to experience and express it. Most of you won't have trouble doing that. Some of you will.

If you do, your first job is to review the list of reasons why people don't want to acknowledge and express their feelings. Read them over with particular attention to your anger. I'll list them here, but not go into great detail about them, although I will suggest a counter-argument for each one. For more detail, return to Chapter 5.

Reasons for not expressing our anger.
1. We were trained to avoid anger as we were growing up.
   (You can always learn how to deal with your anger.)
2. We fear our anger may overwhelm us with its intensity.
   (It won't if you learn how to release it effectively, and to take action.)
3. We stifle our anger because we don't think it is socially acceptable, because we're afraid that people will think we're weak or crazy, or because we think people won't like us.
   (Anger may not be socially acceptable, but it is still necessary to express it. This will be coming from strength and courage. If people don't like you for telling the truth about your anger, that is their problem. Don't make it yours.)
4. We believe that if we keep our anger hidden, maybe it will just go away.

(Anger will never "just go away." It will just go underground and cause a host of other problems.)

5. We believe that it won't do any good to get angry.

(Actually it will. You won't be carrying anger around with you, and you will be in a position to do something about the problem.)

6. We think that acknowledging our anger will just make us feel worse.

(Only in the short run. It is a momentary discomfort that will leave you feeling lighter, and healthier, and in a position to do something about the problem and ultimately enrich your life.)

7. The "Enlightenment Syndrome" folks stifle their anger because they think anger is not enlightened.

(Telling the truth is enlightened. Lying about your anger is not enlightened. It will disrupt your life.)

There's one other reason why some people are reluctant to give up their anger. Giving up anger may seem like condoning or approving of the neglect and persecution that surrounds AIDS and AIDS deaths. Letting go of anger isn't the same thing as condoning.

So get angry, but don't get stuck in it. Get angry, and then go to work and do something about the situation.

Determine what your reasons are for not experiencing your anger. Then develop a new set of more workable beliefs about anger that will assist you in experiencing and expressing your anger.

If you are too afraid to do this, please find someone to help you through it, such as a support group or a therapist. Just make sure that they don't try to make you feel guilty for your anger. (Unfortunately, there are therapists who have as much trouble dealing with anger as you do. They won't be of much help.)

Once you've determined that it is OK for you to start experiencing and expressing your anger, it's time to do it. Don't wait.

There's no Right way to express anger. There is no Right way for you to experience and express your anger. That will be a very individual choice for you. Choose the way that works best for you.

There are three main strategies for experiencing and expressing anger: verbal, written, and physical. You can use any one, or any combination of the three. Again, do what works for you.

Verbal means saying it out loud. Remember that you need to do it with feeling. You need to experience your anger as well as express it. Get mad. Shout. Swear.

You can role-play and pretend the person you're angry with is in a chair in front of you and yell what you need to at the chair. You can just yell into thin air. But yell.

Remember that you don't have to be kind here. You don't have to be fair, understanding, compassionate, loving, or polite. This is just emotional regurgitation. This is just getting it off your chest, out in the open so you can decide what to do about it.

You must say it out loud, not just think it. Remember that your thoughts are much faster than your mouth. Your thoughts can just lead you around in circles, preventing you from objectively evaluating the workability or unworkability of your thoughts.

You don't need anyone else present while you express your anger. Some of you will wonder what the point is if the person you're mad at isn't there to hear you.

The point is that you are dumping out your anger, getting rid of it. The other person doesn't need to be there. In fact, his or her presence could mess up the whole experience, and complicate your life a lot.

Some of you may feel self-conscious and silly yelling into thin air. That's OK too. Who's watching anyway? Give it a few tries before you decide this doesn't work for you.

You won't have to yell for very long. If you're still yelling fifteen or twenty minutes later, you need to check and see what you are really up to. Are you still angry, or are you now just being self-righteously indignant?

Some of us really like feeling so Right while we make someone else so Wrong, and people like Jesse Helms make it so easy.

I must admit that I sort of like feeling self-righteously indignant. Fortunately, I have also learned that there are lots of things that feel better than self-righteous indignation. Consequently, I am much more motivated to let go of it than I used to be.

You may need only a matter of minutes or even seconds to fully express yourself. Then you will know that it is time to move on to the next step and clean it up.

You can also express your anger in writing. Write the letter from hell. Put all of your thoughts on paper, no matter how vile they might seem. Remember to just tell the whole truth about how you are feeling.

This will work even if the person with whom you are angry is not available to you, or if he or she has died. You can still write the letter.

Remember that this is just regurgitation. You are not betraying the person or hurting him or her in any way. You can also use the letter to acknowledge how much you loved him or her.

When you are done writing, burn the letter, or tear it up and flush it down the toilet. Don't keep it around. This is just expression, and doesn't need any further attention.

Some of you may need to express your anger physically. Be sure to choose the way you do that carefully. Don't punch something that is going to hurt your fist. Don't break anything you value.

Many years ago, a client of mine told me that she had finally gotten in touch with her anger at her ex-husband, and that she had broken every piece of her wedding china in the process. I gulped. That wasn't exactly what I had in mind. It turned out that she had hated the china anyway, and was glad to have it gone.

You can beat on a mattress with your fist, or with a broomstick, or even with a beach towel with a big knot tied on the end. You can also buy foam-rubber bats. Some of my clients use cheap tennis racquets.

I have one caution about expressing anger physically. It works much better if you're talking at the same time. You must express out loud what you're angry about, or you won't feel complete.

Expressing anger physically can be like priming a pump and just getting your emotions moving around a little; then you can take it from there by shouting or writing. You'll probably feel a little silly if you're not used to doing this. Feel silly and do it anyway. It will feel good to get this stuff out in the open.

How long after a death should you still be experiencing and expressing your anger? There is no good answer to this one. It's a very individual matter. Don't be surprised if you get angry long after it seemed as if you were through with your grieving. A wide range of triggers can set us off.

The important thing is not to look for the time when you never feel anger again. Just be committed to expressing, experiencing, and cleaning up your anger as soon as it comes up, as often as it comes up.

A client recently told me about being scolded for getting outraged as he watched the preacher Lou Sheldon on the Donahue show spouting more of his hateful invectives about the lesbian/gay community.

My client's well-meaning friend told him that he should be past the anger stage by now. That was not helpful advice.

If anger is there, it needs to be experienced and expressed whether it is in sequence or not. Frankly, I would be more worried about someone who did not become angry while listening to the paranoid rantings of a homophobic bigot.

If anger is present, it has to be recognized and dealt with. Criticizing a person for still being angry is not helpful and won't work. *The presence of anger is not the issue.* The critical issue is learning how to experience and express the anger in ways that are not self-defeating, self-destructive, or carelessly damaging to another person, then being willing to move on and clean it up.

CLEANING UP YOUR ANGER

Step 3 is cleaning it up. Here is where you decide what you need to do in order to deal with the situation that is causing the anger.

Sometimes, there is nothing to be done. You just need to acknowledge that it is time to move on.

Where anger is concerned, cleaning it up will frequently require forgiveness. You may have to forgive other people, and, most probably, you will need to forgive yourself.

It's OK if there are a few people that you aren't ready or able to forgive. I still have trouble trying to forgive people like Helms and Sheldon. While I am not ready to forgive them, neither do I want to have my anger at them run my life and pollute my consciousness.

We'll spend a lot of time on forgiveness in Chapter 7. For now, just know that forgiveness is not about condoning or approving of someone's bad behavior. It simply means giving up resentment and your desire to punish the other person.

Cleaning it up can also mean taking some kind of action. One of the most important actions is to communicate what is going on with you to the person with whom you are angry. Since you've dumped the emotion, you can approach him or her calmly and reasonably. You can remind the person how much you value him or her and your relationship, and then point out that something is getting in the way of that relationship and you'd like to get it out of the way.

The other person may respond well. But give him or her room to have some anger. After all, you have already dumped your anger. The other person may need a little time for dumping theirs.

Dealing with anger by changing your thinking. To be really complete, you will need to examine your feelings and then determine the unworkable beliefs that produced them. Challenge these beliefs and replace them with more workable ones.

You don't need to stay a victim of your anger. If you want to turn it into action, workable beliefs will be necessary.

We have already looked at how your anger was created in the first place by your unworkable belief that the other person had no right to do what he or she did.

It doesn't matter if anyone had a "right" to do what they have done. He or she did it, and if you can't deal with that, you become that person's victim.

This is a hard lesson to learn. Keep reminding yourself that you can give up your anger and still take action to do something about the problem, unencumbered by your anger.

A little anger may be appropriate when you are dealing with the bigots of the world. In most other cases, the anger will just get in the way.

Anger at someone you love frequently comes from your observation that they didn't do something that you wanted, or they did something you didn't like. In our anger we frequently overlook the fact that the other person was approaching the situation with a different set of needs and priorities.

For example, each morning on my way to work, I take a scenic route that is a twisting two-lane road through the hills. I could take a more direct route, but it would be subject to rush hour traffic jams and gridlock.

I don't take the scenic route for the scenery. I take it because I can get to work faster that way most of the time.

I occasionally drive up behind someone who is taking the scenic route for the scenery—the nerve! This person is actually driving under the speed limit, enjoying the magnificent view that I usually ignore in my rush to get to the office.

I have been known to get angry in this situation. But I am a little more patient since the day one of my clients happened to be on the same road, right behind me, watching me shaking my fist and leaning on my horn all the way to the office. After all, the car in front of me was going fifteen miles an hour.

So, which one of us was Right? Both of us were Right. I was right because my need was to get to my office on time. The tourist was right, as his need was to enjoy a spectacular view of the Los Angeles Basin.

It was just that our needs collided. They were not compatible with one another. That doesn't make either one of us Wrong. Neither did it justify my acting like a maniac, although my client assured me that she enjoyed the show.

I am now increasingly able to relax and enjoy the trip behind the slowest of drivers, most of the time. I remind myself that I can either get to the office in a ranting and raving mood, or I can get there later than I should, but having had the chance to enjoy a lovely trip. Of course, I could leave home a little earlier too, but that's another story.

Our anger is caused by our thoughts, attitudes, and belief systems, which are derived from our personal priorities and needs. Other people operate out of their own thoughts, attitudes, and belief systems, which are derived from their priorities and their needs.

When those priorities and needs collide, there is occasion for anger, but it will occur only if one of you insists that the other is *wrong* to have his or her priorities and needs. If you are willing to let the other person have his or her priorities and needs while you hang on to yours, there is an opportunity for coexistence and cooperation, not anger.

Always remember that you can let go of your anger and still resist the other person's priorities and needs, if you think they are harmful to you. Jesse Helms, again, is the perfect example. I am not willing to sit by and let him pursue his priorities and needs at the expense of my community.

I just don't want to waste energy wallowing in my anger. I want to do something about the situation that will produce positive results.

Learn where your anger is coming from. What are your thoughts, attitudes, and beliefs about a given situation? From what needs and priorities are they derived? Refer to the list of unworkable beliefs in Chapter 5 if you need to.

Be willing to identify the unworkable beliefs that are producing your anger. Then be willing to challenge them and replace them with workable beliefs.

Whatever you do, don't get stuck in your anger. Take action to do something to fix the problem.

Dealing with anger by taking action. Finally, action is the answer. Once you have done all you can to clean up the situation, get involved and do something about the larger problem.

If for no other reason, take action so you won't have as much time to sit around rekindling your anger. You'll feel more productive and have the gratification of knowing that you are making a difference. The possibilities are numerous.

You can join a group like ACT UP (AIDS Coalition to Unleash Power), which demonstrates vociferously and commits civil disobedience and other acts of protest. There are other, more moderate groups such as the Human Rights Campaign Fund (HRCF). You can also choose to express your outrage and work for change by lobbying local, state, and federal governments for the support that we need to take care of those who are ill.

In many cases we are still waiting for that support and have forged ahead on our own, taking care of our own as best we can. This creates numerous possibilities for action.

We have educated, fed, and housed our own. We've made sure people with AIDS have buddies, people who are looking out for them. There are people who make sure that they get a ride to see their doctor. Others make sure that they have someone to talk to. Others help them clean their homes.

The possibilities for action are myriad. So get angry, clean it up, and then do something about the problem in whatever way best suits you.

LEARNING FROM IT

This step will be especially important if you notice that you are getting angry at the same thing over and over again. You can keep acknowledging, expressing, and cleaning up the same issue. Why put yourself through the stress?

If he's going to keep leaving his dirty underwear in the middle of the bathroom floor, what good does it do getting angry each time? If you have not been able to convince him to pick them up no matter how hard you've tried, why not just pick them up yourself? Change your belief that those few seconds are unreasonable. Or, you could get a new roommate or partner. This would be especially appropriate where the problem was one of more severe abuse than dirty shorts on the bathroom floor.

I'm willing to accept that Jesse Helms has the right to keep doing what he is doing, but I don't want to waste energy getting stuck in my anger each time he behaves in ways that are absolutely predictable for him. I would rather put my energy into exercising my right to resist his efforts.

If we are willing to learn from our experience, we will have a lot more energy available for getting our job done. See if you have beliefs that need changing, actions that need taking, conversations that need to be held, or just more expressing to do.

GETTING ON WITH THE REST OF YOUR LIFE

This step consists of reminding yourself that you have done all you need to do, or can do, so you might as well move on. Staying stuck in anger is our choice, so let's choose not to stay stuck.

If you're not ready to let go of your anger totally, then go back to Step 1 and go through the process again, seeing what you need to do more of. Hanging on to your anger will only hurt you.

As you grow more willing to deal with your anger, your grief process will go much more smoothly. It will be easier to get beyond the pain. It will be easier to do the things that you must do.

I do the best I know how, the very best I can; and I mean to keep on doing it to the end. If the end brings me out all right, what is said against me will not amount to anything. If the end brings me out all wrong, ten angels swearing I was right would make no difference.
—Abraham Lincoln

say goodbye to guilt

First of all, let me clarify the terms *guilt, shame,* and *blame.* The distinctions between guilt, shame, and blame are unclear in the dictionary, as well as in psychological literature. Through time, different writers have assigned their own specific meanings to the words.

In this book, guilt and shame are considered to be synonymous. I define guilt as a feeling you have about yourself. Blame is a feeling you have about another person or event. You feel guilty for something that you have done, and you blame someone else for what you think they have done.

Is there a more irrational emotion than guilt? No. Is there a more destructive and devastating emotion than guilt? No.

As irrational and destructive as it is, guilt is also one of the most pervasive of feelings. Our society seems to be guilt-based.

In fact, guilt has been viewed as such a normal feeling that people who don't experience guilt are called psychopaths or sociopaths. Trying to tell people not to feel guilty over a mistake that they have made is frequently met with cries of dismay.

I think it is time that we put an end to the confusion about guilt. I think it is time that we learned that there is something that works much better than guilt: responsibility.

WHAT IS GUILT?

If we are feeling guilty, we are saying two things. We are saying that we have made a mistake or done something wrong or bad. We follow that with the notion that we now deserve punishment or suffering. *Both components — acknowledging the mistake, and deserving punishment — are necessary in order to feel guilt.*

If we make a mistake and then feel bad about it, is that guilt? Not by my definition. I don't know how *not* to feel bad if I make a mistake, especially if that mistake hurts another person. I feel sorrow and wish that the mistake hadn't happened. It doesn't become guilt until I add the need to be punished, or the need to suffer for my mistake.

It is crucial to realize that guilt is about judgment, punishment, and suffering. Guilt is *not* about fixing problems or cleaning up damage.

Some guilt is very clear, followed by blatant punishment and suffering. An example of this is someone who physically hurts him- or herself out of guilt to pay for sins or crimes.

Most people don't go that far. They aren't willing to physically hurt themselves, but they do suffer emotionally. They feel guilty, and that means that they feel unworthy, unlovable, and deserving of the scorn of others who know the bad thing they have done.

This guilt can be pervasive, influencing every area of our lives. It can lead to the feeling that we don't deserve to be happy and joyful in life. After all, how can I let myself have a good time when I have done such bad things?

In my experience, most of the guilt that damages people's lives so effectively is guilt over things that just aren't that bad. We're not talking about murder and grand larceny. We are talking about honest mistakes, careless conversation, or just differences of opinion.

The sources of guilt are infinite. Unfortunately, we will never run out of reasons to feel guilty.

We can feel guilty for real mistakes and failures. We can feel guilty for imagined or questionable mistakes and failures. Some people even feel guilty about being successful.

We can feel guilty for things we have done or said. We can feel guilty for things we haven't done or said. We can feel guilty for things we have merely thought about.

All of this is about feeling guilty for our imperfections. This leaps out of our unworkable belief that we should be perfect in every way. When we are not perfect, we must be judged, found guilty, and punished.

Other guilt is much more subtle, and the punishment can be quite indirect. There are myriad possibilities here. You can withhold sexual pleasure from yourself out of guilt for your sexual behavior. You can sabotage success on a project out of guilt over your mistakes or other imperfect behavior. You can withhold joy from your life out of your guilt for things you have done. All this can be done without conscious awareness.

Whether blatant or subtle, guilt is an emotional cancer that will slowly eat away at your self-esteem. Guilt will diminish your sense of personal power. Guilt will deprive you of your chance at happiness in life.

Guilt is never a healthy or helpful emotion. It can always be counted on to make the situation worse, but never make it better.

I can already hear the cries of protest! How can I possibly envision a society without guilt? Wouldn't that mean that people would just be running rampant, taking whatever they wanted, caring for no one but themselves? You could lie, cheat, steal, rape, and murder and not feel bad about it.

That is the way society would look if we didn't feel guilt and *if we weren't willing to take responsibility for our behavior.* I am suggesting that we avoid guilt. I am *not* suggesting that we avoid responsibility. In fact, a big part of living life well requires that we take full responsibility for our life.

Earlier in this book we began the discussion of guilt versus responsibility. Rarely have two concepts been so confused with one another. Common usage holds that guilt and responsibility are really the same thing. It is my firm conviction that they are not.

Am I telling you never to feel guilty? No. If you do something that damages another person, you may indeed feel guilty. However, I don't want you to stay stuck in that guilt, either.

Hanging onto the guilt will not help you clean up the damage. In fact, it will hinder the cleanup, if not block it altogether. Guilt will always get in your way.

Not only that, guilt is a sure-fire guarantee that you will keep making the same mistake over and over again. You don't learn from your mistakes when you are busy feeling guilty. You brainwash yourself with negative comments about yourself, about your competence, about your slim chances for improvement. Guilt will disempower you, and the chances of your making the same mistake the next time will be vastly increased.

We must be willing to let go of guilt as soon as possible. Then we can begin to take responsibility for our actions and clean up any damage. We do not have to suffer just because we made a mistake.

Taking responsibility has nothing to do with guilt and blame. It merely means that I am being presented with this situation, and I must do something to fix it if I can, or accept it if I can't.

THE CAUSES OF GUILT

Like anger, guilt is caused by the combination of a workable statement and an unworkable statement. The workable statement is "I did that." Simple. No fuss here, and no guilt either.

The unworkable statement is " . . . and it's my fault, and I deserve to be punished and to suffer. I am bad and wrong for having done that."

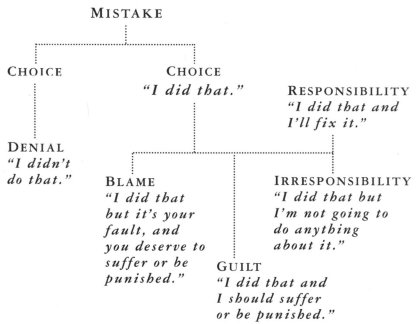

MISTAKE

CHOICE

CHOICE
"I did that."

RESPONSIBILITY
*"I did that and
I'll fix it."*

DENIAL
*"I didn't
do that."*

BLAME
*"I did that
but it's your
fault, and
you deserve to
suffer or be
punished."*

IRRESPONSIBILITY
*"I did that but
I'm not going to
do anything
about it."*

GUILT
*"I did that and
I should suffer
or be punished."*

The diagram starts with the mistake. There are two choice points. The first choice is to own the mistake and say "I did that." The other choice is to deny it.

If you deny it, you will never get to fix it. Most of the time the other person knows you did it anyway, even though he or she may not be able to prove it or be inclined to confront you with it. Your integrity will suffer in the eyes of other people and, more ruinously, in your own eyes as well. You will start amassing evidence that you cannot be trusted.

If you choose to tell the truth and own the mistake by saying "I did that," you are presented with another choice point. There are at least four possibilities.

Blame says, "Yes, I did that, but it is your fault that I did. You are to blame. You should suffer or be punished."

Guilt says, "Yes, I did that, and I deserve to suffer or to be punished. I am bad and wrong for having done that."

Irresponsibility says, "Yes I did that, but I have no intention of doing anything about it. I won't fix it."

Responsibility says simply, "Yes, I did that, and I will fix it."

Which one of those choices do you find yourself making?

The results of your choices. It always works to examine the results of the choices that we make. If we like the results, all we have to do is keep making the same choices. If we don't like the results, it makes sense to make different choices.

What result do you create for your life with your choice between guilt, blame, irresponsibility, and responsibility?

If you choose blame, you will find it tough to keep friends around. No one likes to be blamed for someone else's mistake. No one is really going to accept your blame and hold you blameless.

What is more important, you can't fix a problem that you are blaming on someone else. Blaming someone else gets you off the hook, but it doesn't allow you to learn from your mistakes.

Of course there are those who will jump to take the blame for you, like the soap-opera husband who cries, "If only I hadn't divorced her five years ago when I found out that she was still a working hooker, she wouldn't be a drug addict now, and she wouldn't have had that miscarriage!"

I have worked with people who are just as quick to take blame. Somehow they always end up in relationships with people who like to cast blame. Talk about your match made in hell!

If you choose the irresponsible approach, it also will be hard to keep people around. Responsible people won't find it too pleasant to be around you with your lack of concern for fixing what you broke. You will probably find yourself surrounded by others who are just as irresponsible as you are, and they will drive you crazy. Talk about poetic justice!

If we aren't willing to clean up the damage we create with our mistakes, we will rarely learn how to avoid making the same mistake again. Irresponsible people learn to distrust themselves, smarting under the realization that other people don't trust them either.

Being irresponsible may look like the easy way out, but the long-term costs are high. Solid, nurturing relationships and successful careers and lives are difficult to achieve from a base of irresponsible behavior.

If you choose guilt, you will suffer and suffer and suffer. The job won't get fixed, you won't learn from your mistakes, and you will feel terrible about it.

Responsible people won't find it too pleasant to play with you, either. You will attract those who like to blame others. This is another match from hell. You will meet each other's needs perfectly. But who wants a relationship based on blame and guilt?

If you choose responsibility, you won't waste time suffering. You will learn from your mistakes, and you will clean up any damage that you create. The job will get done. Taking responsibility for your life is one of the most liberating decisions you will ever make.

Responsible people tend to attract other responsible people. They tend to be more productive and have more fun. They know that mistakes are merely opportunities to learn how to do things better. Even if they do make a mistake, those around them know that they will do whatever is necessary to correct the problem. People know they can depend on responsible people. Responsible people have learned to trust themselves.

Responsible people aren't interested in lying, cheating, or stealing. It just doesn't fit their needs or their style. Responsible people always take full responsibility for all of their actions. They will not knowingly do something that damages another person.

Of course, there will still be those who confuse responsibility with blame and guilt. You accept responsibility for your mistake, but they keep on blaming you. They try to make you feel guilty.

I wouldn't waste much time trying to deal with these people. You can't really win with guilt-inducers. A really good one can always find some way to blame you for something.

There is only one way to deal with guilt-inducers. Just refuse to feel guilty. They can't really *make* you feel guilty. That is something that you have to agree to do.

Think about the last time you made a mistake. Which choice did you make? Did you deny, blame, feel guilty, or behave irresponsibly, or did you take responsibility? What was the result of your choice in your life?

Think about another time you made a mistake. Which choice did you make then? What was the result of that choice?

Keep examining the way you have responded to making a mistake until you are clear about the result your choices have on your life. Do you want to keep getting those same results? If you want different results, what would be a better choice to make?

See which choices you have made, and then commit yourself to doing whatever you can to be responsible for your life from now on. If you notice at any time that you are feeling guilty or blameful, stop it. We'll look at how to effectively stop guilt later in this chapter.

GUILT AND MANIPULATION

I suspect that guilt is as pervasive as it is because it is such a potent manipulative device. There are people who have made a fine art of encouraging others to feel guilty.

Many of our commonly used child-rearing practices depend on making children feel guilty for their bad behavior. The same holds true for our school system.

This has created a generation of adults who have learned how to blame and feel guilty. Many adults use guilt to manipulate one another's behavior. People who are guilt prone are sitting ducks for a good guilt-manipulator.

Religion is a major offender in the guilt department. Generations of people have been kept in line by the promulgation of guilt for transgressions. I must plead ignorance of Jewish theology, so I can't say if guilt is theologically correct for Jews. I can say that guilt is *not* a Christian concept, even though it is widely used in both Protestant and Catholic churches.

Encouraging anyone to feel guilty requires that you have first judged that person and his or her behavior as bad and wrong. The New Testament is clear that judgment of others is forbidden. Jesus Christ said, "Judge not, lest ye be judged."

Christians are not to judge one another, or anyone else. Judgment is specifically reserved for God. Nowhere does the New Testament give anyone permission to make someone else feel guilty, and that includes preachers and priests.

The main message of Christianity is forgiveness and compassion, not judgment and guilt. It has never ceased to amaze me how radical born-again preachers consistently ignore this clearly stated concept in the Bible they claim to believe in as literal truth.

Whether you are a preacher, parent, teacher, friend, or spouse, guilt is always there as a possible way for you to manipulate others. It is a powerful weapon that can give you very effective control over the actions of others.

Unfortunately, inducing guilt brings with it a heavy price. No one likes to be made to feel guilty. Even if people allow themselves to be manipulated by the guilt, they will harbor resentment and anger. In the long run, many relationships are destroyed by guilt and guilt-inducement.

Many parents who have always manipulated their children with guilt fail to understand the impact that this has on their relationships. Many such children, as they reach adulthood, decide to cut themselves off from their family in self-defense.

Others choose to remain and put up with the guilt, but they do so with increasing hostility and resentment. They will also tend to put a lot of distance between them and their guilt-inducing parents.

I spent a number of years working in a hospital setting in the department of physical medicine and rehabilitation. Most of the patients were older men and women who had experienced a stroke, heart attack, or other catastrophic illness or accident.

It was always very clear which ones were guilt-inducers. They were the ones with fewer visitors. When their family or friends did visit they usually had to listen to a litany of accusations about their ignoring the person in the hospital by not visiting or calling enough. I could see the visitors backing farther and farther away.

Guilt usually works, but are you really prepared to pay the price? Are you really happy with the result you get? Do you really feel satisfied when someone does something for you only because they know you will try to make them feel guilty if they don't do it?

Think about how you felt the last time you called someone whom you hadn't spoken to in a while, and the first thing out of their mouth was, "Why haven't you called? You know how much your calls mean. How can you be so selfish and ignore me so?"

How does that make you feel? Does it make you want to call that other person again anytime in the near future? Most people will wait even longer before they call again, knowing that they are just going to get another load of guilt thrown on them.

If you are this kind of guilt-inducer, notice the results you get. Do people call you more frequently, or less frequently? When they do call, is it a pleasant, nurturing conversation or one that is distant and cool? Are these the results you want to continue to get? Are you really content with attention that comes as a result of feelings of guilty obligation that you have managed to instill?

Your guilt-inducement may work in the short run, if it helps you control someone else's behavior, but are you willing to suffer the long-range consequences? Do you want people to do things your way (the Right way) or do you really want their love, respect, and support? Guilt-inducement will deprive you of love, respect, and support—that's guaranteed!

If you are a guilt-inducer, don't waste time feeling guilty about it. You must, however, get over it and stop using guilt to manipulate people around you. Learn how to ask for what you want, while granting the other person the right to say no. If someone says no, that doesn't mean that he or she doesn't love you. It just means that he or she has different priorities right now.

GUILT AND AIDS

Guilt following an AIDS death comes in many different forms. Each group of survivors will have its own unique kind of guilt.

Some guilt is understandable, for example when it is connected to the anger and resentment you may have felt toward the one who has died. It is understandable, but still inappropriate.

There is also guilt that defies understanding. I have talked with people who gave up several years of their lives and put their careers on hold so they could take care of their ill partner or friend. All this, and they still felt guilty for not doing enough.

Whether it is understandable or not, inappropriate or not, guilt must be faced and dealt with. Remember that guilt never produces a good result. It only causes needless pain and keeps the real problem from being solved effectively.

Guilt for anger at the one who has died. We can feel guilty for feeling anger and resentment at the person who has died. Death brings with it many reasons for such anger. Remember that anger doesn't have to be rational or kind or make sense. However, such anger must not be an occasion for your feeling guilty.

We can feel angry at the person for getting AIDS. We can blame him or her for the behavior that allowed the transmission of the virus. Remember, anger doesn't have to be fair or make sense.

We can be angry at the person for dying and for abandoning us so that we can no longer enjoy their company or depend on them.

We can feel angry that we have a mess to clean up, that we are stuck paying the bills, cleaning out the apartment, putting up with his family.

We can feel angry because the death has changed our lifestyle in ways that we don't like. Death frequently takes away some of our ability to control our lives.

Some of you as you read this may be shocked, and wonder if maybe a person who feels this anger shouldn't feel a little bit guilty. No. No. No.

All such anger is clearly irrational, but it is not worthy of guilt. It needs to be cleaned up and released as we discussed in Chapter 6. Guilt will only keep the anger under wraps, fermenting away, threatening to break out at the slightest provocation.

If you can make personal sacrifices and not be irritated that you have to do so, good for you. Please don't be judgmental toward those people who feel that sacrifice, even willing sacrifice, is annoying.

The fact that we experienced anger has nothing to do with how much we love the one who has died. It is no occasion for guilt, and must be stopped as soon as you see it happening.

Another cause for anger at the one who has died has to do with his or her behavior while they were dying. It's not uncommon for people who are dying to behave badly. They are frightened and angry. They can easily lash out at those people who are trying to take care of them. They can become stubborn, refusing to take their medication, to eat, or to allow themselves to be kept clean.

They can be verbally and physically abusive. This is particularly true for those persons with AIDS who have experienced AIDS dementia related to neurological damage. These people can become senile and cantankerous. Working with them can be demanding and frustrating. You're only trying to help, but they are fighting you all the way.

Is it OK to feel anger in this situation? You bet it's OK. In fact, I suspect that it is even necessary for most of us, because it means we are telling the truth. Please don't feel guilty about being angry when you are being mistreated by the person you are caring for. If you do feel guilty, we'll discuss how to deal with that later in this chapter.

I have had several clients who became so angry as they were trying to help their friend who was dying that they actually slapped him or yelled at him. They then were overwhelmed with guilt over their actions. Unfortunately, each one had other people around who kept their guilt alive and active.

Before you get too judgmental about this, ask yourself how you would feel if someone shoved a handful of feces into your face as you were trying to change his diaper at four o'clock in the morning.

This is a tough one, I know. Yet feeling guilty over something that has been done is pointless. It is over and done, and it cannot be undone.

Physical punishment is uncalled for, and frankly ineffective, whether you are a parent or taking care of someone who is too old or too ill to care for him- or herself. If you have abused someone physically or verbally, realize that it doesn't work, and it really doesn't feel good. In the long run you may suffer far more than the person you abused.

If the person is still alive, it would be helpful to ask for his or her forgiveness, and to make a commitment to never do that again. If the person is not still alive, you must forgive yourself and make the same commitment. Learn better ways of dealing with your anger.

Accept the fact that taking care of someone who is dying can be a very exasperating experience. Anger is understandable in this situation. Whatever you do, don't feel guilty about feeling angry. Do whatever you can to keep from acting out of anger.

Feeling guilty about it won't keep it from happening again. In fact, the guiltier you feel about it, the more likely that it will happen again with someone else that you care about.

Caregiver guilt. "If he's going to die, why can't he just hurry up and get it over with?" I have talked to a number of devastated people who painfully admitted that they had actually had such a thought. I have talked to more who probably did feel that way but who could never bring themselves to admit it. It just sounded too awful.

"How can I have such an evil thought toward someone I love?" The guilt from this experience is intense and excruciatingly painful. It is also unnecessary.

I have spent many years working with the families and friends of people with AIDS, and people with other chronic illnesses or injuries. Being with someone who is dying is a wrenching, draining, terrifying, awful process. The wish for it to be over is frequently experienced by those people who are caregivers. It is not an evil wish, and you are not an evil person for wishing it.

I understand that there are some people who do not experience that anger. They have infinite patience and infinite control over their own feelings. I have not met many such people and have nothing but admiration for them and the work that they do. Most of us are not that patient or that controlled.

It is quite natural and understandable for people who find themselves unexpectedly in the role of a full-time health care worker to have such feelings of resentment. Their lives have been disrupted.

They find themselves doing things they never imagined they would have to do, such as emptying bedpans, changing sheets at three o'clock in the morning for the third time that night, changing IVs, cleaning wounds, or changing diapers.

You cannot be blamed for wishing it were over. This doesn't mean that you don't love the person. It doesn't mean that you are heartless or cruel. You are simply tired of the suffering, both his and yours. Don't feel guilty about that.

The fact that it makes you angry doesn't mean that you would ever think about stopping your caregiving. It doesn't mean that you would do it any differently, if you had the chance. You love him or her. You are in it for the long run. You aren't going to abandon him or her. It just makes you angry from time to time that you have to do it.

Such caregiver guilt is never warranted, never necessary, and never useful. It must be confronted whenever it comes up. Forgiveness is the only thing that makes sense now.

Survivor guilt. There are those whose friends or partners have died of AIDS, and they feel guilty for surviving. "Why him and not me?"

There is only one answer for "Why me?"

Just because.

I worked with one man, Al, who was consumed with survivor guilt. He had been wildly promiscuous in the seventies and even into the early eighties. Yet he was surviving when most of his peers had died some years before.

He felt guilty. They all had played and played hard. His friends had died, but he had not. He wasn't even HIV-positive.

Why should he be the one to survive? Just because.

Survivor guilt is tough to get to the bottom of. I suspect that it is frequently related to sexual guilt. There is a quiet thought that AIDS is some kind of punishment for sexual transgressions. If I am not punished when others are, I should feel guilty. In Al's case there was not only a long history of sexually compulsive behavior, but there was also a long history of feeling guilty about his sexual behavior.

The same is true for most sexually compulsive men that I have seen in therapy. Although you'd think that their wildly sexual lifestyle would indicate that they have no guilt about sex, I find the reverse to be true. I have yet to meet anyone who calls him- or her-self sexually compulsive who is not subject to some degree of sex-ual guilt. They are in a real no-win ball game. They feel driven to have sex over and over again. Yet they feel guilty for acting on those impulses.

Guilt for sexual behavior will certainly increase the likelihood of survivor guilt. As I keep saying, feeling guilty only perpetuates the problem behavior.

I should also point out that there is a significant difference between sexually compulsive behavior and someone who just loves to have sex. Truly compulsive sexual behavior has a driven quality that is virtually impossible to resist, and usually yields very little real satisfaction. A person's job, or relationship, or the need to sleep takes a back seat to the urge for another sexual experience.

A sexually compulsive individual is going to have sex, no mat-ter what the cost. Someone who just loves sex will be able to choose to act on those impulses if it's appropriate. He or she will have no problem not acting on those impulses if it is not appropriate.

I make this point because too many people are trying now to avoid sex altogether, and are judging those who are still sexually active. Sex is being blamed by some for the existence of AIDS. Again, AIDS is caused by a virus that can be transmitted by unsafe sexual behavior. That does not make sex wrong and bad. That does not say that sex should be avoided.

I deal with far too many people who are trying to avoid ever having sex because of AIDS. Unfortunately, after a time they become so sexually frustrated that they break out of their celibacy with a vengeance and are terrified by the results.

Sex is a beautiful, affirming experience. It can still be embraced, nurtured, and enjoyed. You just need to know about safer sex, and practice it exclusively. Feeling guilty about your sexual behavior will not lead to productive changes.

Survivor guilt may also spring from the thought that you don't deserve the good things that happen to you. If you win the lottery and your friends don't, you feel guilty. If you have a hot new boyfriend, and your friends are still single, you feel guilty. If you make more money than your friends do, you feel guilty.

After all, why should these good things be happening to you

and not to them? There is usually a significant self-esteem problem here, sometimes blatantly clear, sometimes subtly hidden. It's as though you feel you don't deserve to enjoy life.

The truth is that you do deserve to enjoy life and all life has to offer. This is true regardless of how much money you have, or how many friends you have, or how talented you are. You get to enjoy life and all that you have, regardless of what anyone else has.

Know that having more doesn't make you better. Having less doesn't make you worse.

I suspect that there is at least one more kind of survivor guilt. I call this "pseudo survivor guilt."

This is where you say you feel guilty for surviving while others haven't, and you may actually feel a little guilty about that. But the truth is that deep down inside you really don't feel guilty for surviving. You are basically thrilled to be surviving.

It is just that you are watching your HIV-positive friends go through so much fear and struggle that you feel uncomfortable talking about how good your life feels right now. (This can also hold true for those who are HIV-positive and asymptomatic, who are watching their friends start to get sick or be diagnosed.)

I don't mean to imply that you are being mean-spirited or just making it up. It's just that you have trouble appearing to enjoy life while people you love may be ill or dying.

I think this would work better if you were just willing to tell the truth, without rubbing your friends' faces in your good health or in your HIV-negative status. You don't have to lie about feeling good about your life. Just be sensitive about how and when you share that with your friends who may be going through a tough time.

The simple bottom line is that you are surviving. Reject any thought of guilt about that. Don't you believe that the people whom you love who have died would want you to be a survivor? Don't you suppose that they would want you to enjoy all that your life has to offer?

If you are a survivor, make the most of it. Take action and help out however you can. Honor your loved ones who have died, or who are ill, by living your life fully and well.

Partner guilt. People whose partners have died of AIDS will have their own unique reasons for feeling guilty. Some reasons have to do with thoughts that they didn't do enough. Others have to do with feelings of anger at the person who has died.

Some people put their entire life on hold so they can take care of their ill partner. Others aren't willing or able to do that, because if they did, the lack of income could put both partners on welfare or in the streets. They need to continue working full time just to keep the roof over their heads and the bills paid.

You did as much as you could do for your partner. If you feel as though you could have done more, assess that carefully. Do you ever feel as though you do enough? Is this a truly objective evaluation of your efforts?

Either way, what's done is done, and feeling guilty now won't change anything except the quality of your life, which will suffer immensely.

Forgive yourself, make amends, explain yourself to someone if you feel you really need to do that. Many people don't understand the financial pressures that kept you working full time instead of home caring for your partner. Be willing to teach them, and if they aren't teachable, let them go. You don't need their garbage right now.

The toughest guilt to deal with for some people is the anger they may feel toward their partner who has died. Most people believe they are not supposed to be angry at people for dying. This isn't a helpful belief, of course.

Your whole future has been changed by your partner's death. It is understandable that you could feel angry about some of those changes.

You may have to give up your home for one that you can now afford by yourself. This can mean giving up possessions, including pets you can no longer care for by yourself.

There are those whose partners died without wills, with their personal affairs in chaos. Now it is up to the survivor to do what he can to try to clean it up. The responsibilities can be awesome even if the partner has prepared his affairs.

In some of the worst scenarios, families have swooped in on the surviving life partner, kicked him out of his own home, and cleaned the place out. Since there was no will, there was nothing he could do about that. He has a right to feel resentful at his partner for not being thoughtful enough to see that he was protected.

We can be angry over the time and money we spent taking care of the one who has died. Even though we would do it all over again, without hesitation, it can still be hard to accept the fact that our life savings are gone and that we are in worse debt than we have ever been as a result of medical bills.

Some can feel anger because they fear that the person who has died may have passed HIV along to them. In the vast majority of cases, there will be no way to know if that is true, unless you were supposed to be in a monogamous relationship for the last ten years, and you were faithful and he was not. Even then, there isn't 100 percent certainty. Why waste the time worrying about a question that can never be satisfactorily answered? What's done is done and can't be undone. Your job now is to take care of yourself.

Again, your anger is not a cause for guilt. Your anger has nothing to do with how much you loved your partner. Deal with your anger as outlined in Chapter 6, and then move on. Just don't waste time feeling guilty.

Family guilt. Family members have their own kinds of guilt. Some of it can be devastating.

There is frequently a lot of guilt for not having accepted a son's being gay. In some cases that may have involved disowning him or cutting him out of the family circle.

Some families even blame themselves because their son was gay in the first place, and by extension they take the blame for his death by AIDS. This, of course, makes no sense at all.

Other families who had been willing to accept the fact that their son was gay could not bring themselves to deal with the fact that he had AIDS. They kept him at arms' length or away from the family altogether. I have heard so many stories of parents and siblings pushing away the person with AIDS as a means of protecting the children. (Again, I want to point out that there are many families who did not do this, and who stayed right with their child, never wavering.)

It is these tragic rejections that I lay at the feet of those who have persistently sabotaged the efforts to educate the entire population about what causes AIDS and what doesn't. Such fear and rejection are not necessary, and are tearing families apart.

If you are a parent who in some way rejected your son or daughter with AIDS, your guilt will not change anything. What's done is done. Hanging on to your guilt will only damage your life and won't fix anything.

I would strongly suggest that you forgive yourself for your actions, and then get on with it. There are thousands of other brave young men and women with AIDS out there, whose families have also rejected them. They are in dire need of acceptance and tender loving care. Why not volunteer to be an AIDS buddy for such an individual, or get involved in the fight against AIDS discrimination? Do something; don't just feel guilty.

If you are feeling guilty because you shut your son's life partner and friends out of his funeral, or because you cleaned out the house, I don't want you to feel guilty. I do want you to clean up the damage. Give your son's partner what belongs to him. Your son is owed respect for his friendships and relationships. It's never too late to do that.

Friend guilt. Friends can experience all of the same kinds of guilt experienced by caregivers, partners/spouses, and families. In many cases friends have taken on the roles of caregivers, life partners, and families. They have had to do it all.

Unfortunately, there are those who pulled away from their friend with AIDS because they were too freaked out about this reminder of their own mortality. It made them too uncomfortable to be so close to AIDS. They couldn't bring themselves to visit the hospital or their friend's home.

Some were worried about catching the disease by just being in the same room, again ignoring all of the evidence that AIDS is not transmitted that way. Perhaps one of the most painful scenes in the movie *Longtime Companion* was when the young man visiting his friend in the hospital for the first time kissed him hello and hugged him, and then ran into the restroom where he desperately scrubbed his hands and face.

His was an act of fear and ignorance. It was not a mean-spirited act. He, or anyone who has found himself or herself doing the same thing, has no reason to feel guilty. Just get over it, and get back to work.

Other friends who pulled away were defending themselves through denial: "If I don't think about AIDS, or have anything to do with someone who has AIDS, maybe it will leave me alone." Denial won't work. AIDS will eventually break through your defenses, and you will still have to deal with it. Don't feel guilty for being in denial, but make yourself face the truth and do something about it.

If you find yourself feeling guilty over any of these issues, follow the same advice I give to families. There are thousands of people with AIDS who need your help in a variety of ways. Don't waste time nurturing your guilt, just get involved and do something about the problem.

Others of you did manage to stick it out through the worst, and still feel guilty for not doing enough. You might notice if this has become a lifestyle for you. Do you ever feel as though you do enough?

The chances are that you learned that pattern at an early age, and it is now time to break out of it. You can only do so much. You cannot end suffering. You cannot cure disease. You cannot stop a disease process for someone you love. You cannot make him respond to the disease any differently than he has been programmed to do by his own experience of life.

You have to forgive yourself even if your guilt is imagined. Then get back to work.

Sexual guilt. Guilt, which surrounds anything sexual for so many people, will assume enormous proportions with an AIDS death, where it seems as if sex kills. Sex doesn't kill; loving someone gay doesn't kill. The virus kills, and guilt will only make it more destructive.

AIDS is a disease that is frequently transmitted by unsafe sexual actions. This can be a source of shame to many people who buy the absurd and twisted idea that AIDS is the price God is exacting as punishment for sexual freedom.

This raises a number of questions. Why do these people focus only on sexually transmitted diseases as forms of punishment? With this kind of thinking, wouldn't all transmittable diseases be some form of punishment? In fact, wouldn't this make any kind of natural disaster some form of punishment? Obviously that idea is absurd, a waste of time, and a shabbily disguised form of bigotry. Unfortunately, this idea is held by too many people and has consistently hampered the fight against AIDS.

Guilt and AIDS have no connection. There are no guilty persons with AIDS. When well-meaning folks refer to babies and children as the "innocent victims" of AIDS, they need to understand that they are implying that adults with AIDS are *guilty* victims. I prefer to think that *all* people with AIDS, of whatever age or regardless of how the virus was transmitted, are innocent.

People who have more recently converted to HIV-positive may feel guilty. There are bound to be those who will blame them for exposing themselves to the virus when they should have known better. The problem with this point of view is the incredibly long latency period for the AIDS virus. It can hang around for many years before breaking out into the open. You may have been in a monogamous relationship for the last seven or eight years and still test positive based on behavior from nine or ten years ago.

There is a small group of people who have engaged in unsafe sexual practices when they did know better, and have consequently tested HIV-positive after several HIV-negative tests. Should they feel guilty?

What good would that do? What's done is done. It would have been good if they had been more careful, but why should they suffer more? If this applies to you, resist the guilt and put your energy into being responsible for your life and for your continued health.

"But they brought it on themselves. Why should society help them out when they behaved foolishly and badly?" There are those people who feel this way about anyone who has AIDS, such as certain grossly overweight radio talk show hosts and some television commentators.

If we follow this line of thinking, we should withhold medical care from anyone who engages in unwise behavior. We should withhold medical treatment from someone who is overweight and has heart problems, or from anyone who smokes and has a smoking-related disease, or from anyone who refuses to reduce his or her stress levels, or from anyone who is injured while engaged in a dangerous hobby or occupation, or from anyone who has an unhealthy diet, or from anyone who uses alcohol or drugs, or from anyone who drives recklessly.

If we did that, this country could indeed save hundreds of billions of dollars for its health care system. But do you see how absurd this argument is? What good does it do to blame people for their unwise choices, especially when the consequences of those choices weren't known at the time the choice was made?

People who are ill, for whatever reason, deserve to be cared for and offered the best that medical science has to offer. Insisting that they feel guilty for their illness is cruel and pointless.

The above discussion of guilt and AIDS is by no means comprehensive. An entire book could be written on that subject. You need to be aware of any guilt that you are experiencing in your life, then be willing to deal with it.

Every one of us needs to know that guilt never cured or solved anything. Guilt will never work, will never produce good results. Guilt is guaranteed to produce depression and resentment. It must be quickly dealt with.

The next section will cover ways of releasing guilt and reaching a state of forgiveness and acceptance of things that can't be changed, and finding the energy to change what we can.

GETTING RID OF GUILT

There are two basic kinds of guilt. One which is relatively easy to address is here-and-now guilt. This is guilt that is related to something you have just done.

The other is historical guilt. This refers to a pattern of guilt that can reach back a lifetime. This kind of guilt can be pervasive and contain a host of supposed sins and crimes, mistakes and failures, disappointments and shortcomings.

This kind of guilt is tougher to deal with as it is so complicated and interconnected. Yet it can be sorted out piece by piece, and forgiveness for it achieved.

Some situations include both kinds of guilt. For example, a mother who is feeling guilty for pushing away her son with AIDS might be tapping into a reservoir of guilt that she has always experienced for not being as good a mother as she could have been.

A partner who was easily angered and frustrated with his partner with AIDS may be tapping into guilt over being easily angered and frustrated with his partner throughout the entire relationship. He was probably easily angered and frustrated by his parents and siblings as he was growing up.

The solution for each kind of guilt is essentially the same, although historical guilt may require more time and energy to confront.

Be willing to experience guilt. The first step, as with all emotions, is to be willing to acknowledge and experience the guilt. This won't be difficult for many people. They acknowledge and experience guilt in living color and Dolby sound with frightening ease.

There are others, however, who aren't as aware of their guilt. What they experience is depression, lethargy, or numbness. They feel bad, but don't really know why. They constantly criticize themselves without calling it guilt. It seems to them as though they are just being realistic and objective.

Guilt isn't hard to uncover if you are willing to look for it. Once you determine that you are feeling guilty, then you need to say, out loud, what you are feeling guilty about.

Remember that your mind can think a great deal faster than your mouth can talk. At the thought level, you can't evaluate what is going on. Things that really need attention get all mixed up with irrelevant or out-dated stuff. You can't really see what to do about the situation, because you aren't aware of the specifics of the guilt you are feeling.

That's why it is so necessary to express yourself out loud. That way you can evaluate the different components of your guilt. You can sort out what needs attention and action or what just needs forgiveness.

If talking feels funny, write a list of all the things you feel guilty about. Don't let this list depress you. It may look awesome. Remind yourself that this is only the first step toward completion. You can't forgive what you are unwilling to acknowledge.

Clean up guilt by forgiving and taking action. Once you are aware of the thing that you are feeling guilty about, you are ready for the next step: "Clean it up." Some things just need to be forgiven. There will be other things that will require action on top of forgiveness.

Forgiveness simply means to give up resentment and the desire to punish. *Forgive* does not mean the same thing as *approve* or *condone.* It does not require that you agree with the other person's actions.

Forgiveness will liberate you from carrying around lots of unpleasant angry feelings. It is a cleansing experience. It is an important expression of love.

Forgiveness does not keep you from holding the other person, or yourself, responsible for their behavior. For example, while I was completing this manuscript, my home was burglarized. All of my stereo equipment was stolen. I am not willing to go through life harboring anger and resentment at the ones who broke into my home. I am willing to forgive the persons who did it.

This does not mean that I would not hold them responsible for their behavior in the event that they were caught by the police. Stealing is against the law, and the law has prescribed certain consequences for those who are convicted of stealing. I can forgive the thieves, but still allow them to face the consequences for their behavior.

This may seem like a word game to some. I promise you that it is not. Forgiveness just means giving up resentment and the need to personally punish. It means you are ready to take responsibility and put your energy into fixing the situation, which means taking the necessary action to clean it up.

If my actions have damaged another person, I need to apologize to them. If there is anything that can be done to make up for the damage, I should do it as soon as possible. Twelve-step programs call it "making amends."

If my guilt is connected to someone who has died, then I can still make amends by my actions with others who are involved in the fight against AIDS.

If you have discriminated against a person with AIDS, I don't think that you can sincerely ask for forgiveness or forgive yourself as long as you are continuing to discriminate against other people with AIDS.

It would be asking too much to ask a friend to forgive you for your angry words to him if you continue saying angry, hurtful things to him. You can't ask a friend to forgive you for not repaying the debt you owe him if you are not willing to repay the debt.

If your friend is smart, he or she will have already forgiven you for your debt. That means they aren't holding on to resentment because you haven't paid them back. The fact that they have forgiven you doesn't mean that they would then refuse to accept your payment should you decide to make it.

Forgiveness demands that you take responsibility for all of your actions, and that you do whatever you can to keep from making the same mistake again. If you make the mistake again, go through the entire process again. See what you can learn this time so that you can prevent the mistake from recurring. Forgive as often as you need to, and don't forget to take appropriate action.

As with depression and anger, action is the solution to guilt. It is your choice to stay stuck in the guilt or to acknowledge it, to ask for forgiveness from the other person or from yourself, and then take the necessary action to clean it up.

Are you willing to live with the result of your choice?

CHAPTER EIGHT

conquering fear with action

There is not just one epidemic, AIDS, moving inexorably across the land. There are two. The other epidemic is the fear of AIDS, and it is destroying as many lives as the virus. Maybe more.

Fear makes living in the presence of the virus more difficult and much more painful. Fear makes dying in the presence of the virus a horrible process.

Fear creates more personal pain and disrupts people's lives and activities to a greater extent than any other emotion. While anger and guilt can create a lot of damage, fear is perhaps the most disabling and disempowering of all emotions.

There are some people, for example those who follow *The Course in Miracles,* who believe that fear is the basis for all negative emotions. Feelings of anger, for example, could be explained as a cover-up for fear, or as the result of defense strategies that we use to deal with our fear.

I have not found any evidence to challenge this idea. For example, I have yet to meet an angry, hostile person who was not scared spitless underneath the bluster and bluff. Sometimes you have to look very hard, but the fear seems to always be there.

The usefulness of this view of fear is that it can help us understand and deal more effectively with other emotions. Chronically angry people are closer to solving their problem with anger and the mess it always creates if they realize that the root of their anger may be fear. If the fear is uncovered and challenged directly, it will be easier to let go of the anger.

We can be afraid of just about anything. Like the sources of guilt, the objects of fear are infinite in number.

Fear can be attached to virtually any type of object, real or imagined, human or inhuman, concrete or abstract. We can be afraid of other people, of things they do, of things they say, or of things they think. We can even be afraid of our own thoughts.

We can be afraid of events that are happening, of events that will happen, or of events that we think could happen. We are frequently afraid of things we just make up that have little or no chance of happening.

We can be afraid of anything that could cause us pain or discomfort as well as anything that could place us in danger. Consequently, we can fear experiences of failure, rejection, abandonment, taking risks, facing disapproval, being made fun of, or not being liked, among the myriad possibilities.

The objects of our fears are infinite in number. Fear will add unnecessary pain and suffering to already painful situations, unless we understand it and how to deal with it.

WHAT IS FEAR?

According to the dictionary, fear is the feeling of anxiety or agitation caused by the nearness of danger or evil or pain. Psychologists sometimes make a distinction between anxiety and fear. Fear has a specific object: "I am afraid of snakes." Anxiety has no specific object: "I just feel afraid, but I don't know why." Lay people don't usually make the distinction. I will not make that distinction in this book.

The dictionary definition of fear is pretty accurate, but it misses a very important point. While it is true that fear can be caused by the nearness of danger, fear can exist with no danger in sight. Totally innocuous possibilities can still be a source of fear to some people.

The objects of many of our most debilitating fears pose no real threat to us. We can create danger simply with our minds. The danger seems real enough to be disabling, but it doesn't exist in the real world, outside of our minds.

One of the most pernicious forms of fear is the fear of what could happen in the future. "What if . . ." is a frequently used phrase, and will almost always cause fear. Far too many people make today a miserable experience by worrying about what might happen tomorrow, or next week, or next year.

This is especially true where AIDS is concerned. Many healthy people are suffering today because they fear what might happen if the virus in their body is activated or if they start getting sick. That may not happen for years down the road, but they are suffering badly today.

I will never forget the tearful face of one of my clients who looked at me and said, "I don't want to die. I want to stay around and enjoy life." Yet his every day was filled with fear and foreboding. There was no room for joy because of the fear. He hadn't enjoyed life in a long time.

It's important to understand that fear is not automatically bad. It is a normal, healthy reaction to danger or the perception of danger. It warns us to do something differently so we can avoid that danger. Without fear, we would be heedless of danger, and our behavior would frequently be unsafe, perhaps even deadly.

Fear is a clear call to take action in order to avoid danger. Unfortunately, too many people react to fear with paralysis. They stop all forward movement, becoming immobile.

Fear does not mean, "Stop what you are doing immediately." If we did that, all progress would cease. We would still be living in a Stone Age environment if our ancestors had stopped in the face of fear. Progress and success are not possible without fear.

Fear *does* say, "Open your eyes, see what is happening, be careful how you choose to proceed." This produces wise caution, but not paralysis.

It's also important to know that fear is not just an emotional experience. It has very real physical manifestations.

Fear and stress are quite similar experiences. Most researchers believe that stress is our body's response to any change in our environment. The more threatening, or fearful, the change, the greater the stress.

Fear creates stress. Stress results in increased heart rate, increased respiratory rate, and higher blood pressure. Stress causes certain hormones to be dumped into the bloodstream, the chief of which is adrenaline.

Maintaining the body in this constant state of stress is ultimately damaging to the body. It weakens the immune system. It wears out the body parts that are racing because of the stress or the fear. While we can't remove stress and fear from our daily experiences, we must learn how to keep them at healthy levels.

Fear exists on a continuum of experiences. It can be a mild, almost unnoticeable feeling of concern or caution, like a little glitch. It can increase to blind panic attacks at the other end of the continuum, covering the whole range of intensity in between. Some of us slide up and down the continuum many times a day.

Fear can be an acute condition in response to a specific event that has occurred or could occur. Fear can also be a chronic condition that is there every day, grinding away in your mind. It comes and goes, but it mostly comes.

Again, we can't remove fear from our lives completely. We don't even want to do that. If we understand what causes fear, we will be more powerful in dealing with it when it occurs.

THE CAUSES OF FEAR

As with sadness, anger, and guilt, we create our fear by our attitudes, thoughts, and belief systems. Fear is something that we make up with our minds. It cannot exist independently outside of us.

There are no objects that are inherently fearful. We must put fear onto them.

Of course, there are certain things that most people would agree are fearful: snakes, AIDS, nuclear war, tornadoes, earthquakes. Yet there are plenty of people who are not afraid of these same things. They may have a healthy appreciation for the danger that may be represented by each one, but their feeling doesn't get to the level of debilitating fear.

Quite simply, we learn to be afraid. Very small children are not naturally afraid of snakes until someone teaches them to be afraid.

When the father of behavioral psychology, J. B. Watson, demonstrated that he could condition a small child to be afraid of a rabbit, what he was really doing was changing that child's belief system about fluffy white rabbits. The soft and cuddly animal became associated with an unpleasant experience that represented danger. The child came to fear the rabbit.

As Watson reconditioned the child *not* to be afraid of the rabbit, all he was doing was changing the child's belief system about rabbits. Rabbits became, once again, soft and cuddly creatures.

We learn our fears. We also learn to put different values on fear. *This is a vitally important idea.*

I know that some of you reading this book are roller coaster freaks. You would go anywhere at any time in order to ride a faster, steeper, loopier roller coaster.

If you and I were sitting next to one another in the front seat of the front car of a roller coaster just cresting the peak of the first drop—my palms are sweating as I type this—each of us would be having very similar physical experiences. Our heart rates would be increased, along with our respiratory rates and blood pressure. Adrenaline would be coursing through our bloodstreams, causing that infamous "adrenaline rush." Our sensations would warn us that we were about to experience something dangerous: falling, falling very fast, maybe even falling upside down.

Now I guarantee you that while you would be having the time of your life, I would not. I have been on a roller coaster once in my life. I believe that says enough about how I feel about roller coasters.

The vital point here is that we are each having an identical physical experience, with a totally opposite emotional experience. You are having the time of your life, while I am counting the milliseconds until the horrendous experience is over.

It's not that I'm afraid and you aren't. *We are both afraid.* You have learned how to enjoy that fear intensely. I have not. I don't want to try.

The same holds true for sky divers, bungee jumpers, downhill ski racers, and people who enjoy any other activity that can present the opportunity to play dangerously. What they long for and seek out, others avoid assiduously.

We not only create our fear, but we determine the positive or negative value of that experience of fear. The reason that this is important is that it gives us an important clue about how to deal with fear.

We can't live without experiencing fear. We shouldn't even want to live without fear. That would be too dangerous, or too dull.

I did a cable TV show about ten years ago to talk about stress-reduction tactics. I had made several appearances on the same show that year. Each time I was nervous, and I thought that it showed on camera and decreased my effectiveness. I wasn't going to let that happen this time.

I got to the TV studio a half hour early, and found a quiet place where I could be alone. I spent the next thirty minutes doing deep-muscle relaxation exercises. By the time we went on the air, I was relaxed. Was I ever relaxed!

I was so relaxed that when we went off camera at the end of the show, the host looked at me with not a little disgust, and said, "Paul, where in the world were you tonight? That was the most boring interview I've done in a long time."

I have not been asked back to be on that show, and I have stopped doing deep-muscle relaxation exercises before interviews. Fear creates that edge that makes it all more interesting.

We don't want to remove fear from our experience. What we can do is change the value we place on fear, lower the intensity of the experience if that is necessary, and learn to take any appropriate action that will reduce the danger. We do this most effectively if we appreciate how we create the fear in the first place with our thoughts, attitudes, and belief systems.

We create our fear with our belief that something is dangerous. The more dangerous we think it is, the more afraid we are.

If we have a belief that fear is an exciting experience, we get to have a good time with the fear. If we believe that fear is a terrible experience, we will suffer. It's the same fear, just different beliefs.

Our attitudes, thoughts, and belief systems can be appropriate, creating realistic fear. They can be appropriate but exaggerated or overgeneralized, creating unfounded and unnecessary fear. They can be wildly inappropriate, creating unfounded and unnecessary fear.

Some fear is appropriate. Our attitudes, thoughts, and belief systems can be accurate. For example, we can have a belief system that being bitten by an angry rattlesnake can be deadly. Consequently we fear rattlesnakes and choose to keep out of their way. This looks very wise to me.

We can have a belief system that AIDS is a dangerous disease that we would be wise to avoid, if we can. Consequently we can choose to be afraid of AIDS and choose to avoid unsafe sexual or drug-using behaviors. We devise our Wellness strategy, and do whatever we can to stay healthy. This also looks wise.

Some of our attitudes, thoughts, and belief systems are basically appropriate, but are then exaggerated or overgeneralized. This can produce fear that is unrealistic and unnecessary. This fear can paralyze us, prevent us from taking necessary action.

The fear of snakes is a good example here too. I have a home in Cathedral City, California, next door to Palm Springs. We are only a few blocks from the open desert. There are rattlesnakes in the desert. These snakes can sometimes find their way into our backyard.

My belief that rattlesnakes are dangerous is appropriate. I could add the inappropriate belief that I should avoid my backyard, if there is a chance of running into a rattlesnake. That would overgeneralize the fear and rob me of the opportunity of enjoying my backyard. While it is appropriate to fear the damage a rattlesnake can do, it would not be appropriate for me to avoid spending time in my backyard because I might come across a rattlesnake.

Our belief that AIDS is dangerous can be exacerbated by the belief that our being around people who are HIV-positive or who have AIDS is also dangerous. This dangerously inaccurate belief exaggerates our fear exponentially. It can result in our withdrawing from some people whom we love. Our loneliness and guilt will increase our suffering. Such fear and such suffering is needless.

Many of our sources of fear are based on wholly inappropriate attitudes, thoughts, and belief systems. We can fear walking under a ladder or stepping on a crack in the sidewalk, even though we know that such fears are groundless.

Our minds can create fear of objects that really aren't fearful. We can be afraid of flying, elevators, escalators, water, public speaking, or any other thing that we suppose offers some danger. But, while there may be some slight chance of danger, or danger under special circumstances, our fear is out of proportion.

For example, there is nothing to fear about water, in general. If it is over our heads and we can't swim, we are wise to be afraid.

Many people who are afraid of water frequently experience that fear even though they are in shallow water that presents no danger to them. Some can be afraid just looking at a body of water.

There is no real danger involved with public speaking, yet it is one of the most widespread of fears. People react as though their lives were at stake when they stand up to speak before a crowd of people.

The truth is that no one is going to hurt them. In fact, almost everyone will probably be rooting for them, since few people like to watch someone suffer. Yet the person who is afraid of speaking can still be terrified to the point of becoming physically ill.

There is absolutely no reason to fear for the health of our children if we spend time around someone with AIDS. Yet many people have just that fear. There are so many gay men, HIV-positive as well as HIV-negative, who are no longer welcome in their family's home for this very reason. This fear destroys families.

Our fears can sometimes be very selective. For example, my mother lives in central Kansas. She was terrified when I told her I was moving to Los Angeles because, to this day, she is sure that an earthquake is going to get me. This is something she worries about a lot.

Yet she has little fear for her own safety during the Kansas tornado season. When I was in graduate school, I was called home to help her pick up the pieces of five homes that used to be across the alley from her and were now in her backyard. Only their foundations were left. Yet she doesn't fear tornadoes nearly as much as she fears earthquakes, even though she has never experienced an earthquake.

We create our fears with our thoughts, attitudes, and belief systems. We then determine if we are going to place a positive or a negative value on that experience of fear. Our fears can be appropriate, they can be exaggerated and overgeneralized, or they can be completely made up.

If we can learn how to avoid intensifying our fear with inappropriate belief systems, we can minimize its impact on our daily lives.

HOW WE INTENSIFY OUR FEARS

Many of our fears are magnified by other factors. Sometimes it is not the fearful object that causes all the fear. There are other belief systems that can be brought into play that consequently increase our fear.

The fear of certain objects can be accompanied by fear of what someone else will think if they observe us being afraid. This is not to say that the object isn't fearful. It's just that our fear of others' disapproval makes our fear worse.

The first phobic client I ever saw in psychotherapy was a young man who was afraid of elevators. He had a great new job that had necessitated his being transferred to the home office, which was in a high-rise office building. His new office was on the twenty-first floor, and he was terrified of elevators.

We worked on some simple desensitization exercises. First he would stand outside elevators and just watch them; then he might push the button; then he might actually dart into the elevator and dash right back out.

After several days of doing this, he decided he was ready to try a ride. He only had to go up one floor, and he could get right back off. There was an escalator next to the elevator, and he could take that back down if he didn't feel like another elevator ride.

Before too long, he was going up several floors, nervous and sweaty, but still able to do it—as long as no one else was around. If someone got on the elevator with him, he had to get off immediately.

We discovered that he was very afraid of what someone else on the elevator would think about him if they noticed that he was nervous about being on the elevator. He was afraid that they would think he was a wimp or a coward, and he couldn't deal with that. He wasn't able to get completely over his fear of elevators until he dealt with his fear of disapproval.

I have seen some people who are afraid of freeways. In Southern California, this is a debilitating fear. As we investigate the situation, we discover that they are not only afraid of the traffic, the speed, and what would happen if there were an accident, they are afraid of what other drivers will think about them poking along in the slow lane, going under the speed limit.

Their fear of others' disapproval is greater than the more important fact that driving under the speed limit in Southern California is much more dangerous than driving the speed limit in the fast lane.

Some people believe that they are afraid of success or of being loved. I suspect that "fear of success" is just a yuppie euphemism for "fear of failure" when the stakes are high. "Fear of success" sounds more enlightened than "fear of failure," like we're playing at a much higher level.

Although we think we are afraid of success, what we are really afraid of is the risks we will have to take in order to be successful. We're afraid if we once become successful that we won't be able to maintain it. We may also be afraid that we don't deserve to succeed.

The same thing is true for those who think they are afraid of being loved. They aren't really afraid of love. They are afraid of the risks that are associated with allowing themselves to be vulnerable enough to love another person. They, too, may feel as if they don't deserve to be loved.

Many men I have worked with who were diagnosed with AIDS certainly were afraid of the disease. They frequently were able to come to grips with that fear. Unfortunately, they would also hold on to the fear of others' disapproval and fear of them because they had AIDS.

Dr. Albert Ellis talks about two other processes that are guaranteed to increase the discomfort of our fear: *heaping* and *catastrophizing. Heaping* is where we put a whole string of events and possibilities together and end up reacting to the whole mess. We are afraid of having AIDS, going bankrupt, being shunned by some of our friends and family, losing our health, suffering pain, and dying.

All of this together would indeed create a very fearful experience. This accumulated fear can appear nearly insurmountable. It is all too easy to become a victim of this kind of fear.

Catastrophizing is looking at a potentially negative event and making it into a catastrophe.

Being rejected is an unpleasant experience. It is not a catastrophe, although there are many people who still choose to react to any rejection as though it were a catastrophe. For them, in fact, rejection becomes a catastrophe.

We can catastrophize about the possibility of failing at something, instead of recognizing that while failure is unpleasant and to be avoided when possible, it is not a catastrophe. We can remind ourselves that we don't even have to think in terms of failures. We can realize that they are only *results,* which we can change as we learn more. (This idea comes from motivation expert Tony Robbins.)

The point is, *we* decide what is a catastrophe and what is just an unfortunate thing that we wish hadn't happened. Our level of fear and our level of suffering will be completely dependent on which choice we make.

Fear is just another emotion. It is not all-powerful. It is not a stop sign. It is not a signal to turn back. It is not a signal to give up. As the book title says, we need to learn to *Feel the Fear and Do It Anyway.*

We need to know that bravery is not the absence of fear. It is the willingness to feel fear and still do what you are afraid of. A brave person is not someone who is never afraid, but someone who doesn't let fear stop him or her from doing what he or she has to do. Like a bungee jumper, he or she may actually relish the fear.

AIDS FEAR

Any death usually creates fear, because it reminds you of your own mortality. An AIDS death can produce terror as you contemplate your future, especially if you are HIV-positive.

Added to the terror of possible impending death, there is the fear of potential suffering, and there is terror of the discrimination, societal judgments, and alienation that accompany AIDS most of the time. Even those who are HIV-negative will not be immune to this terror. They are tarred with the same brush and subject to the same discrimination.

Their AIDS fear has turned many gay men into victims. These men have become depressed and paralyzed as they await their own death. I have held their hands and tried to get them to see that they had other options and other choices. In some cases I was successful. In others, I was not.

I have watched too many men wrap themselves up into tighter and tighter balls, so that even therapy or the best efforts of their friends could no longer reach them. I have seen otherwise healthy HIV-positive men whose lives were destroyed by that fear.

You don't have to be HIV-positive to be terrified of the AIDS virus. Many HIV-negative men are terrified of AIDS even though they repeatedly test negative. They are just as much a victim of AIDS as someone who is HIV-positive and overrun by fear.

Some people are now talking not only about being HIV-*infected,* but being HIV-*affected.* That includes an even larger group of people whose lives are touched by AIDS or the fear of AIDS.

Fear of death is a major source of AIDS fear. Ironically, the fear of death has become so intense for some that they end up committing suicide.

I don't know how to deal with the fear of death except by realizing that we will all die one day. That fact is guaranteed, and nothing will prevent it.

Whether that death will happen tomorrow, next week, or many years from now, we must accept its inevitability. We must not waste any energy fearing that. We must put all of our energy into living today as well as we can. We must make the most out of every hour we have to live, and live it to the fullest.

One of my favorite authors is Wayne Dyer. He wrote *Your Erroneous Zones, Pulling Your Own Strings, The Sky's the Limit,* and others. His books and audiotapes have had a major influence on my own growth process. He has a very important idea about living today well.

Most of us can remember the poster that was really popular during the sixties, "Today is the first day of the rest of your life." I had always thought that was an appealing idea, until I heard Dyer point out its danger. We are not guaranteed to have a second day. None of us is guaranteed to have a tomorrow.

Today is the only day we have, and Dyer asserts that we should live it as though it were our last day. Why not live it as fully, as joyfully, as passionately as we are able? When and if tomorrow comes, we will live that one as well as we can also.

I know many people who have been able to deal with their fear of death but have a debilitating fear of the suffering that they know they could experience before dying.

The answer here, too, is live today well. We don't know how we are going to die, or what will be involved in that process. We must not give dire *possibilities* (sorry, Wayne) time to disrupt our experience of today. We must remind ourselves as loudly as we can to live today well. Deal with tomorrow, tomorrow.

Fear of living life without your loved one, without his support, without his strength, also must be faced. You may be feeling devastated now, at a loss and without hope, believing that you don't have the resources to face this fear, too.

Know that as your grieving process progresses, you can find the necessary resources. You *can* find the support and the energy to confront your fears, all of them. Don't hesitate to ask for that support, and if it isn't forthcoming, go somewhere else and look for it.

Caregivers are especially vulnerable to dealing with fear. While they were busy taking care of their friend or family member, there wasn't a lot of time to think about being afraid. After they said goodbye, there was more than enough time. Fear can then mushroom.

Don't be alarmed if this happens to you. Understand that it is part of the process. It may seem overwhelming because you have been storing up fear for a long time, unable to look at it while you were taking care of your loved one. You will have a lot of un-heaping and de-catastrophizing to do.

Fear can keep people away from the person who is ill, as well as away from the death and any memorial service. I have spoken to a number of men whose life partners or friends had been diagnosed and admitted to the hospital, and whose friends subsequently disappeared, except for the rare message left on the answering machine when it was certain no one would be home.

This scenario creates guilt for the ones staying away, and anger for the ones who are left. The person in need feels abandoned and uncared for.

That is not the problem. The real problem is fear, and this is where the solution must lie as well: in learning how to confront fear, yours and your friends'.

Give your friends time to adjust to the news, time to have their fear. Often, they will get over it and come back to you. Try not to punish them for their desertion, and put your energy into welcoming them back. Enjoy their support now, without wasting time worrying about their lack of support in the past.

If they don't come back, don't waste time worrying about it. You might even find some sympathy for someone who is such a victim of fear that they cut themselves off from the people they love.

Life partners may fear discrimination and persecution by landlords, by the family of the deceased, by society in general. There may be the fear that no one will ever be able to love them again, knowing their partner died of AIDS. With that thought, dating again will be a nightmare.

Some of these problems are potentially real, but don't let them heap up on you. Sort them out. Deal with each as best you can. Focus on getting the job done as well as you can. Seek out support from empowering people. Don't wallow in blaming others for their lack of support.

If you lose your home, it's a heinous and unjust act, to be sure. Don't allow yourself to become a victim of your landlord's fear, however. Get on with your life as best you can. Do whatever you have to do in order to protect yourself and to get a roof over your head.

Family members, friends, and coworkers may have their own fear that is generated by an AIDS death. In spite of massive education efforts, there is still too much misinformation out there about AIDS. There are far too many people afraid of "catching it" in spite of the absence of any high-risk behavior in their lives.

Education is one of the most powerful antidotes to fear. If you know the stuff intellectually but are still needlessly frightened, I'd strongly advise you to seek professional help. You don't need this suffering.

AIDS fear is unlike any emotion that any of us expected to have to experience. It's virtually impossible to avoid it. This is especially true if you know you have the viral time bomb ticking through your bloodstream.

AIDS fear can kill you just as surely as the virus. It must be confronted as part of your grieving process, or your process won't be complete.

DEALING WITH FEAR

"Don't be afraid!" This is perhaps one of the silliest things we can ever say to anybody about any fear. If you are afraid, you are afraid.

Knowing that you shouldn't be afraid will not free you from your fear.

If we are to be of assistance to someone who is afraid, we must take their fear seriously. Then we will be able to help them start to challenge it effectively.

We have already hinted at some of the ways to deal with fear. We can let fear energize and challenge us instead of paralyzing us. We can feel the fear and do it anyway. We can sort out the sources of our fear so that we aren't "heaping," and we can learn to change our thinking in ways that will "de-catastrophize" our fears.

To deal with fear, we can follow the Victim-ectomy Formula.

Deal with fear by being willing to experience it. Most people don't have any problem experiencing and expressing their fears. Fear isn't as frequently repressed and suppressed as anger.

While we may be successful at keeping others from knowing about our fears, we are rarely able to hide our fears from ourselves. The easier ones to hide from are the more indirect ones, such as the fear of disapproval or rejection.

This may take some sleuthing. We may know better than to say we're afraid of disapproval or rejection, yet our actions clearly indicate that we must fear disapproval or rejection, otherwise we would seek it out more vigorously in the pursuit of our goals.

If you are in the midst of your grieving process, you may not be ready for the techniques that follow right now. You may just need to try to hang on for a while. If you know that fear is making your grief harder to bear, then gently push yourself toward the following exercises. They will get results.

Start your fear-coping process by listing on a piece of paper all of the things you are afraid of. Remember to put them all down. Nothing is too petty, or too awful, or too silly. If you're afraid of it, list it. If this task starts to be upsetting, remind yourself that it is just the first step in the process.

Once you have a good list, take a highlighter and mark through those things that you really want to deal with. Don't be overwhelmed by this either, if you have checked a lot of items. You won't be working on all of them at once.

Make it easy on yourself and select only a few items to start with.

Pick easy ones. As you get some successes under your belt and you understand how the system works, you can tackle some of the biggies.

Sometimes just acknowledging and quickly expressing your fear is all it takes. I have clients who are HIV-positive and still asymptomatic who must periodically shout out loud, "I am afraid of AIDS. I am afraid of suffering. I am afraid of dying." Just getting that out of their system is all they need to do. Then they just get on with it.

There are others who have no problem listing their fears. They are stuck in their fears. They shout over and over again, "I am afraid of AIDS. I am afraid of suffering. I am afraid of dying." They are stuck in that litany of fear. They aren't able to get on with their lives. Their fear has paralyzed them.

If you see yourself here, I strongly urge you to seek out a support group or a psychotherapist experienced in dealing with AIDS fear. Just be sure that your support group or your therapist does not support you in being stuck in your fear.

Once you have listed and expressed your fears, you are ready for the next step, which is "Clean it up." Here is where we examine our belief systems, un-heap, and de-catastrophize. This is where we examine the negative value we are putting on our fear and see if we can't turn it around to our advantage.

Deal with fear by changing your thinking. Now, pick a fear to work on, and then see what unworkable beliefs support it. Go back to Chapter 5 if you need to, and examine the list of unworkable beliefs. See which ones contribute to your experience of fear. Then find a way to challenge each one. Be prepared to make that challenge over and over again, as long as the fear continues to reoccur.

The A x B = C formula works very well here. A is the event or object. C is the fear. B is the belief system that helps create the fear. Note what you have to be thinking or believing in order to create and maintain your fear.

Be on the lookout for heaping and catastrophizing. They will frequently be important factors in your belief system.

The solution to heaping is sorting things out, then tackling them one at a time. Your mind may be screaming, "But look at all this stuff. How can I ever cope with that?"

Don't be intimidated by your mind chatter. If you can just get started on dealing with one issue, you will quickly see that this task is not as insurmountable as it first appeared.

Catastrophizing is almost always part of every belief system we have that produces strong negative emotions. Suffering can be a catastrophe, or it can merely be something that we must bear if that's what's on our plate right now.

People who catastrophize will suffer more. People who have learned how to just get through a bad situation, no matter how awful it is, don't suffer as much.

Once you are willing to de-catastrophize and challenge the unworkable beliefs behind your fear, you are ready to face the object of your fear. ("Oh, rats. You mean I'm going to have to face it? Can't I just deal with it in my head?")

You could do that. However, until you are willing to face the object of your fear, you won't really be in charge of your own life. That fear will run you.

No matter how much good work I do with a client who is afraid of AIDS or of dying with AIDS, our work is incomplete if he or she is unwilling to go face AIDS.

How do you do that? It's easy, actually. Become an AIDS buddy. Work on a hotline or at a food bank for people with AIDS. Deliver food if your community has a Project Angelfood or something like it that provides free hot meals to people with AIDS who are too disabled to get up and fix their own meals. Visit people in AIDS wards. Go to a funeral or memorial service.

Don't start with the hardest task first. Most people would probably find working on the telephone to be an easier first step than visiting a hospital.

Decide which step in facing AIDS would be the easiest and which would be the hardest. Then start with the easiest action and work up to harder ones.

Change the negative values you place on fear. Instead of looking at your fear as a stop sign, or as an indication that it is time to retreat, remind yourself that fear is just a sign to look around, scope out the danger, and take effective action.

Fear can be a powerful motivator if you don't get stuck being a victim of it. Fear can be seen as a kind of electricity. Electricity is just energy. How it is put to use makes a vast difference in the result. Electricity can kill. Electricity can also run a life support system.

Fear can kill, too. It can also provide the motivation to take aggressive, effective action in dealing with a problem. Facing the fear and the object of our fear can be turned into a challenge. Life will be more exciting and less painful, with less suffering, if we are willing to do that, no matter how hard it may seem at first.

I believe that the human spirit is capable of overcoming almost any challenge if we don't allow ourselves to become a victim of our fear.

Let your fear energize you as you embark on a program to do something about the problem. Where the fear of AIDS is concerned, this means embarking on your own Wellness program.

Action and a wellness program is a great antidote to fear. The market is full of books that contain powerful and fascinating ways for you to combat your fear of AIDS with an aggressive Wellness program. My first book, *Pathways to Wellness: Strategies for Self-Empowerment in the Age of AIDS* is one such book. The reason I chose the word *pathways* is that it seems to me that there isn't just one right way to face AIDS. There are many ways that are working for many people, and not working for others.

One of the startling discoveries in Michael Callen's book *Surviving AIDS* is that the long-term survivors he interviews are all on different paths and programs. I know several long-term survivors who don't really have a program at all. They are just surviving.

No one can tell you precisely what you have to do in order to design your own Wellness program. The only way for you to do that is to read a lot, go to a lot of workshops and support groups, and talk to a lot of people. See what looks promising and interesting to you and then give it a try.

Make a real commitment to designing your own Wellness program. Remember to be flexible. Trial and error is always an effective way to learn.

Don't waste time on programs that you already know you can't stick to. You may know a dozen people who are doing well on macrobiotic diets. If you know that there is no way you could realistically stick to such a program, then don't choose that one.

Your commitment to your own Wellness will be the most powerful thing that you can do to combat your AIDS fear. Knowing that you are doing everything that you can possibly do to stay well and live today well will empower you to turn your fear into motivation for even bigger and better things.

PART TWO   **AIDS grief**

The next three chapters address the specific problems that are
faced by life partners, family members, and friends, with emphasis on practical suggestions for how to deal with a wide variety
of problems.

I urge you to read all three chapters and not just the chapter
addressing the form of your relationship to the person who has
died.

Much of the information listed in the chapter for life partners
is relevant for family members as well as friends. The chapter for
family members has information that is relevant for partners and
friends, and so on. The information won't be repeated in detail
in each chapter.

Finding appropriate support during this period of grief is of
maximum importance. Life partners, family members, and friends
can be powerfully supportive of one another. If each has a better
understanding of what the others are going through, that support can be even more effective. Reading the other chapters can
lend to that understanding.

when your life partner has died

If your life partner has died of AIDS, you have experienced one of the most painful events a human being can endure. The impact on your life has been profound. It's likely that your emotions are still in a state of chaos. Your own sense of personal power in your own life is being severely tested.

If you have been able to pick up this book and start reading, you are probably already on your way to healing. You may have a way to go, but at least you have begun your journey.

While your partner's struggles have ended, yours are continuing. You must begin thinking about putting your life back together. I know that it can look overwhelming now, but you can survive. It will begin to look less overwhelming.

The fact that your partner died of AIDS will, in many cases, make your grieving more complicated and difficult. As we have discussed, AIDS will add extra components to your grieving: dealing with fear, societal prejudice, AIDS rage, and guilt.

If you are gay, the complications multiply. You will have to face the same issues as a heterosexual person who has lost his or her spouse. In addition, there will be the question of the legitimacy of your relationship to your partner. No state will recognize you as the legal spouse, at least at the time of this writing.

You have no guarantees about your part in burial, funeral, or memorial services. Your own jointly held properties are not guaranteed to you. You may find it difficult to find safe places to share what you are going through with others.

The list of potential difficulties can look overwhelming, I know. It might seem kinder for me not to point them out. Yet, the problems will still be there, even if we don't talk about them. *If we ignore them, they could get worse, much worse.*

Some of the problems will need immediate attention for your own protection and safety. By the time you feel ready to handle them, it may be too late and you will suffer loss or other unpleasant consequences.

Sometimes there isn't the luxury of time in which to grieve. There is work that must be done. As daunting as it may look, I know that you can rise to the necessary tasks.

If you can, at least, be aware of some of the pitfalls surrounding an AIDS death, then you can learn how to devise more effective strategies for dealing with them.

I know that some of you may not be experiencing all of these negative circumstances. There are many families who respect their child's life partner and friends. There are enlightened employers and landlords. There are magnificent friends who will be with you every step of the way.

If you are fortunate enough to have any or all of these resources, cherish them. They will make your grieving process that much more bearable.

If you are not fortunate enough to have these resources, don't waste time bemoaning the fact. Put your energy into moving through your own grief process as well as you can. Your job may be tougher, but it won't be impossible.

This chapter will address the more practical issues that you may have to face following an AIDS death. Dealing with your feelings will not be addressed in this chapter. If you're still having difficulty with your feelings, go back and review Chapters 1 through 8. Do the suggested work as best you can.

You may not feel ready to face "work" on these practical issues at this time. I really do understand that, but *I still advise you to read through this chapter.* There are undoubtedly some things that will require your immediate and thoughtful attention, no matter how upset you are feeling. To put them off would complicate your life and possibly jeopardize the integrity of your home. Identify those tasks that just cannot be put off and then set about to get them handled as soon as you can. Don't hesitate to ask for help if you need to.

I would also urge you to read the following two chapters. The chapter for parents will perhaps help you understand more of what the family is going through, and help you deal with them more effectively. The chapter for friends also includes a section on caregiver burnout. This is a concept that could be very valuable for you, particularly if you have been helping take care of other friends as well as your life partner.

YOUR NEEDS, RIGHT NOW

There is no adequate timetable or schedule for you to try to follow. Your grief process will be as unique as you are.

For some of you, this is the first time you have ever gone through an experience like this. You are facing uncharted territory. It may look terrifying, but know that you can get through it. I hope this chapter will give you some ideas about how to handle some of the stuff you will be facing in the weeks and months to come.

Others of you have been grieving for a lot of people in the last ten years. This is nothing new, except for the fact that the person who has died was your life partner. Some of you may have already lost several partners.

For some of you, dealing with death may be easier now. You are not in totally foreign territory. You have a good idea about what to expect, and know how to prepare yourself to meet it more effectively.

For others, it never gets easier. Each death is just as painful as the last one, maybe more so. The fact that you have been through this before doesn't make it any easier to bear.

Some of you have been so busy taking care of your partner and possibly your friends that you didn't begin grieving until it was all over. Others of you have been grieving since you first discovered that your partner was HIV-positive. Your grief process has been going on for a long time.

The important thing for you to realize is that you are exactly where you need to be right now. Your needs, *right now,* are different from anyone else's needs. Your needs, *right now,* are different than your needs were a month or a year ago. Your needs, *right now,* are different than your needs will be in a month or a year.

Don't make the mistake of comparing this death to the last one. Your relationship to this person was different than your relationship to anyone else you have lost. The circumstances are probably very different, as well.

Don't compare your experience to anyone else's experience. Your history as a human being is different. Your needs as an individual are different. The way you deal with emotions is your own, and may not correspond to the way your friends deal with their emotions.

Don't try to figure out which stage of grief you are in. That won't produce useful information, and your feelings will probably change anyway, perhaps momentarily.

Just know where you are *right now,* and do what is appropriate for *right now.* Above all, don't even think that you will be in the same place next month, next week, or even tomorrow. *You will not always feel this way.* This too shall pass.

Later is now. Many people have been so busy taking care of their partner that lots of things had to be put off. "I'll deal with that later." Well, later is now.

It would be nice if after a death you could just quietly go away for a while and heal. Some of you may be able to do that. For others, that can't happen, no matter how much you need it.

There are things that just will not be put off any longer. This can include issues with your home or with your finances, such as getting around to paying the bills. It may look easier to put them off now, but you don't really need to deal with the stress of bill collectors and angry phone calls from creditors. A few minutes spent here can help you avoid lots of painful and annoying stress later.

Your job may also need some attention. Many of the people with whom I have worked have tended to let their jobs sort of slide during the last days of their partner's illness. Even the most understanding boss will not let you continue to do that for very long. Again, you don't need to be dealing with the stress of being unemployed on top of everything else.

Putting more energy back into your job will also provide you with a more powerful feeling of rejoining life. It will help you avoid falling into a deeper state of victimhood.

You will probably need to be concerned about your own health. This is important regardless of your HIV status. Even if you are HIV-negative, the stress of the illness and death could have a deleterious effect on your own health.

If you are HIV-positive, you will definitely need to deal with your fear of your own future. You will need to know how to handle the worries that you may have been stockpiling during the illness.

It's time to put some energy into taking care of yourself. It's time to begin thinking about living today well.

Later is now, and there may be an awesome list of duties crying for attention. Again, I suspect that more than a few of you reading this don't want to hear about more responsibilities right now. I understand that.

However, I also know that there are things that still must be done, not matter how hard we are hurting. Not to do them would cause us more massive problems later.

Make a list. As overwhelming as it may seem, I'd suggest that you start by making a simple list of all of those things that need to be done. Nothing is too big or too small for this list.

Don't let the list get you down; it's just a way for you to begin to prioritize your responsibilities and use your time more wisely.

You don't have to dive headfirst into the list. You are merely going to use it to be certain that you aren't forgetting something that must be done right away.

If this is really tough for you to do, ask a friend or family member to help you. Just grit your teeth and do it.

As you create your list, remember that you don't have to do everything now. Neither do you have to do everything yourself. You don't have to be noble here. *Be willing to utilize your support network.*

If you have lost part or all of your support group because of the presence of AIDS, don't waste time worrying about that. Put your attention to finding replacements. You deserve help.

Be prepared to do what has to be done. Be willing to ask for the help you need.

Don't be afraid to utilize your support network. What is a support network? It is the people around you who care about you. This could mean your family and friends. It could mean people in a support group that you regularly attend. It could be people from your church or temple. It could mean people in the community who contribute their time and energy helping out however they can. Your support network can also involve professionals such as your physician or a psychotherapist.

If you are in one of the major cities, you will have little trouble finding some kind of support network. If you are in a city where such services are not available, you may need to be willing to travel or use the telephone.

No one deserves to go through this situation alone. Don't be afraid to ask for help from whatever resource you can find. No task is too small or insignificant to ask for help with.

Please don't make the mistake of waiting for your friends to offer their help. They may not know what needs to be done. They may not want to intrude on your grief and may be waiting for you to let them know how they can best support you. If you don't ask for what you want, you likely will not get it.

Asking for help is not the same thing as being rescued. You are not being a victim by asking for help. You are not asking someone to take over your responsibility; you are just asking them to be with you and help out. You are still the one responsible for your life and what is happening in it. *There are too many people who have become a victim of their unwillingness to ask for help.*

Being told no does not mean "I don't love you." Don't be afraid to ask for exactly what you want. At the same time, however, be willing to let the people from whom you are asking help to say no. If that happens, try not to worry about it or waste time feeling resentful. Just find others who are willing and able to help you.

Don't let "no" mislead you. It doesn't mean that people don't love you. It doesn't mean that they aren't there for you anymore. It just means that *right now* they don't have the resources to help you.

They may have sources of stress going on in their life that you know nothing about. With so many of us grieving for people we love, there may be times when it just isn't possible to find the strength to support someone else who is also grieving.

Respect the grief process of others and be sure to clear the way for them to be able to come back into a relationship with you when they are ready.

I know you are the one who is hurting and who is wanting help. The idea is to put your energy into finding that help wherever it is, instead of resenting where it isn't.

I have worked with too many people who have crossed off names of friends they felt let them down. While it seemed understandable at the time, they later regretted their action, as it deprived them of a meaningful friendship.

Many will be willing to help, if you ask for it. Not everyone will say no. Many will be willing to be there for you, if you are willing to tell them what you need. It will be far easier for some of them to make phone calls regarding a memorial service or to help make burial arrangements. Their help will be invaluable when it comes time to begin to reorganize your home. Just hanging out with people can be a wonderful comfort.

One of the most frequent mistakes that I encounter is people's unwillingness to ask for what they want from their support group. They inappropriately assume that everyone knows how to support everyone else. This would require mind reading.

There are lots and lots of ways one person can support another. Support can look like sitting and holding your hand for hours while you cry. If you need someone to do that with you, that's fine, but you need to be willing to ask for that kind of support.

Tell them that you just need them to be there, that you aren't expecting them to solve the unsolvable or accomplish the impossible. You just need someone to cry with. That's OK.

Support can also look like going out to a movie together, or going for a walk on the beach. (If that's something you used to do with your partner, you may want to put that off for a while. Give yourself a little more time to heal.)

The point is, your friend can support you by just going out somewhere with you. At the least, it can be distracting from your grief. At best, it can begin to ease you back into the flow of life a little faster.

Ask for what you want. Decide how you want to be supported. Then ask for that. Don't hesitate to let your friends know if they are supporting you in a way that doesn't work for you. *That is not unkind or ungrateful.* If you were trying to support someone in a way that wasn't working, wouldn't you want to know it?

I see a lot of people who just need a bodily presence in the room with them, watching TV, reading the paper, or just listening to music. They don't want to be held or cuddled. They cringe at the thought of someone all over them physically. They don't want to be waited on. Taking care of themselves feels good to them.

I see others who want it all. They want to be held and cuddled. They want to be waited on. They want to be catered to. They would most definitely not be satisfied with someone who just wanted to sit on the sofa with them watching "The Simpsons."

Don't make a value judgment about which one is wanting support the Right way. Each of us gets to do it our own way.

Of course, there are tricky gray areas with each choice. The "I'll do it myself" types can go too far, so that they are actually running from much-needed support. They likely have trouble trusting other people to take care of their needs. They may be afraid of intimate relationships. If you see yourself here, I'd urge you to get some assistance in dealing with your fear of being supported.

The other group, the "do it all for me" folks, can easily lapse into victimhood, demanding everyone around them take care of them and do it all. This would be a rescue, and it won't work.

This group will have trouble keeping people around to help them. Their friends will wear out quickly and run screaming for the woods.

If you see yourself here, please consider seeing a therapist. Be aware of your tendency to enter therapy expecting your therapist to do it all for you. He or she can't. They can share insights with you, they can make suggestions, but they can't do it for you.

Trial and error support. Asking for support, or giving support for that matter, is really just another trial and error situation. You may not know just how you would like to be supported. You won't know until you try.

There's nothing wrong with changing your mind and letting

your support group know that you'd like to try it differently. Always remember you are the one being supported. You get to ask for what works for you.

I can still hear some of you worrying about telling someone that they are supporting you in a way that you don't like. You may fear that they will accuse you of being ungrateful. Some of them may do that. If they do, notice that they are now playing persecutor to your victim.

A real source of support will want to support you only in the way that works for you. A rescuer will support you the way they think is the Right way. You don't need rescuers at this time in your life. Rescuers will only complicate your life and string out your grieving process.

Types of support groups. There are many types of support groups available to you, both professional and peer groups. Some deal specifically with grieving issues. There are others that deal with a range of HIV issues, including grief. There are still others that deal with a wide range of human issues, including HIV issues.

Just because you have lost your partner doesn't mean that you need to go to a grief support group. You need to choose one that feels good to you.

I have had clients who felt worse after each support group they attended. They would be doing fine, then the support group would come along and they would find themselves getting depressed or angry all over again.

Other clients are alive today because they belonged to a support group. The comfort they received was invaluable and life-sustaining.

Again, the point is to do what works for you. Don't fall into the trap of choosing what has worked for someone else that you know.

Twelve-step programs can also be a welcome source of support. Codependents Anonymous and groups for Adult Children of Alcoholics are widely available. I have had clients who were not co-dependent and who were not adult children of alcoholics who found marvelous and effective support from these groups. If you can't find a listing for either of these groups, call your local Alcoholics Anonymous number for information about Twelve Step programs.

If you are heterosexual and your spouse or lover has died of AIDS, you may have a much tougher time finding a support group with other heterosexuals. If you can, that's good. If you can't, you aren't all on your own. I know of a number of gay men's support groups who have welcomed heterosexuals into their groups with very open arms.

If you have some homophobia to deal with, do that. Don't let it stand in your way of getting support. Don't be surprised if some lesbian or gay people get angry with you for your homophobia. We have all been putting up with it for way too long, and many of us just won't stand for it any longer, and have very little patience for dealing with it when we encounter it. You will be welcome; your homophobia won't be.

If you have trouble working with a group and would prefer individual work, seek out a therapist. Money may be an issue here, but most major cities have therapists who reserve a certain number of slots for low-fee clients in their time schedule. Look for them. Call the nearest Lesbian/Gay Community Services Center or AIDS Project for lists of these therapists.

Be cautious about choosing support groups or therapists. As I have stated over and over, don't let yourself get involved with a doom-and-gloom group. You don't need any help feeling worse than you already do.

Be sure that your therapist is not homophobic. Don't ever assume that just because someone is a credentialed therapist they can't be homophobic. This includes lesbian or gay therapists. Unfortunately, homophobic therapists are all too common, even among those who are gay and lesbian. If your therapist is lesbian or gay and still "in the closet," I would advise you to question him or her carefully to be sure that their closetedness isn't connected to subtle homophobia.

Incidentally, anyone who has the notion that gay and lesbian citizens are second-class citizens is homophobic. They may not be as dangerous as Jesse Helms, but they are still not affirming your wholeness as a person, and that is damaging.

Be willing to confront your therapist if you feel, however vaguely, that he or she might be homophobic. If your therapist is homophobic, you are frankly nuts to keep going to him or her. How can anyone help you if he or she won't accept you as you are?

Watch out for the victim triangle in your support network. Try to explain to them that you don't want to be a victim, and you don't want to be rescued. You just need assistance or company as you do what has to be done.

If the person or group persists in working on the victim triangle, run for the woods. You'll be better off without that kind of "help."

There is another reason for caution with formal support groups. I firmly believe that each therapy group needs a strong leader or a powerful group bonding that includes very clear rules and agreements about how the group is going to function, and how it will deal with anger and personal attacks among group members.

I have listened to too many stories of people who came away from support groups hurting more than they did when they went in. This is usually because there was no leader to defuse and redirect anger and hostility, or because, if there was a leader, he or she refused to intervene.

People who are grieving are frequently angry and lash out at those around them. This often occurs in support groups. They don't intend to be mean; they are just hurting and angry. A strong leader, or at least a strong group bonding that can help turn aside such angry thrusts, is essential.

A person who has a need to attack others certainly needs to be allowed to deal with his or her anger. That can mean supporting him or her in the appropriate expression of it. That can mean lovingly stopping him or her when they are on the attack, and helping them redirect their anger in more appropriate directions.

This is not about being rescued. It's about being protected from unnecessary meanness.

If you feel damaged by someone in your group, say something about it as soon as possible. If you can't do that, at least be willing to talk to the leader if there is one. He or she will be able to help you bring it up in the group.

Qualities to look for in a support network. The following is a list of characteristics that I'd suggest you look for in choosing a support group. It should also apply to any individual therapist that you are working with, and to your friends, as well.

1. The group will recognize and honor your individuality. That

means that they can make suggestions but will respect your personal needs and styles. They won't insist that you grieve the same way that they do.

2. The group will support you in being powerful in your own life. They won't let you stay stuck in the awfulness of the situation. They will remind you that you can be a powerful person in the face of the most dire circumstances. They won't try to rescue you, nor will they wallow in the awfulness with you.

3. The group will encourage you to hang on to hope, for yourself and for your community. They will know that the situation is certainly serious, but not hopeless. They will not allow doom-and-gloom baloney to go unchallenged.

4. The group will be willing to let you cry if you need to do that. There is no time limit on tears.

5. The group will be willing to let you be angry if you need to do that. Stifling your anger will just make you depressed. The group will support the appropriate expression of anger in ways that aren't hurtful to other group members. There is no time limit on anger.

6. The group will help you confront any guilt feelings that you may be having. Guilt has no positive place in grieving. It will only muck things up and keep the grieving constant and painful.

7. The group will encourage you to start to play and have fun when you feel ready to do that. Remember that your having fun again has nothing to do with how much you loved the person you have lost.

8. The group will encourage you to start dating again, if you want to, when you are ready. They won't accuse you of being disloyal to your deceased partner. Neither will they put undue pressure on you to start dating if you don't feel ready to.

9. The group will share your commitment to taking action to do something about the problem. They won't be into hiding out, or dropping out.

10. The group will share your commitment to rejoin life as soon as you are ready. They will appreciate the meaning of living today well.

If you have trouble finding a good support group that meets the above suggestions, be powerful enough to start your own. You can do this with a group of your friends who are going through similar experiences. You could even advertise in your local lesbian/gay newspaper or newsletter.

You can form a leaderless group, or you can form a group and then seek out a therapist to lead it. Most therapists I know would respond with joy to a group of men and women approaching them with the idea of leading a group.

Groups are cost-effective and won't have to cost you an arm and a leg. Many therapists work on a sliding scale based on your income and financial resources.

If your community does not have a low-fee referral list of psychotherapists, create one. Ask the nearest Lesbian/Gay Community Services Center to help you, or the local lesbian/gay newspaper, or do it yourself. Be willing to do whatever it takes.

You won't have much trouble forming your own group in one of the larger cities. You may have to work harder in some of the smaller towns across the country.

Don't despair. You are probably not that far away from a large city. If you are willing to travel, you can find the support you need.

Most large cities have some kind of lesbian/gay newspaper. You can find them in most lesbian or gay bars. If you don't know how to find any lesbian or gay bars, look in the phone book for an adult bookstore. There you can find several different "bar guides" that list all of the lesbian and gay bars in cities and towns all over the world. One of the best known is the *Damron Guide,* but there are others.

Once you find a lesbian/gay newspaper, you will be more aware of the resources in that community. If there is nothing, go to the editor and ask for a story about the need for more HIV-related resources. Take out your own ad, asking for anyone who is interested in forming a support group. If you don't want your address in the ad, get a post office box.

In other words, do whatever you have to do in order to get the support you need. There is no reason for you to go through this crisis alone.

Most of the AIDS support organizations, such as AIDS Project Los Angeles, were started by people who were grieving AIDS deaths and wanted to do something about the problem, as well as find support for themselves. They looked, they found the need, and they were then willing to do whatever they had to in order to meet that need.

As we look at some of the more practical matters, don't hesitate to utilize your support network to help you get through the tough times. Be willing to let them love you. Be willing to love them in return.

As you face the list of things you need to do, and as you are willing to utilize the support of your support network, you will probably notice that you have a number of decisions to make.

MAKING DECISIONS—WHEN?

If you haven't made your list of things that need to be done, I'd strongly urge you to do that now. If you need help or emotional support, don't hesitate to ask someone in your support network.

Once your list is complete, you can decide what has to be done immediately and what can wait for a more opportune time. This way, nothing will be overlooked.

Decide what you, personally, need to do. Decide what you can ask someone in your support network to do for or with you.

If it doesn't have to be done now, don't worry about it until you need to. Put it out of your mind.

Put off major decisions, if you can. I would caution you against making any decisions that don't need to be made right now. If the decision is a major one, such as changing jobs, moving to another city, or making other major changes, I'd advise against making it at this time.

While there is no Right way to do this, I'd recommend that such major decisions be put off for at least six months to a year, if you can do that. (If the promotion that you've been working for comes through, go for it if you think you are ready. Otherwise, let it wait.)

One of my clients, Brad, was so distraught by the whole AIDS crisis, and the injustice that goes along with it thanks to people like Sheldon and Helms, that he quit his job and put his home on the market the week after his partner died. He didn't think he could stand living in Los Angeles any longer, and he wanted to go someplace where AIDS wasn't a part of daily life and conversation.

It only took a few weeks for him to begin to seriously regret his decision. He had loved his job and had a large group of friends who were very special to him. He realized that he didn't really want to leave either his job or his home. Fortunately for him, the house hadn't sold and his boss was willing to give him back his old job.

I have worked with several others who weren't nearly as lucky. They added incredible stress to their lives as they tried to adjust to new jobs or new cities while they were still working through their own grief process.

It's understandable that you might just want to cut and run. That is a decision that you can always make at any time. Just be sure that you are thinking clearly before making such an important decision. Remember that your emotions are in a state of turmoil right now. The world looks very different in such a state. You aren't in the best position to evaluate the results of significant changes you may want to make. Don't make decisions that you will possibly come to regret.

YOUR HIV STATUS

One of the most important decisions that you do have to make is to take care of yourself, especially if you know that you are HIV-positive. If you are like many of my friends and clients who have spent long weeks or months taking care of someone they love who was dying, you have probably been neglecting your own health.

Now it is time to do something about that. Don't put it off.

If you are HIV-positive and have not been to your physician in a long time, make that appointment. It is now undeniable that early intervention is important. If your blood studies indicate the need for intervention, you need to know that, and be willing to take appropriate steps.

One of the most common fears is that you will have to go through the same thing that your partner went through. With that thought, it is easy to want to avoid finding out what has been going on in your body.

People respond differently to the AIDS virus. Courses of illness are different for different people. Don't allow your partner's experience to predict your own.

Remember, too, that every day is one day closer to our knowing more about how to take care of people who are HIV-positive, and one day closer to a cure. Whatever you do, don't give up hope. Hold on to every possibility for a rich and full life that you can. Do whatever you need to in order to maximize your health and vitality.

If you belong to a gym and have been unable to get there, now is the time to start back. Exercise is not only healthy for your body, but it is also a great stress-reducer and anxiety-reliever.

Begin paying attention to your diet again. I know too many who have existed on fast food and the microwave throughout their partner's illness. That's not healthy. Do what you can to get back on a healthy nutrition program.

If you've never been to a gym, don't let that stop you. I worked with one man, Dave, who had always loathed the idea of going to a gym and working out. He thought it was strictly for Neanderthal morons. However, he was lonely without his partner, and they hadn't had many close friends. He decided to give the gym a try. It took about four sessions for him to be hooked on the physical, emotional, and social benefits of working out regularly.

We've already discussed the advantages of a personal Wellness strategy. If you don't have one, create one. Use whatever resources are available to you. An aggressive Wellness strategy can empower you as you continue through your grieving process. Take a look at my first book, *Pathways to Wellness.*

While you are taking care of yourself, and while you are utilizing your support group, it will probably be necessary to give some attention to your friends. Friends can be an invaluable source of support. They can also be a pain in the butt.

DEALING WITH FRIENDS

Dealing with friends should be easy, but sometimes it's not. I have heard stories that at first I couldn't believe about the insensitivity of friends.

When the vultures start to circle. One of my clients told me about an incident that happened during the reception following the memorial service for his life partner. The woman who lived across the hall, and who had been a good friend to both him and his partner, walked through the living room carrying his partner's answering machine. When confronted with what she was doing, she replied, "You don't need two anymore." My client was in such a state of shock that he allowed her to leave with the machine.

His friends were not as understanding, and went to the woman's apartment and retrieved the machine. She couldn't understand what was wrong with her taking it.

One of the most loathsome happenings following a death is when the vultures start to circle, with their wish lists in hand. This is certainly not unique to an AIDS death.

If there are vultures circling above you, get prepared to say "not now." This is regardless of who is circling, family members or friends. By definition, a vulture will not understand your reluctance to part with the object of his or her desire. Tough.

There will come a time when you will be ready to part with some of the things that belonged to your life partner. Until that time, *part with nothing.*

Another of my clients, Larry, was approached after his partner's memorial service by his partner's sister. She wanted to have some photographs of her brother. In his distraught state, he just handed her the photo albums that contained the pictures taken throughout their long relationship. At the time, he didn't think he could ever bear looking at them again, so he gave them to her.

After several months, he realized he had very few photos of his partner and contacted the sister in an effort to get them back. She categorically refused to give them back, and said that she had thrown most of them out since she didn't know any of the people in the photos.

Remember, the time will come when you will be ready to part with some of your partner's belongings. Until then, if someone asks you for something, think hard, very hard, before you give it away.

You don't have to say no. You can just say, "Not now. I'm not ready to deal with that yet."

Another of the frequently reported problems with friends is their desire to tell "war stories" about the good old days. This is pretty common following a death. People like to remember the good times as their way of honoring the person who has died.

If that feels good to you, then go for it. Join in the discussion. In fact, such conversations can be a valuable part of working through your grief process.

If it doesn't feel good to you, then don't do it. Let your friends know that it is just too painful for you right now. There may come a time when you will be able to do that, but not now.

By the same token, let your friends grieve their own way as well. Don't begrudge them their grief process. If it isn't compatible with yours, let them know that, lovingly.

We have already discussed what to do with those people who pull away from you following your partner's death. Don't rush to judgment. Remember that they have lives of their own, and they just may not have been able to be there for you in the way you would have liked. Their own resources may have been stretched too thin. Their own fear may have been overwhelming.

To be sure, some of those who pull away don't deserve your continued friendship. When that is absolutely clear, then do what you must.

There may be other cases, with people who are truly your friends, where the relationship can be salvaged. Good friends are hard to come by. Don't throw them away unnecessarily. In a time when so many of us are grieving for so many deaths, there inevitably will be some times when we can't offer the same support we may have offered at another time or under other circumstances.

The possibilities for upset generated by friends are myriad. There's no way to cover them all.

For example, a friend of mine had just lost his partner to AIDS. At a party several weeks after the memorial service, one of his late partner's old boyfriends had tried to cheer him up by reminding him how good his partner had been in bed.

He asked me what I thought he should have said. My suggestion was not kind or gentle. The bottom line in dealing with friends is to simply tell them the truth, the whole truth, and nothing but the truth, lovingly and respectfully. If they are doing or saying something that you don't like, tell them. If they are doing or saying something that you do like, tell them that too.

Also, do whatever you can to make it safe for your friends to tell you their truth as well. This two-way truth-telling is the only way a relationship can really work.

PRACTICAL MATTERS

This section will look at some of the practical matters that may be facing you. You may have difficulty with some or all of them. Some will be relevant right now, and others won't have to be addressed for a while yet.

Who do you tell and when? I wish there were an easy answer to this one. Obviously, if every one of us who is grieving for an AIDS death were to tell all of our family and friends, a vast number of people would realize that they have a closer investment in AIDS issues than they had thought.

This could lead to a ground swell of support for AIDS services, legislation, and funding. It could lead to a decrease in AIDS-related violence and lesbian/gay-bashing. It could lead to a more compassionate approach to dealing with people who are HIV infected as well as HIV affected.

I wish it were that easy. Unfortunately it is not.

Having people know that your life partner has died of AIDS could have possibly serious consequences in your life. Know what those consequences are and be sure that you are willing to face them before you disclose the nature of your partner's death.

Not all employers, landlords, and families are terrified of AIDS. There are those who will stick by you and do whatever they can to help.

Unfortunately, there are others who will not. Your job, your insurability, and your home could be affected. You don't need this when you are dealing with the death of your life partner.

Choose wisely whom you tell, and what you tell. There may be a time later when you will be ready to risk your job or other relationships by coming out about being lesbian or gay, or about the fact that your life partner has died of AIDS. Be sure it's your choice and that you are willing to face any consequences.

Don't sell your family short. Many are more able to deal with the knowledge that your partner has died of AIDS than you might think. Many others will eventually come around after they have had some time to digest the information.

Finally, recognize that you can handle whatever rejection you may experience, whether it is losing your job, or your home, or your family. While you may want to avoid it, or at least delay the possibility of that rejection, you can still deal with it if you have to.

There is no job, no career, no home, and no family that cannot be replaced if necessary. If you find yourself rejected, don't waste time beating your head against a brick wall. Create a new job, find a new home, or create a new "family."

Before AIDS, many lesbians and gay men had to create their own "families" after their biological family kicked them out for being lesbian or gay. These new "families" can provide an amazing source of support if you'll let them. Being with friends who love you and support you totally just as you are is frankly more enriching than being with a biological family who treats you like an outcast or "pervert."

Blood may be thicker than water. That doesn't mean you should allow yourself to be belittled or demeaned by homophobic family members. You do not have to put up with their hatred and disapproval.

Legal issues. It had been my naive hope to be able to provide at least a few suggestions here for the legal problems you may face after your partner has died. It only took a few conversations with attorneys to know that it would not be a service for me to do that.

AIDS-related laws vary widely from state to state, even city to city. Some states are quite enlightened. Others are almost Nazi-like in their suppression of the rights of persons with AIDS and of lesbian or gay citizens.

Even within the same state, there can be widely varying local laws that may affect you. For example, in the state of California, if you live in Los Angeles, you have protection by city ordinance from discrimination against you if you are lesbian or gay, or if you are a person with AIDS.

If you live in Palm Springs, California, you have no such protection (at least at the time of this writing). The City Council and Mayor Bono in Palm Springs agree with former Governor Deukmejian that there is no such thing as discrimination against persons with AIDS or against lesbian and gay citizens. They believe this in spite of listening to hours and hours of ranting and raving by "born-again" bigots. Go figure.

The point is that the only way you can be sure of your rights and protection under the law is for you to contact a local attorney who is familiar with AIDS-related laws and ordinances. You may have more rights than you think.

You can find such an attorney by contacting your local Lesbian/Gay Community Services Center or your local AIDS Project.

Be sure that any attorney you contact isn't AIDS-phobic or homophobic. Be sure he or she is experienced in dealing with AIDS cases.

The will. If your life partner left a will that will stand being contested, you may not have any trouble. But it won't be a guarantee.

There are increasing numbers of families challenging wills. They claim that their son named his life partner as his sole heir as the result of undue influence, or they claim the partner was not mentally competent to sign a will.

In the vast number of cases, this is sheer homophobia in action. It is clearly an unwillingness to grant legitimacy to loving lesbian and gay relationships.

Since lesbian/gay relationships are not legally valid, we are at risk when our partners die with or without wills. We could be shut out by vindictive and greedy families, and all too frequently we are.

The only solution is to make the best-constructed will you can. If you do not have a will and are HIV-positive, you might even consider asking your attorney about having a complete physical and psychological exam to indicate that at the time of the making of the will you were in full possession of your decision-making capabilities. That won't stop an angry family from challenging your will, but it could give your designated heirs a bit more strength in their resistance to that challenge.

If your partner died without a will, all is not lost. Many families will honor your relationship and your possessions. If they do not, you need to contact an attorney to see what your legal rights are.

Whatever you do, don't just give up and let the family have it all. It is not your fault that lesbian/gay relationships are not legally recognized. If you and your life partner had a deeply committed relationship, you are morally and ethically every bit as much his spouse as if you were heterosexual and legally married. Don't just walk away from that right.

If you have exhausted all legal recourse, then all you can do is to simply walk away with as much dignity as you can muster. Starting over again isn't a pleasant thought, especially if you are walking away from a home that you and your partner lovingly put together.

Don't let that victimize you, however. If you have to start over, don't waste time being bitter and resentful, even though you have a right to feel bitter and resentful.

Try to remind yourself that you always have a choice about how to feel. You can enjoy the moment, work toward putting your life back together, or you can resent the vindictive family. Which do you really want to do? Which will yield the more desirable results?

Give some consideration to the possibility of making a legal case for your rights as a "longtime companion." If enough of us would do that, we might be able to effect some change.

It is time for society to recognize that two men or two women can love each other just as deeply as a man and a woman can. Our love for our life partner is no less strong, no less deep, no less binding because he or she is of the same sex.

Taking care of your partner's things. This can be a very tough situation. Cleaning out the closets, desk drawers, and garages can be a very painful task. It can cause enormous upset and pain.

Don't be talked into doing it before you are ready. I've had a number of clients whose well-meaning friends forced them to do the cleanup too soon. The anxiety and depression caused by such action was horrible and could have been avoided.

One of my clients, Harry, waited over six months before doing anything about the cleanup. Even the medical equipment that his partner had used was still in the house. He used to sit in his partner's favorite chair, wearing his partner's favorite old sweater.

His friends were distressed. They viewed his behavior as abnormal and unhealthy. I suggested that he not listen to them. He would know when he was ready to begin taking care of some of the things.

After about six months, he did feel ready to do that. It was still tough on him, but not nearly as tough as it would have been if he had given in to his well-meaning friends' demands that he "get a grip, right away."

He began dating again, and even started a new relationship. He was not damaged in any way by refusing to clean out the house immediately.

Others of you may want to clean out the house right away. Having your partner's things around to look at is just too painful. Don't feel guilty about that either. Do whatever you have to do in order to feel more comfortable. Remember to be cautious about parting with anything right now. Box it up and store it for a while. Later you will be in better shape to decide what you want to keep and what you want to let go of.

Some people need to leave their home for a new home that is just theirs, and not associated with their partner. This is one of the issues I would advise waiting at least six months before deciding, but if you are absolutely certain that it is what you need to do, then do it.

Others have told me that it worked just to do a major rearranging of the furniture and artworks, putting their individual stamp on it. Do what you have to do to make it your home.

Then there is the garage sale from hell. If you are going to go this route, be sure you are up to walking around the garage watching total strangers buy a pair of your partner's shoes for $1.50.

I'd strongly urge you to ask your support network to handle the garage sale if they are willing. You can help them get ready, but before people arrive at the sale, take off for the day. Come back when it's all over. This is not cowardly. It just looks sensible to me.

The same holds true if you are going to give your partner's things away to a charity for resale. Let your friends help you do this one too.

Requests for mementos. What about mementos? Many of your friends and your partner's family may want mementos. If what they are asking for is clearly appropriate and you are absolutely sure that you won't regret giving it away, then give it to them.

However, if you are not certain, don't say yes, but don't say no either. Just say, "Not now." Ask for some time to heal before you start giving things away. Be sure that you don't part with things that you will regret not having later as a way for you to remember your partner. A reasonable friend or family member will understand.

Don't feel guilty about resisting vultures. One of my clients told me about being in the kitchen with his partner several months before his partner's death. They were listening to his partner's mother and sister dividing up the spoils of the living room furniture and artwork, unaware that they were being overheard. The mother and sister were destined to be very surprised and disappointed.

Once again, I want to point out that all families are not homophobic vultures. Many are wonderfully supportive and respectful of relationships. But I do feel I must address the pain that is caused all too frequently by homophobic vultures, because I don't want you to become their victim.

The point is, worry about your partner's belongings when you are ready to do that. Don't let well-meaning friends rush you.

At the same time, if you have been clinging to any remembrance of your partner, holing up inside your home, and avoiding other people in your grief for too long, try to listen to your friends and see if maybe they are right about this one. You may need to seek professional help to get through your grief.

Mementos for yourself. Be careful that you don't give away things that seem trivial now but that could seem more meaningful later on. When I lost one of my best friends, I couldn't think about asking for something to remember him by. I didn't want to seem like a vulture.

Several months later, I deeply regretted that I had very little to remember him by. There were several rather insignificant items that meant a lot to both him and me, but they were now gone and irretrievable.

I can practically guarantee that the time will come when you will want those mementos. There's nothing wrong with that. Just be sure you haven't already disposed of them.

Starting to date again. This is one of the tough ones. There is no right formula for deciding the right time. When it seems comfortable, give it a try. You can always back off if it seems too soon.

Some of you will want to do it right away. Part of dealing with your grief will be to find someone else to be with, perhaps sexually, perhaps romantically. There's nothing wrong with doing this. It's not more noble to go into seclusion for months or years. It doesn't mean that you loved your partner any less.

If you do want to wait months or even years before you start dating again, that's OK too. Just be sure you aren't hiding.

When do you tell a prospective date that your partner died of AIDS? This is one of the most frequently asked questions I hear.

Most people who have asked it wanted to hear that you don't have to tell them right away. They were disappointed with my answer.

I feel the same way about this as I do telling a prospective date that you are HIV-positive. Do it at the earliest time, definitely before you go to bed.

I know that this could result in your new friend running scream-ing into the woods. So be it. Think about it. Why would you want to spend any time at all, in or out of bed, with someone who is so terrified of AIDS that he wouldn't knowingly go out on a date or choose to have safer sex with you?

If he can't handle it on the first date, why would you think he would handle it any better by the third or fourth date, or the tenth? I come to this advice after listening to a lot of horror stories told by people who waited several weeks or months to tell their new friend about their partner's death.

There have been a lot of times when the new friend did run for the woods but didn't run because of the AIDS death. He ran because he felt he had been lied to. He felt that he should have been given the chance to make up his own mind about whether or not to date or have sex with someone whose partner had died of AIDS.

Once you start to date again, other issues will come up. How much do you talk about your deceased partner? Obviously, you don't want to spend all your time talking about him. Yet you don't need to totally avoid him either. The two of you had a life together. It is very much a part of who you are. Trying to avoid talking about him totally would mean ignoring a large part of your life.

Be moderate about it, be thoughtful, and if you aren't sure, ask your new friend if he is bothered by it. Don't try to read his mind, or expect him to read yours.

Above all, don't let the fact that your partner died of AIDS cause you to be afraid to love again. I know that the prospect of losing someone else can seem awful, yet it is not as awful as living the rest of your life alone and afraid to love.

You deserve to love and be loved.

Sex. Don't be too worried if you notice that having sex, especially for the first time after the death, turns out to be difficult and anxiety provoking. This happens to a lot of people.

If you have no trouble having sex again, enjoy it. Don't waste time feeling guilty. There is no reason to do that.

If you do have trouble, whatever you do, don't start to obsess about it. The more you let yourself worry, the tougher it will be the next time.

If you have already told your new friend that your partner has recently died of AIDS, he will likely understand if you don't function like gangbusters. If he doesn't understand, you should probably question the wisdom of getting involved with someone so insensitive.

Your problems will very likely pass with time, especially if you find a sensitive sexual partner. If they do not pass, seek out professional help. These kinds of problems are usually not that difficult to deal with.

If the AIDS death awakened some old feelings of guilt about gay sex, this may require more time and energy to deal with. But it can be dealt with if you are willing to put out the time and energy.

Getting away. If you can afford to get away and have taken care of those things that absolutely must be done, then going away for a while can be healing. The experience of my friends and clients would suggest that you may want to choose someplace new, as opposed to somewhere you used to love to go with your partner.

If the two of you had your favorite little bed and breakfast up in the wine country in California, you may want to go somewhere very different. This doesn't mean you can never go back to the bed and breakfast, but you will likely find the memories too painful at this time. It would probably be more healing to be somewhere that is not filled with memories of your partner and the things you used to enjoy together.

If you are sure that you want to go back to your favorite places right now, and are sure that you have adequate support, then go ahead. Don't feel like you have to tough it out, however. If it's too tough, cut your trip short.

If you find it to be healing for you, then that's great. As with all else, always be sure you are grieving in your own way.

Memories. You will always have your memories. There will be times when they are nurturing, warm, and healing. There will probably be times when they are painful and agonizing.

Try not to be afraid of your memories. If they are wonderful, enjoy them. If they are not wonderful, then try to replace them with other thoughts as soon as you can.

Be aware that your memories can and often will trigger some grief. Even if you are long past acute grieving, a memory can pull you back into the old pain. You don't have to stay there, but the brief trip can be awful.

If you are like many people, there will be certain times of the year when your memories will likely surface with three-dimensional reality. This will almost always happen around times of birthdays and anniversaries. It will frequently happen during special holidays, or at the beginning of favorite seasons.

Every one of us will have our own special set of circumstances that will remind us of our loss. Something as simple as cutting the first rose of the year from the garden the two of you planted together can recall a lot of warm memories, or a lot of pain. I have heard from several people that a simple trip to the supermarket turned into a hellish experience when they went past the frozen food section and saw their partner's favorite Häagen Dazs ice cream in the freezer.

There are unlimited possibilities for events and places that will trigger your memories. Some can be predicted and prepared for, such as birthdays and holidays. Look ahead as often as you can and be sure that you have planned activities for yourself that will offer you support and nurturing. Don't hesitate to include your friends and family here.

Whatever you do, don't try to tough it out alone, unless you are absolutely sure you want to do it that way. Don't try to be noble or super strong here.

The first Christmas will most likely be tough, no matter how well you are dealing with his death. Plan for this and surround yourself with loving support.

Other possibilities that trigger your memories will be sudden, coming at you from out of nowhere. You might hear a favorite song on the radio, or hear a line in a movie, or see someone walking down the street who walks just like your partner.

These surprises can be crippling. There's no way to avoid them. You just have to be prepared to deal with them as best you can.

Remember, the pain will pass. In many cases, the memories will get sweeter and less painful. Do what you must, and don't forget to ask for support from those who love you.

Take action. Finally, take action. One of the constant themes of this book has been to focus on action as the solution. Do something about the problem. Becoming involved in making a contribution to your community in whatever way you are able will be a great assist to your grief process.

When you are ready, get out of the house and find someplace to invest some time and energy. Chapter 14 will go into detail about how to do this, and how to find a group that works for you.

Don't allow yourself to become a victim of your grief. Get involved. Be willing to be powerful in your own life and in your community.

When your life partner has died, allow yourself to grieve your own way. Don't be afraid of your feelings; they will likely be chaotic for a while.

Remember, you won't always feel this bad. It will get better. Life will look worth living again.

He would want you to be living today well.

when a family member has died

The family member who has died of AIDS could be a son, a daughter, a parent, a sibling, a cousin, an aunt, or an uncle, and so on. For the sake of simplicity, I will most often refer to the family member who has died as the son.

This is not to overlook other forms of relationship, or to downplay their importance or the frequency of their occurrence. In the first draft of this chapter I tried to address all of the above possibilities for relationships to the one who has died. The result was cumbersome to read.

So please bear with me. If the one you have lost was not your son, but another member of your family, the suggestions in this chapter will be just as relevant.

I strongly urge you not to skip the previous chapter. Whether your son had a life partner or not, there is valuable information in that chapter for you that will not be repeated in this chapter. It will also help your grieving if you have some understanding and empathy for your son's friends and partner.

The loss of a child or a sibling is one of the most devastating experiences a human being has to endure. Parents don't expect that they will ever outlive their children. Siblings assume that they will all grow old together.

AIDS has changed all of that. AIDS has ripped apart families, leaving gaps that can't ever be filled. They can only be endured.

Our job as survivors is to somehow get through our grief as best we can, and rejoin the flow of life as soon as we can. At first it may not seem likely or possible that we will ever be able to do that, but we will.

All of the extraordinary circumstances that surround an AIDS death can create as much pain for the family as it does for the life partner and for others who loved him. In addition to the loss represented by any death, the AIDS death of your son will probably be accompanied by extra portions of fear, guilt, and rage. You could be subject to the same shabby treatment and fearful exclusion. You could be subject to the same ignorant discrimination and bigotry. You could find it just as difficult to find support and nurturing for yourself. You will have to deal with "coming out" about the fact that your son died of AIDS.

This isn't easy to do in a small town in the Midwest. Frankly, it's not a lot easier to do in a big city like Los Angeles if you've been in the closet about having a gay son all along. But at least in a big city, support groups for family members are more readily available.

You may have an additional source of stress and complication: you may not have known your son was gay until you found out that he had been diagnosed with AIDS. Some families have not known that their son was gay or that he had AIDS until they were notified of his death. All of this information given in one fell swoop can be overwhelming. It can create emotional chaos.

Dealing with your son's sexual orientation may create an extra burden for you if you have had a difficult time accepting your son and his lifestyle. As difficult as it may seem to you, accepting your son's sexual orientation is still important for you to do, even though he has died.

I believe that grieving well requires that we learn how to honor our loved one for the person he was. To honor someone means accepting his lifestyle and how he died. To honor someone is to be willing to accept who he was, completely, without exceptions, without conditions, without resentment.

Honoring our loved one can include our disappointment in his shortcomings, whatever they may have been. Honoring our loved one can include his mistakes and failures.

I know that can look very tough, if not impossible for some. Yet it must be done. Refusing to accept who he was will not allow us to complete our grief. We will become a victim of our resentment, a victim of our denial, a victim of our judgment.

Later in this chapter we will address how you might be dealing with your own unique feelings about your son's sexual orientation. Whatever you do, don't try to deny or repress your feelings, and don't feel guilty about them, either.

If you are willing to express your feelings fully, then you will be in a powerful position to release them and challenge any unworkable beliefs you may have operating. This way you won't become a victim of unexpressed emotions.

I won't be repeating the information about dealing with the emotions of grief in this chapter. If you are still having trouble with your feelings, please return to Chapters 1 through 8.

While I don't want to repeat each of the sections from the last chapter written for life partners, I would like to review several. I strongly urge you to refer to the last chapter for a more complete discussion of these issues.

IF YOU WERE THE PRIMARY CAREGIVER DURING YOUR SON'S ILLNESS

If you were your son's primary caregiver while he was dying, you will have to face many of the same issues as a life partner. You'll have to deal with your own fatigue and stress. You'll need to take care of the necessary arrangements, in spite of that fatigue and stress.

You will need to face a lot of the same here-and-now stuff we talked about in the last chapter. Later is now. All of those things that you have been putting off are still waiting for you, and you must get to them as soon as you can.

Grieve your own way, in your own time. As always, experience your grief your own way. While there may be things that have to be dealt with right away, don't worry about keeping to some kind of time schedule. Your schedule and the way you move through your grief, even as you take care of necessary business, must be your own, no one else's.

People who are grieving should not have to put up with the ignorance and insensitivity of well-meaning friends, and even some professionals, who will insist that you grieve the Right way. I know that they are really trying to help, but they are not helping. Since such people exist, it will be up to you to educate them. You must tell them about what you need from them as you experience your own unique grief process.

Tell the truth. Don't even think you need to apologize to anyone for the way you are experiencing your grief.

A group of Mothers of AIDS Patients I spoke with in Orange County told me about losing several members of their support group. The women left because they were all seeing the same therapist, who told them that it had been six months since their loss and they should be over it by now. It's hard to imagine that any professional could be that stupidly and dangerously ignorant, but unfortunately such professionals exist.

If you find out that you are hooked up with one, I'd advise finding another therapist. You don't need to waste your time and energy trying to educate a professional who should know better. Call your nearest AIDS Project and ask for a referral. If the person you are seeing came from their referral list, let them know about your unhappy experience.

Grieve your own way. Don't worry about how other people choose to grieve. Don't worry about how your spouse is grieving. If you try to force yourself to grieve someone else's way, you will probably not get through your grief as effectively or as well.

The rest of your family may be needing you. In the case of many families that I have spoken with, the other children and the spouse of the caregiver, frequently the mother, have been doing without her tender loving care since the beginning of their son's illness. She has been so wrapped up in taking care of her son that she wasn't able to spend the usual amount of time with the rest of the family.

The mothers I have spoken with are pretty evenly divided between two groups. The first group consists of those who were painfully aware of the problem and feel terribly guilty for neglecting the rest of their family. This kind of guilt is unnecessary.

The other group is made up of mothers who are furious that the rest of their family doesn't understand that they only did what they had to do. They didn't like having to neglect the rest of their family, but didn't see that they had a choice. Their son was dying and needed them.

If this is going on in your family, please do what you can to help heal hurt feelings. Loving communication will be the most powerful healing strategy.

Gather the entire family and let each one have the opportunity to talk about his or her feelings. Be sure that people don't just talk about sadness, but also any anger or resentment.

Younger children will probably have a harder time understanding why you were spending so much time with their older brother. They only see the abandonment, not your needs or your son's needs. Try to be patient with them. Explain what you can to them.

You can say, even to a young child, "I certainly understand that you may have missed Mom while she was taking care of your brother. I would understand if you felt a little mad about that. What I want you to know is that I still love you. I have always loved you, even when I had to spend lots of extra time with your brother."

Reassurance of being loved is critically important for adults as well as children. It's always very dangerous to assume that your loved ones know that you love them. Such reassurance is necessary, especially when the entire family has just gone through an emotional upheaval. I don't believe that we can reassure one another too much, ever.

The rest of the family needs to understand that the mother or father was only doing what he or she felt was necessary. The fact that a parent chose to be with the one who was ill doesn't mean that he or she loves that child more. It just means that that child needed his parent more while he was ill. Caregivers deserve understanding, forgiveness, and compassion.

Of course the most powerful demonstration will occur as you are able to resume your former role in the family. Small children need even more reassurance and reminding than adults do. Tell them often how much you love and value them. Frequent hugs can go a long way to promote healing as well.

Don't be surprised if your other children start acting out by creating needy situations or showing attention-seeking behavior. They saw you take care of the child who was in need. They may feel as if they need a problem for you to take care of too. Let them know, repeatedly and constantly, that they don't have to have a problem for you to love them or care about them.

It wouldn't be unusual if your spouse showed some resentment for the time you had to spend with your son as he was dying. Sure, your spouse understood the need, but that didn't make it easier to get along without you and your tender loving care. Your spouse missed you and maybe was even jealous. I know such jealousy doesn't make a lot of sense, but human feelings are fragile where love and attention are concerned. Give your spouse as much reassurance of your love as you can.

Be careful, however. Before rushing back to take care of the rest of your family, be sure that you get some rest and recuperation. This is the hardest thing for a lot of mothers and fathers to do. Now that your responsibilities to your son are complete, the urge will be for you to dive headfirst back into family business and try to make up for lost time.

I know they need you, but explain to them that you need a little time to rest and heal. Remember, you won't be able to take care of your family if you overstress and overwork yourself.

Taking the time to take care of yourself will probably feel selfish. It is not. It is only sensible and necessary.

You do deserve a break today, and tomorrow too. Just be sure to give your family the reassurance that when you are rested, you will be back.

Emphasize the need for family communication. I addressed this issue above, but it merits further attention. Remember what we talked about in earlier chapters on grief. Our society doesn't prepare us well to deal with grief. All too often, people don't talk about their grief with one another.

This is especially true for families that didn't communicate well with each other in the first place. While I keep saying that there is no Right way to grieve, there are a few principles that hold true for most people. The need to communicate about feelings is one of those principles.

You don't need to do this for hours or days at a time. In fact, you'd be amazed at how much communication can occur in just thirty minutes or an hour.

Encourage each family member to talk about how he or she is feeling. Be sure to make it very safe for each person to say anything he or she wants to say, even if you don't like it. If you punish people for saying something rude or ugly, you teach them not to communicate truthfully. You teach them to lie in order to avoid punishment and your anger.

Make an agreement with the family group that anyone can say anything that he or she wants to without being jumped on by anyone else. Each one must be allowed to express fully what he or she is feeling.

If you aren't absolutely certain that you can keep this agreement, then don't make it. Making it and then going back on your word will damage your relationship with your family. They will learn that your word isn't to be trusted.

I would urge you as strongly as possible to make and then keep this agreement. Your family needs to learn to express their feelings of grief. It must be safe for them to do that.

If you can't make it safe, seek out a family therapist who can assist you all to talk about your feelings. Such an investment in time and energy will be worth it.

If anyone says things that are untrue or inaccurate, it is OK to correct the inaccuracies. Please do so lovingly, patiently, and oh so gently. Try to do this after that person has completely expressed him- or herself. Jumping in too soon could cut short that person's expression of feelings.

Don't hesitate to find professional help. If your family is having a lot of trouble talking about their feelings, you may want to find a support group or other professional help. Your physician or minister may be able to help you or make an appropriate referral.

I believe that it is most important that any support group or person that you utilize must be comfortable with the fact that your son was gay and that he died of AIDS. A judgmental person or a bigot will not be of much help to you. You don't need that kind of input right now. I would also suggest that you read the previous chapter to see how to evaluate the effectiveness of a support group or a therapist.

If you have trouble finding such a support group, you can always call your local Lesbian and Gay Community Services Center or your local AIDS Project. In most cities that is what they are called. In other cities, they may have other names. For example, in New York City one of the main AIDS groups is called Gay Men's Health Crisis. If your town is too small to have such an organization, the nearest large city most likely will have one.

If your telephone Directory Assistance can't help you, you might call your local city councilperson, state senator, or assemblyperson, or even your United States Senator or Congressperson.

These elected officials have staff members whose responsibility it is to find local resources for their constituents. Make use of them.

At the back of this book is a list of names and phone numbers of regional AIDS resource centers. If you call any of them, you will find a helpful resource. If you aren't satisfied with the person you talk to, call back another time. Most of the people on the telephones are volunteers. Some may not be as effective as others. Keep trying. Do what it takes to find the support you need.

Don't be afraid to utilize your personal support network. This could mean the rest of your family. It could also mean friends from your job or church.

You don't have to be going through this alone. It's not weak to ask for support. Don't be afraid to learn as you go along about what is supportive and what is not. Trial and error works well, if you don't beat yourself up for your errors. If a way you thought would be supportive turns out to be uncomfortable, find a different way. Communicate this to your friends.

Be willing to allow anyone you ask for help to say no. That doesn't mean they don't love you. It just means that they aren't available right now.

Just be sure that your friends fully support your expressing all of your feelings. You don't need anyone telling you that it is time to stifle your feelings. You'll get a lot of such advice. It may be well meaning, but it is highly inappropriate and won't help you at all.

In fact, it will make your job much tougher.

One mother I spoke to told me how angry she was at some of her friends who would offer to take her out to dinner and would tell her, "We don't want any crying tonight. Let's just try to have a good time." She knew that they meant well, but they were telling her to deny her feelings, and that will never work.

She had a lot of crying to do, a lot of grief to express. Covering that up will only cause more depression.

Even if you find yourself crying a lot, know that it will get better, eventually. The tears will begin to dry. You won't always hurt like this. If you feel you're hurting too much and for too long, then seriously consider some kind of professional assistance.

TAKING CARE OF NECESSARY BUSINESS

I know that you may have been doing this for a long time. Right now you probably feel more like holing up and resting for a while. I want you to do that. I just want to be sure that you don't put off things that must be dealt with right away, in order to avoid messy complications farther down the road.

Make the list. You would benefit from making a list of things that need to be done. You won't have to do them all right now, and you probably won't have to do all of them yourself. The list is just to help you prioritize and be sure that what absolutely must be done gets done.

If you make a list you will be able to consciously put off a lot of things that can be done later at a more appropriate time, when you are feeling stronger. Free yourself up to do only those things that must be done right now.

Pace yourself and be sure to give yourself time to recuperate. Enjoying keeping busy is one thing; trying to hide by overworking yourself is quite another.

Don't hesitate to ask your support group for help. Don't try to do this all by yourself.

Put off major decisions, if you can. You need to be aware that right now may not be the best time to make major decisions. No one in a state of emotional chaos will make very good decisions. If the decisions can be put off, please try to do that.

Ask your friends for a reality check if you are unsure about any decision. Someone more distant from the loss will have a much more objective view of the circumstances that surround the decision.

I have spoken with several couples whose marriages were sorely tested by their son's illness. Divorce loomed high in the picture. Fortunately, they were willing to wait, and discovered that a divorce would not have been a good solution. They had just been experiencing an extreme response to the stress they were under.

The anger associated with grieving is easy to dump on your spouse or other family members. Things get said that no one means or even wants to mean. They just come out. Try to remind each other that emotions are running rampant. You don't need to take too seriously the things you say to each other when you are in a state of high emotion.

Be kind to yourself and to your spouse. Don't make any major decisions that aren't absolutely necessary right now.

Dealing with difficult friends.

Friends can be just as cruel to parents or family members as they can be to life partners. Most of them don't mean to be.

It will be up to you to set boundaries and limits for what you will tolerate from well-meaning friends. It will be very helpful if you can just get used to telling them the truth about how you are feeling.

I have heard unbelievable stories about the insensitivity of friends. Some parents and especially some children have suffered through a friend telling anti-gay jokes or jokes about AIDS shortly after the death of their family member.

You don't have to tolerate anti-gay jokes, now or ever. You don't have to be afraid or ashamed of who your son was. You don't have to be afraid to stand up for your right to have your son respected. Speaking out may seem frightening, but it will make you feel a lot better. We'll look at how you might deal with possible homophobia of your own later in this chapter.

In talking with some parents, I have heard a number of hurtful things that have been said by religious friends who were trying to use their son's death as a way of converting them to the Right way of thinking. These are the same religious folks who proclaim that people die of AIDS as direct punishment by God for their sinful lifestyle.

No grieving parent needs to tolerate this kind of abuse. Such friends should be asked to keep their judgments to themselves, even if this means losing their friendship.

Unfortunately, cautioning these zealous folks won't always change their insensitive, compassionless manner. Don't get too upset if you can't change their minds. Their belief systems are often set in stone. If you disagree with them, they will only brand you a heretic or a Godless pagan. The fact that you may consider yourself to be a devout Christian won't mean anything to them, as long as you are disagreeing with them.

Don't feel guilty for being angry with these people. Why would you want to be friends with those who loathe and persecute your son and his community?

Don't feel guilty for letting go of such destructive friendships. You don't have to be ashamed of who your son was, and you deserve to have him respected for the person he was.

When the vultures start to circle. Vultures can attack families, too. Siblings and family friends can cause major pain if they try to get a share of your son's possessions. I don't know why some people become so greedy and grasping following a death, but they do.

You don't owe them anything. Don't hesitate to say, "Not now," if not a flat no.

Don't let people rush you to part with anything that belonged to your son, no matter how badly they say they might need it. Don't allow them to make you feel guilty or weak for not giving in to their demands.

You do not need that kind of intrusion and that kind of stress. You don't have to feel guilty, and it's not weak to say, "No" or "Not now." If saying no threatens a relationship, then so be it. Who really needs friendship with vultures?

Respect your son's life partner and what rightfully belongs to him. Some families have a hard time dealing with their son's life partner claiming ownership of their home and belongings. Before you get upset, please, please ask yourself, what would you do if this were the spouse of a heterosexual child?

If your son had been heterosexual, you wouldn't think of trying to take the home and belongings away from his wife. Please give your gay son's partner the same consideration. Chances are he paid for as much of it as your son did, even though they may not have thought it necessary to keep records about who spent what for what. Even those things he didn't pay for should still be treated as property of the relationship. We'll talk more about this later.

Who do you tell and when? While you may not be at the same level of risk as your son's partner, you may be subject to discrimination and rejection if people find out that your son died of AIDS. This won't always be the case. Many of you will find helpful, thoughtful responses to your loss.

You don't have to be embarrassed about the fact that your son was gay. You don't have to be ashamed that he died of AIDS. Too many people are ashamed, and that causes untold misery.

Standing up to such bigotry and ignorance is a magnificent way to honor your son. It is also a powerful way for you to work through your own grief, instead of becoming a victim of hatred and ignorance. We'll look at ways of resisting homophobia later in this chapter.

The more people who know about your loss, the better it will be for the fight against AIDS. While you certainly deserve to consider the consequences of others knowing how your son died, I would urge you to be as honest as you can be.

Parents of people with AIDS have powerful voices when they are raised in the service of compassion and caring.

Taking care of your son's things. If you were the primary caregiver you will find yourself with the duty of taking care of your son's belongings. This can never be an easy task. Don't hesitate to ask your support group to help you or at least to be with you.

Don't rush to dispose of anything. Give yourself time to heal. Be sure you don't get rid of things you will regret not having later. Box-and-store may be the kindest solution here, so that you don't have to endure too much stress too soon after the death.

I have talked to several mothers who were shocked and embarrassed to discover their son's erotic video collection, or erotic photography magazines, along with various sex toys. Some gay men have agreements with friends to go into their home and remove materials that they don't want their parents to know about. Others haven't thought to do that, or figure that it will be your problem to deal with.

If you have developed a good relationship with your son's partner or friends, let them help you out with this one. Try to understand and respect that your son may have had a different set of sexual values than you have. Try not to be judgmental about this.

Getting away. Getting away could be a great idea for you. You may want to go alone, or with your spouse and even your other children.

I'd suggest thinking hard before returning to a favorite family vacation spot. Going somewhere new, where you will not find painful memories at every turn, is something you would be wise to consider.

I have talked to several families who found that getting away was a major help in breaking out of some of their grief. Of course the sadness was still there, but when they returned home, they were a little closer to being able to put their life back together.

Guilt. Parents can feel guilt for a lot of things. They can feel guilty for the fact that their son was gay. They can feel guilty for things that were said or done during the illness. They can feel guilty for not taking better care of their son. They can feel guiltier if they had rejected their son because of his sexual orientation.

Guilt will only hurt you. It won't help your grieving or your peace of mind.

If you need to, review the chapter on guilt and learn how to take responsibility instead. Do what you can about the problem. If you can't "make it up" to your son, "make it up" to other sons who are still fighting AIDS.

Guilt about feeling angry. A lot of parents feel guilty because they were angry with their son for getting AIDS. Clearly that kind of anger will accomplish nothing and is best worked through and let go of. Don't waste time and energy feeling guilty about it.

Some parents feel guilty for getting angry with their son if he was rude and abusive when he was ill. It's hard for mothers or fathers to understand that they can become safe objects for their son's anger and frustration. He can't rage at his physician, who is the one keeping him alive. His friends may not stand for it. Good old mom and pop are easy targets.

Knowing that probably won't make dealing with his rage any easier. It's OK for you to feel anger at the abuse, even if your son apologized after he abused you. There is nothing that says that mothers and fathers have to silently endure their ill son's rage.

I tell parents who are taking care of their sons that it is totally acceptable for them to set limits for their son's behavior. If dementia sets in, however, there isn't much to do except endure.

Other parents are angry because of the sacrifices they had to make while they were taking care of their son. Feeling resentful about making sacrifices is not an occasion for guilt. It's a pretty normal response unless you are some kind of saint.

Whatever you do, don't feel guilty about your anger. It will prolong your grief.

Mothers and fathers sometimes have different ways of grieving. Don't feel guilty if you are handling the loss better than your spouse. I have talked to both mothers and fathers who felt very guilty and wrong because their spouse was so much more upset than they were. They were hurting, and they missed their son too. They just handled their grief differently.

Remember there are many different styles of grieving. You will grieve in the way most suited to you and your history. The loudness or the length of your grief has nothing to do with how much you loved your son.

If you are concerned that your spouse isn't grieving as hard as you are, don't be quick to assume it means he or she isn't hurting as much as you are. Talk to your spouse about it. Give your spouse the right to grieve in his or her own way.

Memories. You will have to be on the watch for memories. Some will be sweet and gentle. Others will be agonizingly painful.

Expect that special occasions, such as Christmas or Passover, his birthday, or other significant dates in his history with you, will bring up a lot of painful memories. If you know that, you can effectively plan for those holidays. Ask your support network to be there for you. Don't let these occasions surprise you and devastate you.

You would be wise to expect that it won't be just the first Christmas or birthday that will be upsetting to you. This can go on for years. If it does, it's not your fault. It's not a sign of weakness or instability. Plan for it as best you can, get through it as best you can, and try to enjoy the special occasion with the rest of your family.

Some memories you won't be able to plan for. Something out of the blue will remind you of your son. When that happens, just hang on and try to get through it. This pain, too, will begin to fade with time.

I think some mothers have an even harder time in the supermarket than partners do as they pass their son's favorite cereal on the shelf. If this is true for you, don't feel weak or unstable. It happens to the strongest.

Such surprises will probably keep happening for a while. There is nothing wrong with you if they do.

Your only defense is to plan for what you can predict will be upsetting. Ask for support from your network. Know that you can endure even the surprises. Whatever you do, don't blame yourself for being weak or unstable.

Taking action. You, too, can benefit from getting involved in the fight against AIDS. You may not want to do that right away. You may need time to rest.

When you are able, however, get involved. There won't be a finer way for you to honor your child.

Mothers of AIDS Patients is a support group that was started by people who wanted to make a difference, and who wanted to honor their sons by helping out other families whose sons were ill or whose sons had died. Fathers and other family members are welcome too.

Taking appropriate action may put you up against any homophobic ideas that you have. You will suffer far less if you learn how to confront homophobia whenever you find it.

DEALING WITH HOMOPHOBIA

What is homophobia? The term actually means the fear of homosexuality. Popular usage expands that to any type of negative feelings about homosexuality.

Gay bashing, or any kind of violence against lesbians and gays is homophobic. Using terms like *faggot, queer,* or *dyke* in a pejorative way is homophobic.

Homophobia can be even more subtle. It can refer to well-meaning attempts to accept your son's being gay while still believing that he is not as good as your heterosexual children. Viewing gay and lesbian citizens as second-class citizens is homophobic. Not accepting the validity and the meaningfulness of gay and lesbian relationships is homophobic.

Feeling responsible for your son's being gay, believing that somehow it is your "fault" that he chose this lifestyle, is homophobic because it makes being gay a mistake or makes it a lifestyle that needs to be justified. There is nothing wrong with being gay. I have heard of a number of families who tried to forget their son was gay, that he had AIDS, and that he died of AIDS. *It never works.*

Your silence and your hiding from the truth will exact a terrible price from you. It will vastly increase your level of depression and the length of time you grieve.

No matter how hard you try to deny that your son was gay, deep inside you will still know the truth. You will never be able to totally escape that knowledge. You may find it difficult to forgive yourself for your rejection of your son and of his life.

The only way for you to honor your son's memory is for you to be able to honor him and love him for all that he was. If this looks impossible to you now, don't give up. It is possible. It may just take some time, and not as much as you might fear.

If your son was gay, he was gay. Your disapproval caused you and your son a lot of pain when he was alive. Your continued disapproval will continue to cause you pain and intensify your suffering.

Isn't it easier to accept him the way he was, instead of demanding that he be the person you wanted him to be? Do you really want to be in partnership with those who have discriminated against and persecuted your son and his community?

If you have homophobic feelings, please don't waste time feeling guilty about them. Take responsibility for your beliefs and your feelings and challenge them.

There is another reason for you to be willing to let go of your homophobia. Your negative feelings about the lesbian and gay community will deprive you of the possibility of support from your son's partner and friends.

The lesbian and gay community opens its arms to parents who are willing to have a relationship with them. Let them be there for you.

Every year in most major cities in the country, there are gay pride festivals and parades, usually held in June, to commemorate the Stonewall Riots, which are honored as the birth of gay and lesbian liberation. Millions of men and women, lesbian and gay as well as heterosexual, participate in these pride events.

An organization that marches in every parade is Parents and Friends of Lesbians and Gays: PFLAG. They are one of the most enthusiastically received groups that has ever marched in any parade.

Many times I have stood in the crowd that lines the streets of West Hollywood to watch the Christopher Street West Gay Pride parade. I cannot watch the contingent of marchers from PFLAG without tears in my eyes — tears of pride and tears of gratitude.

Here are people who have embraced their gay sons and lesbian daughters, unconditionally loving them. There is virtually no person along that parade route who does not have the same reaction. I am not the only person with tears in my eyes as the parents and friends walk down the street, beside their children, carrying their signs, "I love my gay son," "I am proud of my lesbian daughter."

I have spoken with a number of parents who marched in the parade who were in a state of shock by the end of the parade. One father, newly aware that his son was gay, looked at me with tears running down his cheeks and said, "Do you know what it's like to be cheered and applauded and loved for six miles, every step of the way, by hundreds of thousands of people?"

He said he was convinced that Michael Crawford, stepping out on the stage at the end of another triumphant evening of *Phantom of the Opera* to a tumultuous standing ovation, could feel no more pride than he did during that march.

If you are willing to turn to the lesbian and gay community, you will receive overwhelming love and support. Many of us want our parents back, and if we can't have our own biological parents, we'll be delighted to borrow someone else's.

How do I get rid of homophobic thoughts? The first step is to acknowledge all of your homophobic thoughts and ideas. This is easy for some. It is harder for others, because it means voicing some unkind and ugly ideas. If ugly ideas are there, they must be expressed before you can let go of them. Then you can get on with accepting your son for exactly the person he was.

Challenge each homophobic thought. Remind yourself who your son really was, and challenge yourself to be willing to include his being gay along with the rest of it.

If you slip back into a homophobic thought, quickly challenge it. Be willing to do this as often as you need to.

Neither should you be willing to tolerate homophobic baloney from anyone else. If you wouldn't listen to racial putdowns, don't listen to anti-gay putdowns either.

If you try to understand your son as a gay man, if you try to understand what the lesbian and gay community is really all about, you won't have any trouble dumping your homophobia. Everyone wins if you are willing to do that.

My dear friends, you have a choice. You can choose to give in to your fear or possible hatred of the gay and lesbian community and live your life with bitterness and resentment. You can also choose to accept what is, and come to value each person for just who he or she is, regardless of whom they choose to love.

WHAT YOU NEED TO KNOW ABOUT THE GAY AND LESBIAN COMMUNITY

The more you know about the gay and lesbian community, the easier it will be for you to accept your son's lifestyle. The more you know and understand, the less you will be misled by the myths and lies told about the lesbian/gay community, especially by "born-again" bigots.

AIDS discrimination and discrimination against the gay and

lesbian community is based on ignorance and on fear. People can hate as long as they don't understand.

If you are willing to learn, and if you are willing to understand, you will be able to honor your son for exactly the person that he was. The information that follows will address as many of the aspects of being gay as possible, given the limitation of space.

Why do we say gay and lesbian? First of all, why do we say *lesbian* and gay? Why not just say *the gay community?*

For many people, *gay* has the connotation of *gay male.* The lesbian community prefers to be called lesbians as a means of distinguishing themselves from gay men. They have their own community and their own needs, which are different from the needs of the gay male community. For years, lesbians and lesbian needs were tacked on after gay needs and gay social-service programs.

A lot of consciousness has been raised, and now the lesbian community is dealt with on their own terms. This is not to say that all is well. It is not. There are still many deficiencies in social-service programs for lesbians. Inadequate attention is paid to their health care questions. Inadequate information is available about sexually transmitted diseases for lesbians, and facilities for their treatment are also inadequate, in spite of the astronomical rise in sexually transmitted diseases among women, lesbian as well as non-lesbian.

Lesbians are one of the lowest-risk groups for AIDS. Very few lesbians have contracted or died of AIDS. This tends to poke a few significant holes in the idea that AIDS is God's punishment for homosexual lifestyles.

In spite of this, lesbians have been in the forefront of the fight against AIDS. Most AIDS service organizations have received significant support from the lesbian community. Lesbians were among their founders, and remain as mainstay supporters of those programs.

The gay community owes a great debt of gratitude to the lesbian community. The lesbian community now deserves our support as they work on their own health-care battles with breast cancer, cervical cancer, and other health problems.

What does it mean to be "in the closet"? Being in the closet refers to hiding the fact that one is gay or lesbian. Some people are in the closet in every area of their lives. The only people who know they are gay or lesbian are their occasional sex partners.

Others are quite open about being gay, in a gay context. They would have no problem walking down the street in West Hollywood, or going into a gay bar or restaurant. But outside of a gay environment they are reluctant to have anyone know that they are gay. They usually haven't told their boss, coworkers, or family members yet, either.

Then there are those who are out of the closet to everyone they know. They usually report feelings of incredible freedom. They don't have to hide who they are from anyone.

Staying in the closet is unhealthy. It requires self-denial. It means buying into the homophobic prejudices. It's difficult to have a healthy level of self-esteem if one is denying a large part of who one is.

Why didn't my son tell me he was gay? There are lots of reasons why your son may have hidden his sexual orientation from you. Probably the most common one is fear: fear of rejection, fear of disapproval, fear of being hurt in some way.

The fact that your son didn't tell you he was gay may have been because of things you or your spouse may have said about gays at one time or another. A close friend of mine told me about a time in high school when his father said that he would rather have a murderer for a son than a faggot. He has never come out to his father. Is it any wonder?

Your son may not have come out to you, even though you have tried to make it safe for him, because he was just too influenced by societal homophobia. No matter how much you say you love him, he just couldn't bring himself to risk losing your love and support, no matter how small that risk might have appeared.

I have even talked to some parents who knew that their son was gay, and who told him as much only to have him deny it. The fear of parental rejection and societal punishment can be overwhelming.

As always, if you think you gave your son reason to think you would reject him for being gay, don't waste time feeling guilty. What's done is done. Make whatever amends you can and get on with your life. Doing something about discrimination against lesbians and gays will be a very powerful way to handle your guilt. As always, action is the solution.

What is the gay and lesbian community really like? The gay and lesbian community includes those people who choose to love members of the same sex. Beyond that, the gay community and the lesbian community are far from homogeneous.

In fact, the gay and lesbian community is just as diverse as the heterosexual community. We have our conservative Republicans, even Birchers. We have our flaming liberals. We have everything in between, including those who don't give a damn one way or the other.

We have our very wealthy. We have members of our community who sleep on the streets in cardboard boxes. We have everything in between.

We have our wildly promiscuous. We have those who are involved in long-term monogamous relationships. We have those who have been in numerous relationships, and those who have never been in relationships. In this we are no different from the heterosexual community.

We have gay men and lesbians who are committed to raising their own children. We have gay men and lesbians who will never have children and don't want to.

We have gay men and lesbians who are profoundly religious, Protestant, Catholic, Jewish, and a variety of other religions. There are lots who are evangelical fundamentalists, even though they are not welcome in those churches. We have gay men and lesbians who are into various New Age beliefs. We have gay men and lesbians who are atheists and agnostics.

We can't even agree on language. I have indicated that I refer to homosexual women as lesbians, and that is the current politically correct term, but there are women who prefer to be called "gay women."

For decades the term *queer* was loathed and hated by gay men and lesbians. It was a derogatory term used by bigots. Today, the group Queer Nation has embraced the term with their slogan, "We're here, we're queer. Get used to it." They are angry about prejudice. They are angry about AIDS and governmental neglect.

There are plenty of gay men and lesbians who are still not comfortable with the term *queer*. Nor do they approve of the angry tactics of Queer Nation.

(I wouldn't advise heterosexuals to begin to use the word *queer* in their conversations. It would not be well accepted. I suspect this is something like it being OK for black comedians to refer to "niggers" in their stage acts, while it is still considered prejudice for whites to use that term.)

No business, no career, no occupation is beyond the reach of the lesbian and gay communities. We, indeed, are everywhere, even in stereotypically unlikely places—for example, gay men are policemen and construction workers, and lesbians are flight attendants.

Quite frankly, we defy the stereotypes. We haven't been too interested in correcting those stereotypes until recently. That's because it's easier to hide as a lesbian or gay man if everyone thinks that all lesbians are truck drivers and all gay men are interior decorators and hairdressers.

There are effeminate gay men. There are macho gay men. There are "masculine" lesbians. There are "feminine" lesbians.

Given these differences, there is still a sense of lesbian and gay community. Nothing has fostered the sense of community more than the AIDS crisis. AIDS has created a more powerful, more effective, and more nurturing sense of community than we have ever had.

Not nearly enough has been written about the magnificence of the lesbian and gay community's response to AIDS. This community has faced a horrible crisis with heroic courage, tireless efforts to take care of their own, and selfless giving.

The lesbian and gay community is today a community of heroes. They deserve praise, acknowledgment, and assistance as they continue in their fight against AIDS and against continued discrimination.

Why is someone gay or lesbian? Frankly, no one really knows. The consensus among professionals seems to be that being gay and lesbian is a matter of innate sexual orientation, as opposed to preference.

I know of no lesbians or gay men, and I have worked and played with thousands, who feel as if there was a point in their life when they simply made the choice to be gay or lesbian. As far as I can tell, the only choice we have is whether or not to accept our sexual orientation.

I did not choose to be a gay man. For as long as I can remember, I have always been more drawn to members of my own sex. I resisted this for years, not wanting to subject myself to persecution and discrimination and harassment.

This had nothing to do with how I felt about women. I found women attractive. I successfully dated a number of women and even planned to marry one. I cared for her a great deal, but it would have been tragic for me to have tried to deny who I really was while I tried desperately to play house for the sake of appearances.

I needed to recognize that something was missing. I didn't realize what that was until I fell in love with another man. We spent the next ten years together. While we are no longer lovers, he is still my closest friend on the planet outside of John, my life partner.

I don't know how to explain any of this. I don't know why. I just know that it is. I know the pain that I suffered trying not to be gay. I have observed the pain suffered by other gay men and lesbians as they tried to resist being what they were.

Is it genetics? Is it social learning and conditioning? Is it fate? I don't know. I don't really care. Gay just is.

Is it the parents' fault when a child is gay or lesbian? Is it your fault that your son was gay? No. It's not a question of fault. No parent ever needs to feel guilty that their son is gay or that their daughter is a lesbian.

If we don't know why anyone is gay or lesbian, why should parents feel guilty? Many parents are sure that they must have done or said something to their child that made him or her turn out to be homosexual. I can guarantee that whatever you said or did, there are other parents who have heterosexual children who said or did the same thing.

Some are sure that being gay is the result of having a weak or absent father, and a powerful, perhaps overpowerful, mother. I know a number of gay men for whom that is true. I also know a lot of heterosexual men who experienced the same thing, but have never had a gay experience.

I have known gay men who have powerful fathers and weak or

absent mothers. I have known gay men who had very normal and loving fathers and mothers.

Nothing you could have done would have made any difference about your son being gay. If you accepted him as gay, then you at least made his journey easier. If you rejected him because he was gay, then you did make his journey more difficult, but you didn't make him a homosexual.

Could my son have been recruited to be gay? About the only people who spend a lot of time thinking about recruitment are those "born-again" preachers. They harp on it constantly. The fear of homosexual recruiters seems to be a potent weapon in their hands as they try to pass laws against gay and lesbian citizens.

I have been a therapist working with gay men and lesbians for the last twenty years. I have led workshops and seminars for thousands of gay men and lesbians. I have yet to meet a gay man or lesbian who feels that he or she was recruited to be a gay man or lesbian. If they do exist out there somewhere, I have neither seen them nor heard about them.

According to the earliest Kinsey studies, 40 percent to 50 percent of American men have had a homosexual contact to the point of orgasm, yet only 10 percent are considered to be gay. That means the vast majority of men who have an experience of sex with someone of the same sex don't continue in the gay lifestyle.

It takes more than one experience with someone of the same sex to make someone a homosexual. Since we don't really know why some people are heterosexual and others are homosexual, the concept of recruitment is vacuous and grossly misleading.

Incidentally, there are plenty of gay men and lesbians who have had heterosexual sexual experiences. That didn't make them heterosexual.

Frankly, recruitment is only a figment of the "born-again" preachers' hyperactive, hypercurious, and somewhat sleazy imaginations. They resort to those same imaginations when they berate gay men and lesbians as child molesters.

In doing so, they willfully and knowingly ignore research study after research study that shows that the vast majority of child sexual abuse cases involve a heterosexual adult, usually a friend of the family or a family member.

There are some homosexuals who are child molesters, but they are a very small number. The vast majority of lesbians and gay men have never, and would never, molest a child.

Such child sexual abuse is wrong, regardless of the sexual orientation of the abuser. It should be dealt with appropriately by the legal system. However, it cannot be used as a means of indicting an entire community.

Gay men and lesbians are not recruiters. They are not child molesters. They are not rapists. When "born-again" preachers say different, they are simply lying. Willful ignorance from the pulpit is still a lie.

Why are gay men only interested in sex? They are not. Gay men, in my experience, are no more obsessed with sex than their heterosexual counterparts. One of the great myths of all time is that gay men are hyper-sexual sex fiends who will stop at nothing to have sex, anywhere and anytime. This just isn't so.

There are gay men who are asexual or almost asexual, having sex never or very infrequently. There are gay men who have had sex with only a few other men.

Yes, there are gay men who have had sex with thousands of other men in their lifetime, but as near as I can tell, that's not the norm.

The media frequently presents gay men as walking down the street groping one another, staggering from one gay bar to the next. Some do. Most don't.

When was the last time you spent any time in a heterosexual singles bar, or in a heterosexual locker room, listening to the sexual banter going around? One visit is all it would take to show you that homosexuals don't have the corner on the sexually active market.

I don't believe that gay men think about sex any more than non-gay men. They just have more opportunity to act on their impulses, possibly because women are less sympathetic to male promiscuity than other men.

We have an interesting double standard. It's all right to be sexually active if you are a heterosexual male. That just makes you a stud. If you are a heterosexual female, or a gay or a lesbian, you're just sleazy and easy.

Gay men and lesbians may be more comfortable with and less guilt-ridden about sex. This doesn't make them perverts.

Gay men and lesbians are just as committed to their careers, their relationships, and their community as are heterosexuals. Being gay or lesbian is about a lot more than what one chooses to do sexually, or how often.

Doesn't AIDS mean that gay sex is bad and wrong? No, it does not, no matter what the "born-again" preachers are saying. I don't believe that any disease is a punishment from God. I don't believe it makes sense to single out AIDS and say that it is punishment from God.

When most people who are HIV-positive were exposed to the virus, no one knew the virus existed. No one was aware of the dangerous consequences of certain sexual acts. It makes no sense to blame anyone for something they had no way of knowing about.

There is another lie about AIDS and sex and the gay community. The idea is trumpeted loudly, widely, and dishonestly by the right-wing preachers and politicians. They would have everyone believe that the gay community is continuing to have rampant and undiscriminating sex, willfully transmitting the AIDS virus to one another.

This just isn't so. Statistics regarding sexually transmitted diseases indicate that the vast majority of gay men are having safer sex. If the right-wing preachers were willing to look they would see that this is true, but they would then lose one of their best selling points as they try to drum up fear and loathing in their search for financial gain and political power.

When your son contracted the virus, it is highly likely that he did not know that what he was doing would cause the transmission of the virus that killed him. Your son is not to blame. His partner is not to blame. The lesbian/gay community is not to blame.

Then who is to blame for my son being HIV-positive? Who do you blame for the fact that your son was HIV-positive? No one. There is just no way to know how any one person received the virus. Long latency periods and the inherent trickiness of the virus makes it impossible to know. It could have come from anyone that your son had sex with in the last ten years. The last article I read on the subject indicated that the latency may be as long as eighteen years.

Pointing the finger at your son's lover or his friends won't help, won't work, and is useless. There's no way to know and no reason to need to know.

I have clients with AIDS who have had thousands of sexual partners over the years. I have had clients with AIDS who have had sex with very few other men in their whole lifetime.

There is no one to blame for your child being HIV-positive. Don't waste time and energy on this one.

Why couldn't my son "go straight"? Can a gay man or lesbian switch to being heterosexual? Frankly, I doubt it. Some try, and suffer immeasurably by so doing. They pay the huge price of their personal integrity and personal happiness.

"Going straight" or becoming straight is very different from acting straight. Acting straight is easy. Most of us spent a lot of time doing that before we accepted who we really were.

There are those who claim that they have truly "gone straight." It's my best guess that some of them weren't really gay in the first place. They misinterpreted momentary feelings or occasional experiments as being gay.

There are a number of others who claim to have "gone straight" who are really just acting straight. Some do this as a way of pleasing someone else. Others do it because they were never able to get over the guilt they feel about being gay or lesbian.

Still others try to "go straight" because they believe the lie that gay men and lesbians cannot have warm, wonderful relationships. They believe that to be gay and old is to be alone and miserable.

Some gay men and lesbians do have trouble having relationships. It's my notion that they would also have the same trouble having relationships with someone of the opposite sex. Their trouble isn't with being gay, it's with intimacy and relationships.

There *are* older gays and lesbians who are alone and miserable, but aren't there also heterosexuals who are old, alone, and miserable? A person's sexual orientation has nothing to do with how he or she is going to spend his or her old age.

As might be expected, radical "born-again" preachers have programs that are supposed to "cure" homosexuality. Frankly, if a gay man hates being gay so much that he is willing to subject himself to such a program, and if he is able to put together a warm, supportive lifestyle as a heterosexual, then I wouldn't try to deny him that route. I sincerely hope it works for him.

As a former fundamentalist, I can say that the fundamentalist church is riddled with closet homosexuals. I grew up in a fundamentalist church and went to an evangelical college. I know there are many closet homosexuals because I had sex with a number of them.

I also know the pain, guilt, and misery that they experience, and that I experienced. The only time I ever felt peace of mind and satisfaction with life was when I accepted the fact that I was a gay man whose sexual, romantic, and emotional attractions were for other men.

Most gay men and lesbians that I know have no interest in making any attempt to change, even if it were certain that they could. Happiness comes from personal integrity, not from being socially acceptable.

Honor your son by fighting discrimination. If you are feeling guilty about the way you dealt with your son's being gay, don't continue to hurt yourself by hanging on to that guilt. If your son has died, there is nothing more you can do for him. There is a great deal you can do to honor who he was. Joining the fight against discrimination will be a powerful way for you to honor your son.

Discrimination has been with us since the dawn of civilization. Human beings have always had a tendency to distrust and be fearful of anyone who was appreciably different from themselves.

Discrimination has never produced a good result. It has always produced pain and suffering. This is as true for those who do the discriminating as it is for those who are discriminated against.

Over the last thirty years we have made a lot of progress in the area of civil rights. Even so, we have long way to go before we live in a society based on equality of its citizens.

It's no longer socially acceptable to publicly voice prejudiced, bigoted ideas. That does not yet include anti-gay, anti-lesbian, or anti–people with AIDS. In our society, it is still OK to discriminate against lesbians and gay men and against people with AIDS.

If you find yourself doing this, don't waste any time feeling guilty about it. Just stop it. You must realize the danger created by discrimination in our society.

As long as any one group is allowed to discriminate against any other group for any reason, then no group is safe. No member of society is safe.

Until minorities are granted equal rights with whatever prevailing majority group there is, no member of the majority is really safe.

The balance of power could change tomorrow. The person who used to be part of the majority could find himself or herself in a minority group subject to the kind of discrimination they approved of when they were members of the majority.

For example, white Anglo-Saxons used to be in the majority in the state of California. By the turn of the century, they will be a minority. What would happen if the various minorities united and decided to pass laws discriminating against Anglos the way Anglos discriminated against them?

The brilliant concept on which this country was based came from the fact that the people who founded our country and wrote our Bill of Rights and Declaration of Independence wrote those documents from firsthand experience of bigotry and discrimination, particularly of the religious variety.

They wrote those documents with the intention of creating a society of freedom and inclusion. One of my more conservative friends told me, "Yes, but they didn't mean to include homosexuals." That's right. They didn't. While their intention was good, their practice was not consistent.

They also didn't think that women were equal to men, and they believed that a white man had a right to own a black man as personal property.

Over the years we have overcome much religious and racial discrimination—not all of it; it is still with us in certain areas. Now it's time for discrimination based on sexual orientation to be outlawed.

Making us illegal and casting us out of the churches hasn't diminished the number of homosexuals. Our numbers increase with the population. Our influence is growing, and our presence is increasingly felt. This is in spite of the tens of thousands of us who have already died of AIDS.

Regardless of Jesse Helms's disapproval, we aren't going away, and we aren't going back into our closets.

Please join us. Honor your son by honoring his community. Bitterness and resentment, or pride and compassion: the choice is yours.

Honor your son by honoring his friendships and relationships. It's also important for you to honor the relationships your son had. This includes his friends and especially his life partner.

Lesbians and gay men love their partners no less deeply than any heterosexual ever loved his or her spouse. Some of you may find this unbelievable. All I can do is assure you that it is absolutely true.

For over six years now, I have shared my life with my life partner, John. He is the very center of my life. He is an integral part of the very structure of my life. The gap in my life created by his leaving would be immeasurable. I cannot imagine that any human being has ever loved another human being more than I love him.

It saddens me to think that there are people who can't comprehend that. I urge you, if your son had a life partner when he died, to consider the fact that he loved his partner just as much.

If you would truly honor your son, how could you not honor his relationship with his life partner?

If one of your heterosexual children had died, it is likely that you and that child's spouse would form a partnership in grieving, being there for one another, helping one another cope with your loss. I beg you not to deprive yourself of this means of support.

One support group is an organization called Mothers of AIDS Patients (MAP). Most of the parents I have talked to in this group have found incredible support and love in their relationships with their son's partner and friends.

RESOURCES

Whom do you ask for support? You may find yourself in the same position as gay partners and friends. You may be subject to the same disapproval and rejection. You may need advice about dealing with your own "coming out" to friends and neighbors who don't know you had a gay son, or that he died of AIDS.

To date, many families have to grieve alone, with too few resources available for them. There still aren't enough resources, but there are more than ever before.

Fortunately, you have at your disposal two major sources of support. They are found in many cities and towns in the United States and across the world. At the end of the book, there will be names and phone numbers for PFLAG and MAP.

Either Parents and Friends of Lesbians and Gays or Mothers of AIDS Patients can offer you a fine support group as you come to grips with your son's death.

Both groups were founded by parents of gay men and lesbians. Both groups are run solely on volunteer time from mothers, fathers, other family members, and friends who are choosing to do something about ending discrimination and finding support for other parents who are just going through the "coming-out" process or the grieving process.

They are literally just a phone call away. Please let them support you.

If a member of your family has died of AIDS, you have an awesome task before you. Telling the truth, acting out of compassion and caring, and refusing to become a partner to those who hate and discriminate against persons with AIDS will make your process much easier.

when your friend has died

If your friend has died of AIDS, you may be facing many of the same issues as partners and families. You may have the same responsibilities, face the same tasks, have the same sense of loss.

The information in Chapters 9 and 10 will be just as relevant for you as for partners and families. If you haven't already read those two chapters, I'd strongly urge you to do so now. This will be even more important to do if you were the primary caregiver for your friend.

Please know that friends may grieve just as strongly as partners and families. Frequently friends have been around a lot longer than partners. They have spent much more time in the adult lives of those who have died than their families. In fact, in our community, friends have frequently become our surrogate families. The loss of a long-time friend can be just as wrenching as the loss of a partner.

There is no competition for grief. There is no protocol for who grieves more painfully. The only thing you can do is feel however you feel, regardless of your relationship to the one who has died. You don't have to apologize for hurting so much because you were "just a friend."

Just as with life partners and family members, friends have their own sadness, depression, anger, fear, and guilt to deal with. You will have to grieve your own way. You may have vultures to fend off. You may have personal belongings and property to help dispose of. You'll need to return to taking care of business, because later is now. You'll have your own varieties of homophobia to challenge and resist.

In this chapter, I will concentrate on other practical issues that might be affecting you.

IF YOU ARE NOT GAY OR LESBIAN AND YOUR FRIEND HAS DIED

There is an increasingly large number of people who are not gay or lesbian but who are grieving for gay friends who have died of AIDS. You will definitely experience the same grief issues as family members and gay and lesbian friends. You may even be subjected to the same persecution by AIDS bigots who will be suspicious of your friendship with a gay man.

I also encourage you to read carefully Chapter 10, which was written for family members. Even though this chapter addresses those issues faced by gay and lesbian friends, you will find helpful information for yourself as you are grieving for your lost friend.

As do some family members, you may notice that an AIDS death revives some of your own negative judgments about gay sexual behavior. I have spoken with a number of non-gay/non-lesbian people who reluctantly admitted that they had had some harsh judgments about sexual lifestyles, such as "Didn't my friend bring this on himself?"

Please remind yourself of the often-overlooked fact of the very long latency period of the AIDS virus. It can hide in the blood, not causing any damage, for ten years. One journal article recently suggested an eighteen-year latency period for the AIDS virus.

Most of those people who have died of AIDS did not know they were engaging in behavior that would transmit the virus at the time they were exposed to the virus. At that time, we didn't even know there was such a thing as the AIDS virus.

Please remember that it was the gay and lesbian community who started intensive safer-sex education programs, long before the government did. In many cases, our efforts are still being sabotaged by elected officials such as Senator Helms and Congressman Dannemeyer, as well as AIDS bigots like Lou Sheldon and others.

In spite of their opposition, we have continued our efforts to promote safer sex. The plummeting statistics for sexually transmitted diseases within the gay male community are solid evidence of the effectiveness of our efforts.

As a non-gay/non-lesbian person, you can have a powerful impact on how the government continues to deal with the AIDS crisis. As unfair as it is, your voice is louder than ours. When heterosexuals begin to insist on aggressive intervention against the disease, and on the compassionate treatment of those with the disease, elected officials who have turned a deaf ear to the gay and lesbian community will have to listen.

Please consider getting involved in the fight against AIDS. Can there be a better way for you to honor your friend who has died?

You might also remember that AIDS is not just a gay phenomenon as its numbers increase in the heterosexual community. In other countries, AIDS is a predominately heterosexual disease. Your own community has its own needs.

The incidence of teenage pregnancy and the statistics for sexually transmitted diseases in the heterosexual community are clear indicators that the heterosexual community is still not practicing safer sex. The need for safer sex education for heterosexuals, particularly teenagers, is great.

The "just say no, abstinence is best" mentality is absurdly naive. This mentality has been and will continue to be responsible for the AIDS deaths of heterosexuals, particularly teenagers.

Teenagers and young adults have always had sex before marriage, no matter how violently society and the churches have urged against it. It is a fact that won't be denied. It is a fact that won't change. Neither do I see an end to adult heterosexuals having sex outside of marriage.

The "born-again" preachers and some Catholic clergy who have so vehemently blocked efforts at safer-sex education in our schools will someday have to account for their responsibility in the deaths of people who could have been informed about the dangers of unsafe sex. I would like to feel some satisfaction in the fact that history will not treat them kindly, but that is small comfort when people are dying.

Again, your voice raised against those who are blocking lifesaving safer-sex education will be louder than ours. Won't you raise it as loudly as possible?

Find out who your local, state, and federal elected officials are. You can do that by calling your local city hall. They will give you the necessary information. Make a list with phone numbers and addresses of these elected officials.

Then write or call every one of them and let them know that you fully support the fight against AIDS, the fight against discrimination against people with AIDS, and the fight for widespread public education about safer sex, especially in the schools.

One very easy way to join the fight against AIDS is to become part of the Speak Out program of the Human Rights Campaign Fund (HRCF). HRCF is the only nationwide political action committee working for the civil rights of gay and lesbian citizens as well as people with AIDS, and for women's health issues.

If you become a member of the Speak Out program, you will be asked to authorize a certain number of mailgrams to be sent in your name to targeted elected federal officials. You decide how many to authorize at a cost of $3.25 per mailgram (at the time of this writing).

These mailgrams will support legislation that fights AIDS, and will oppose legislation that seeks to punish those with AIDS or otherwise hamper the fight against AIDS. With very little effort on your part, you can have a significant impact on your federal elected officials.

Many people also have chosen to become a Speak Out volunteer and sign up friends and neighbors in this very important program. Some have reported signing up entire hospital staffs while they were visiting friends who were hospitalized.

You can reach HRCF at 202-628-4160. You can reach Speak Out at 800-787-HRCF. (See Resources.)

If your friend has died of AIDS, grieve well, and then consider getting involved. Is there a finer way to honor your friend?

GRIEVING WHILE YOU ARE STILL TAKING CARE OF OTHERS

Friends frequently have the added complication that while they are grieving, they are still taking care of other friends who are ill. They don't have the luxury of time to let go and grieve. They have too many responsibilities to the people who are still living.

They may also be worrying about friends who are HIV-positive and still healthy. How long will it be before they may become ill?

This creates a picture of potential loss after loss, taking care of one person after another only to lose them too. This can seem a devastating future to look toward: more illness and more death. If you are HIV-positive, it might look like this can only end with your own illness and death.

This can be terrifying and potentially overwhelming. Psychologists' offices are filling with people trying to cope with this desperate scenario.

As devastating as this picture can be, we must not allow ourselves to become victims of our losses and victims of our fear for the future. We are still alive, and life is still there for us to live as fully as we can.

We must know how to grieve well. We need to know how to constantly express our feelings fully, no matter how frightening they might be. We need to make a commitment to take care of ourselves, of our physical health. We must not forget how to love and play. We must nurture hope and keep it alive for our ill friends as well as for ourselves.

We must be prepared to handle the details and necessary tasks awaiting us. We must not allow our sadness to keep us from getting the jobs done.

FRIENDS ARE SOMETIMES PRIMARY CAREGIVERS

Many of the people who have died of AIDS did not have a life partner. In some cases they had also been abandoned by their families. Consequently, the responsibilities for taking care of them were exercised by friends.

These friends worked just as diligently and selflessly as life partners or parents would have as they took care of the one who was ill. After the death, it was the friends who were left with all of the responsibilities.

As a primary caregiver, you may have had to put up with abuse and mistreatment from the one who was ill. You may have risked other relationships, even your job, as you took care of him. You may be currently experiencing great fatigue and a sense of burnout.

Some of you have become amateur health-care workers, and are exhausting yourselves as you take care of one friend after another. It is truly wonderful that this is taking place, but I have seen too many who are burning themselves out and putting their own health at risk.

There is far too much to be done for you to allow yourself to burn out. The end to all of this is still a long way off, and the only way we can survive is to make a firm commitment to taking care of ourselves.

If your friend was abusive. This is a frequent occurrence. People with AIDS are often frightened and angry. This can cause them to lash out at those closest to them.

I believe that this causes them as much pain as it does you. They know they are being difficult or inappropriate. They may just be too ill to do anything about it.

If this has happened to you, you will need to take care of your own anger in response to the abuse. If you didn't get angry, that's great. If you did, it was perfectly understandable. There is no reason for guilt.

If you are currently taking care of someone who is being abusive, it will be very important for you to talk to him about the abuse. Let him know that you understand his anger, but that you don't want to be the brunt of it. Let him know that you still love him, and that you forgive him.

If you were angry back at him, explain that too. Apologize and then forgive yourself also.

If your friend has already died, there is nothing you can do directly to clean it up with him. You can still honor him by learning a valuable lesson about your feelings, and by learning how to deal more effectively with other people you are caring for.

Learn to set limits. Taking care of someone else, especially if you are also grieving for someone who has died, will be a lot easier if you can become comfortable setting limits. If you are willing to learn from your experience, you can begin to set limits for what is acceptable behavior.

The fact that your friend is ill doesn't mean that you have to tolerate being abused without expressing yourself to him. The more lovingly and calmly you can do this, the greater your chances for success.

Whatever you do, don't feel guilty about setting limits for appropriate behavior. You're not insulting him or abusing him. You are just letting him know that you don't want to be the object of his anger. You are just setting limits, and most people who are ill are able to respect those limits.

Some of us are pretty good at setting limits for other people's behavior. Others of us find it very difficult.

When I was working in a rehabilitation hospital with catastrophically ill or injured patients, I noticed that there were some staff members who never seemed to experience much abuse from patients. There were other staff members who always seemed to be abused by angry patients.

I suspect the difference is that those who were not abused were more effective at setting limits. They may not have been aware that they were setting any limits, but they just weren't willing to put up with abuse and somehow communicated that, directly or indirectly.

Those staff members who were abused seemed to feel guilty setting limits. After all, the person was ill, or severely injured. Didn't he have the right to be angry?

Yes, people who are ill do have the right to be angry. They are also, in most cases, capable of learning how to deal with their anger without resorting to the abuse of their caregivers.

Learn to lovingly set limits for abusive behavior, and to lovingly and compassionately enforce them. It may be difficult and your friend may get angry with you, but that doesn't make you a bad person.

In fact, you will be doing a favor for your ill friend. At some level, he knows that he is being abusive and probably feels guilty about it. He knows it's not a good thing for him to do, but he just can't seem to help it. He will be increasingly anxious that you may decide to leave him rather than put up with more of his abuse.

If you are willing to set limits with him, you will actually increase his level of security. Even though he initially may be angry, at some level he will see that you aren't going to abandon him, and that you, in fact, care enough about him to tell the truth about his troublesome behavior.

Your friend may pull out the stops to try to make you feel guilty for having the nerve to set limits. If you don't confront this, you are going to be building lots of resentment toward him. Being around him will become more and more difficult. You may start to find excuses not to be around him.

If you start to avoid him, you will probably start feeling guilty. Your friend is left without support. No one wins.

You can avoid this unfortunate situation if you are willing to lovingly set limits and stick to them, no matter how much your friend tries to manipulate you.

Keep reminding yourself that he is terrified and outraged by what he is going through. Don't take what he is saying or doing personally. It's about his fear, not about your worth as a friend.

If your friend had a hostile family. One of the great tragedies of AIDS is the way it can tear apart groups of people who would ordinarily be supportive of one another. Families are sometimes not able to handle their son's gay friends.

They often don't understand the depth of the friends' grief. Some families are openly abusive and hostile to friends and partners, who are left out in the cold to grieve on their own.

Hopefully your relationship with your friend's family was a good working relationship that allowed you to share the care he needed. Such a relationship will now provide you with the support that you need as you are grieving.

If you aren't fortunate enough to be facing a supportive family, your job will be tougher. Your first responsibility will be to try to talk to the family. Explain your love and caring and ask to be included.

If they still don't welcome you, frankly, there's not much you can do. I know this isn't fair, or just, but if it is happening to you, the only thing you can do is accept it and find a way to take care of yourself.

It's OK if you are angry, but don't allow yourself to get stuck in resentment. That will only make you a victim of his family's hatefulness.

There are a lot of friends who have been shut out after an AIDS death. I know of several who were threatened with grave bodily harm if they showed up at the funeral or memorial service. They weren't even allowed to see their friend's body and say goodbye.

As unfortunate as this is, it doesn't mean that you can't be involved in the honoring of the one who has died. You just don't get to do it with his family.

A lot of friends who felt excluded from a funeral or memorial service have proceeded to organize their own memorial service. It was just as meaningful a way to say goodbye as the service held by the family.

In the last chapter, we'll look at other issues of saying goodbye. You don't need the family's cooperation and inclusion in order to do that.

Memories. Since you most likely spent more time with your friend as an adult than his family did, you may find yourself even more plagued by memories. There will be numerous places that will carry memories that may possibly cause you pain.

Of course there are the holidays and other special occasions that you used to share together, like the Gay Pride Parade each year, or the Gay Rodeo. Annual parties you used to attend together, favorite bars and restaurants, fund raisers, organizations for which you may have volunteered together, or your church or temple likely will bring up memories.

The songs you used to dance to, the gym where you worked out together, the support group you may have attended together will also make you think of him. That will usually create some sadness, maybe a lot.

If this is happening to you, it doesn't mean that something is wrong with you. It is a normal occurrence. I don't know of any way to avoid it, nor do I think we should try to avoid it. If painful memories come up, we need to be willing to face our sadness.

We must then be willing to move on, without castigating ourselves for being weak or unstable. Too many people I talk with tell me that such sadness over memories makes them feel inadequate, as if they're not handling it.

They are handling it. *"Handling it" doesn't mean never feeling sad again.*

Let the memories come up. Just don't get lost in the pain. Memories can be sweet as well, as you remember the wonderful times you had together.

YOUR HIV STATUS

Dealing with your friend's death will almost always raise issues about your own HIV status. Your fear may be intensified by the experience of his death.

Your friend has died, but that doesn't mean that you will soon die too if you are HIV-positive. In today's situation, being HIV-positive is not an automatic death sentence. By the time this book is published that will undoubtedly be much more apparently true.

Be prepared to confront the fear when it comes up. Fear that isn't expressed can't be challenged. Fear that isn't challenged will create immense stress and do a lot of damage, both physically and emotionally.

Be sure you are taking care of yourself. No matter how many people you are taking care of, you must take time for yourself. You must find some time to get away and relax. Keep reminding yourself that you aren't going to be of much use to the people you are caring for if you are burning yourself out.

Consider formulating your personal Wellness strategy as a powerful means of combating the fear of AIDS. Rest, nutrition, guided imagery, exercise, hugs, and challenging unworkable beliefs are all important options for you to consider.

Just as there isn't a Right way to grieve, there is also no Right Wellness strategy. The reason I called my first book *Pathways to Wellness* was because I am convinced that there is no one right way to challenge AIDS.

Long-term survivors have taken many different pathways. There are long-term survivors who have taken completely traditional medical approaches. There are those who have taken very metaphysical or New Age approaches. There are those who have not followed any program at all. Your duty is to find the one that works for you.

What if you're HIV-negative? I have spoken with a number of HIV-negative men who have lots of guilt over being the ones who are surviving. There is no justification for survivor guilt. *Your friend would have wanted you to survive.*

Some who are HIV-negative are angry at being subjected to the discrimination created by AIDS even though they are HIV-negative. This isn't fair, of course, but it is happening. If you are gay, you will be subject to discrimination even if you are HIV-negative. Your HIV status doesn't matter to Helms and Dannemeyer.

Don't allow discrimination to victimize you. Choose to take action that will do something about the problem instead.

There are some who feel guilty about having their own problems not related to HIV. It's as though they are saying, "How can I have problems when my HIV-positive friends are dealing with life-and-death issues?"

You are entitled to have your problems, whatever they are, even if you are HIV-negative. There isn't a competition for whose problems are more valid. Your HIV-positive friends may indeed be dealing with life-and-death issues, but that has nothing to do with whatever is causing you trouble. You don't have to apologize for the fact that your problems are not life-and-death matters.

Be aware that there are HIV-positive people who will not understand why you are so upset when the problems you are dealing with have nothing to do with life and death. Such people do exist, but you don't have to buy their beliefs. You have as much right to ask for support and nurturing as someone who is HIV-positive. There is no weakness in that.

Being HIV-negative and feeling excluded. Some HIV-negative men have told me that they feel left out and excluded by their HIV-positive friends.

I doubt that HIV-positive men mean to exclude HIV-negative men. It's just that there is a lot of commonality among people facing the same challenge. They may feel as if an HIV-negative person can't understand or relate to the panic that is experienced with the appearance of a strange rash, blemish, or cough.

They may feel as if you wouldn't be interested in listening to long conversations about research information regarding new forms of treatment, or comparing symptoms or experiences with the various diseases that frequently accompany AIDS.

If you are feeling left out, say something about it to your HIV-positive friends. Realize that if you do it in a challenging and critical way, you may not get what you want. Just lovingly and gently explain that you feel excluded.

Before talking to your friends about feeling excluded, be sure that your friends truly are excluding you. I have talked to several HIV-negative men who were actually excluding *themselves.* They were the ones who felt different and alienated. They were the ones putting barriers up between them and their HIV-positive friends.

Some HIV-negative men withdraw out of their fear of being around people who are ill or dying. Blaming it on their HIV-positive friend seems to help take some of their guilt away. If you see yourself here, don't waste time feeling guilty, just do something about it.

Being HIV-negative—and morally superior (?) The most inappropriate thing that HIV-negative people can do is to become judgmental of those who are HIV-positive. Being HIV-negative is indeed something to be thankful for. It means that you haven't been exposed to the virus, period.

Being HIV-negative has nothing to do with moral superiority. It makes no one any better than someone who is HIV-positive.

If you find yourself feeling that superiority, please realize that you are just buying the baloney from the "born-again" preachers that AIDS is somehow a punishment for sinful behavior and that a person with AIDS is of sleazy character without any sense of morals.

Feeling morally superior for being HIV-negative is really just another form of homophobia. Please be willing to challenge it.

At the same time, you don't have to hide the fact that you are HIV-negative, and you don't need to apologize for being HIV-negative. Just be thankful. Most of your HIV-positive friends will be happy that you are HIV-negative.

GUILT ABOUT STAYING AWAY

We have already talked about people who have stayed away from their friends who were ill or dying. They tend to experience a lot of guilt about that. Of course guilt won't help. Neither will staying away from your friends who need you.

A lot of people are so afraid of AIDS that they avoid being with someone who has AIDS. I think that this was more common in the early days of the epidemic, but it is still happening. Everybody loses in such a scenario.

If you are avoiding someone who is ill, please realize that you need to confront your fear, or whatever else is keeping you away. Continuing to stay away will only damage you. It won't do your friends much good either.

Such a level of fear is dangerous to your health. It will create a lot of stress. It needs to be dealt with for your own good.

One of the most effective ways to confront the fear of AIDS is to spend time with someone who has AIDS. A lot of my friends and clients who have volunteered many hours of their time working for other people with AIDS have shared with me that their own fear tended to diminish as they spent more time around people with AIDS.

That doesn't mean that their fear disappeared totally. I don't know how to make that happen. But their fear did diminish, and it no longer prevented them from being around their friends who had AIDS.

If you are currently avoiding a friend with AIDS, make a commitment to work through your fear. Reread the chapter on fear, Chapter 8. If that isn't enough, seek out professional help.

Then go to your friend and explain about your fear. He very likely will understand. If he doesn't and gets angry, try to understand what he's up against. Try to hang in there with him. Let him know that you are doing whatever it takes to get on top of your fear so you can be with him.

If your friend has died, there is nothing you can do about repairing that relationship with him. If he had a life partner, you could go to him and explain about your fear, and apologize for not being there.

If your friend's lover refuses to accept your apology, don't give up. He is in the midst of his own grief and may not have the resources to treat your apology with more kindness.

Don't give up on the relationship. You don't have to buy his condemnation. Neither do you have to condemn him. Remind yourself what he's been through and give him some time to heal.

If there is no one to apologize to, then you can still do something about it. You can learn from the situation. You can conquer your fear and get involved helping others who are ill.

This kind of action is the basis of the twelve-step-program idea of "making amends." If your friend has died, you can't make it up to him, but you can make it up to someone else who is fighting the disease. Take care of another friend or begin doing volunteer work with people with AIDS. You will feel better. You will help diminish your fear. The world will truly be better because you are here.

Whatever you do, don't just hide out, a victim of your guilt and fear. Take action.

YOUR PARTNER OR BOYFRIEND MAY BE NEEDING YOU

You may find yourself in the same boat as the parent who has been the caregiver. You may have your own life partner or someone that you are dating who has been missing you.

I have heard of more than one relationship biting the dust because one of the partners was spending too much time taking care of someone who was ill. Neglecting your relationship will ultimately result in more stress. You don't need that.

Part of avoiding caregiver burnout is knowing how to nourish yourself. Your relationship can be a major source of support for you.

Be sure you are in constant communication with your partner or friend. Tell them what you are going through. Tell him how important it is for you to be able to take care of your friend. Explain how much you love and miss him. He will appreciate the reassurance.

Be sure to allow him to express himself to you. Try not to get angry at him for being angry. Understand that he misses you very much and may be feeling jealous and unimportant to you.

If the two of you are willing to communicate fully, you will probably get the support that you need, and he won't feel threatened. Just tell the truth. Make it safe for him to tell the truth.

Unfortunately, there will be those people who are too needy to be willing to share you with anyone else, even an ill friend. They may expect you to choose between them and your friend.

If this happens, I am pessimistic about the future of the relationship. If you do give in on this one, you will feel as resentful toward that person as you will feel guilty about leaving your ill friend.

I suspect that this won't be the last demand made on your time and energy. People who force such a choice are usually so very needy that they are always devising tests and gathering other evidence that they are loved. Unfortunately, they will never get enough evidence to feel secure.

Be sure that you are not spending too much time taking care of your friend. Being a caregiver can be an all-consuming experience. You won't be healthy if you are sacrificing everything to take care of your friend. Learn how to effectively ask for help.

If you don't take care of yourself, how can you ever take care of other people? You will burn out, sooner rather than later.

DON'T BE AFRAID TO LOVE AGAIN

With so many dying, there are a lot of people who have already experienced so much grief that they have begun to withdraw from relationships. This may help them avoid more grieving, but it will cost a lot in terms of loneliness and a sense of alienation.

Don't ever be afraid to love again. Of course, it may mean that you will again experience a loss of someone that you love. I guarantee you that the time you spend in a loving relationship will be worth the grief.

Living without friendships and love may seem safer, but the quality of your life will be severely damaged by that effort. Human beings were not meant to live solitary lives. The human spirit does not do well in isolation.

Be willing to love again. Be willing to be loved again. It's worth it.

caregiver burnout

This chapter is for anyone who has been or is taking care of someone who has AIDS. The more people you have taken care of, the greater the likelihood that you will be approaching burnout. The more friends you have lost, the more likely it is that you will experience burnout.

Burnout and grief are a pernicious combination. Suffering is multiplied. The combined emotions can seem overwhelming.

Burnout is a fact of life that we all must face, but it can be avoided. You can prevent burnout.

If you're already in it, it can be reversed. You can recover from burnout.

Burnout is what happens when you are functioning under too much stress. It feels as if your resources have run out, as if you just don't have what it takes to keep going. It can create a sense of helplessness and hopelessness. You can begin to question your values, your decisions, your abilities.

Burnout can take place in your career as well as with your family. It is especially likely when you are taking care of someone who has been ill for a long time.

Burnout happens when we ignore our own vital needs as we are trying to meet someone else's. Burnout is usually created by the inability to say no, coupled with the unwillingness to take time off for yourself. After all, your friend is in need, and you don't want to be selfish.

Unfortunately, too many people think that the solution for selfishness is to be totally selfless. This will get you into trouble. It will practically guarantee caregiver burnout.

It's really never a question of a choice between being totally selfish and totally selfless. Neither way will work.

Dealing with caregiver burnout means making sure that you have balance in your life. You need to spend time with yourself and with people who are important to you while you are taking care of someone who is ill. You need to take care of your own needs while you take care of someone else's.

PROFESSIONAL CAREGIVER BURNOUT

Caregiver burnout is not just limited to family members or friends who have been taking care of someone who is ill. It is also experienced by professional health-care workers as well. Physicians, nurses, psychologists, social workers, and any other therapists who take care of people who are living with AIDS are all potentially at risk for caregiver burnout.

Before AIDS, many physicians rarely had to deal with the death of large numbers of their patients. If their patients did die, it was usually from old age, or the various maladies that afflict older people.

AIDS has changed that. Most physicians who are taking care of persons with AIDS have experienced more death in the last ten years than many physicians used to experience in their entire careers. This creates unbelievable stress.

Some professional caregivers I know about have formed their own support groups in order to deal with their stress, their grief, and their feelings of helplessness. They are the wise ones.

If you recognize the symptoms of caregiver burnout in yourself, please consider finding an effective support network. It can be formal or informal. Just be sure that it helps you empower yourself as you continue to take care of people. Whatever you do, don't let your pride get in the way. Physician, be willing to heal yourself.

I know there are a lot of people who need you. However, if you ignore your need for support, your need for rest and recuperation, you are setting yourself up for caregiver burnout. You and your patients will suffer.

RECOGNIZING CAREGIVER BURNOUT

This is not always easy to do. Each of us reacts to stress in different ways. Some of us experience it physically. Others of us experience it emotionally. Still others just ignore it as long as they can.

Physically, frequent indications of caretaker burnout will be a series of minor illness or other uncomfortable physical symptoms such as headaches or back pain.

You may feel too weak and too fatigued to want to do much. You just don't have any energy.

Stress can be manifested with stomach and digestive system upsets such as ulcers or colitis, or in any other way that you traditionally respond to too much stress, such as herpes outbreaks or other skin problems.

You can also notice drastic changes in your eating habits, such as loss of appetite or a sudden increase in appetite. These can result in sudden weight gain or weight loss.

You can have sleep disturbances such as not being able to get to sleep, not being able to stay asleep, or sleeping too much. Your sleep can be interrupted by nightmares or bad dreams. You can wake up feeling tired or cranky.

Emotionally, caregiver burnout can show up as increased feelings of fatigue and apathy, or depression. You may have no motivation to do much of anything. Nothing looks satisfying or fun. Life becomes boring, and that seems to be OK with you.

One of the most frequent symptoms of caregiver burnout is increased irritability. If you find yourself short-tempered and impatient with friends who didn't used to cause you trouble, this could be a sign of caregiver burnout. You may find yourself snapping at people, or losing your temper over small incidents that wouldn't have bothered you before. Driving can become a nightmare, as every little infraction takes on major significance.

You will have no patience and no tolerance for frustration. Camels' back-breaking straws are everywhere.

Anxiety or unusual panic attacks can also occur. These can be in response to something that is actually happening, or they can come out of nowhere.

Others will notice that they have a hard time concentrating and focusing their attention. They will experience memory lapses. They will become highly distractible.

One client calls it the "lights are on, nobody's home" syndrome. He just doesn't feel as if he is able to connect with other people.

Some people will turn to their friends for extra support. They may need much more support than anyone else can give.

Others will tend to pull away from their friends. Dealing with people will seem more of a drain than a support. They don't have the energy for small talk or schmoozing. Social events seem like a major burden or an imposition.

Some people lose all interest in sex. Others may find themselves needing more and more sex. Some who are interested in sex will find themselves unable to function well. I have heard of a number of people who lose interest in the middle of having sex. Their sexual energy just disappears and they need to run for the woods.

Increased consumption of alcohol or drugs is often a good indicator of burnout. The temptation will be great, but please realize that drugs and alcohol actually increase stress in the long run, in addition to the damage they do to your body in the meantime.

Running through all of the above symptoms may be a pervading sense of helplessness and hopelessness. This can create feelings of despair and pessimism.

Any or all of the above symptoms can be experienced by someone who is going through caregiver burnout. If you see them in yourself, please take action to take care of yourself. Be willing to listen to your friends. They may spot your burnout before you do.

WHAT DO I DO ABOUT CAREGIVER BURNOUT?

If you are well into caregiver burnout, you may feel as if the only solution is to run away. You may just want to get away from it all. You may want to hole up and hibernate.

Unfortunately, that won't work too well. Running away and

abandoning your friends would probably cause of a lot of guilt and that will only add to your stress level.

If you can spot caregiver burnout early enough, you won't have to resort to such extreme measures. The fact that you are burning out doesn't mean that you have to stop everything you're doing. If you are right in the middle of taking care of someone you love, you won't have to abandon them.

You *will* have to make a firm commitment to taking better care of yourself. You will have to find more time to nurture yourself and allow yourself to be nurtured.

Schedule time to relax. If it's possible, you may want to try to get out of town for a week or two to just relax and recuperate. This break will truly empower you to return and take care of your friends.

If that's not possible, at least try to find some weekend time for yourself. It will pay off.

Whether you go away or not, be sure to schedule time for yourself *on a daily basis.* Even thirty minutes of relaxation time can be very rejuvenating.

Do whatever is relaxing for you. You can take a nap. You can just veg out and watch TV. You can take long soaks in hot baths with a good book. You can catch a movie or play. You can meet friends for coffee or a drink. You can do deep-muscle relaxation exercises or guided imagery.

Physical activity is a very powerful way to reduce stress. Go for a walk or a swim. Do a workout at the gym.

If you are in a relationship or dating someone, spending time with them can be important. Some people are so busy that they have to make appointments to spend some time alone together. If that's what it takes, then do it.

Go for walks together. If you have access to a Jacuzzi, be sure to spend time each day in it with your friend, just talking, just being with each other.

Some of these things you can do every day. You can also create special stress-reducing events.

One of the most relaxing days John and I spent last year involved apples. We spent the morning in a pick-it-yourself orchard in Yucaipa, California. We spent the afternoon canning apple butter.

We hadn't known how to do that, but it was fun learning and the results were magnificent, if I do say so myself.

The important thing is for you to *make* the time, every day, for yourself. I know that there may still be a lot of people depending on you. You don't have to totally abandon them. You do have to explain to them that you need a little rest and recuperation time so you can take better care of them.

Get physical. Being touched can be wonderfully relaxing as well as healing. Don't be afraid to touch and be touched.

Virginia Satir, a world-renowned psychotherapist and author, (see Suggested Reading) has this advice about hugs: four a day for survival, eight a day for maintenance, and at least twelve a day for growth. If your friends don't know about this, share it with them. Make a firm commitment to get your twelve hugs a day, no matter whom you have to ask.

If you are involved in taking care of someone who has been ill for a long time, I suspect that it may take more like twelve hugs a day just for survival.

Some people will have a tough time being hugged. It is too intimate for them. If you are one of those people, try to push past your fears. You may even want to discuss it with a therapist. You are depriving yourself of a magnificent form of support and nurturing.

Some people are worried that hugs can become sexual. Of course they can, but that is totally within your control. If all you want is a hug, and someone else wants more, gently let them know what you want.

If you are the one who wants more and they say no, respect that. Hugs are too wonderful to avoid because of the fear of possible sexual agendas.

Massages can also be wonderful and renewing. If you can't afford to hire someone to do that, find a friend and teach each other how to give massages. Being touched releases a lot of stress and tension.

Like hugs, massages can become sexual if you want them to. There's nothing wrong with that. But they don't have to be sexual, if you don't want them to. You can enjoy just being touched.

Create a caregiver team. Too many people try to do it all by themselves. I know that in some cases there really isn't anyone else around to do it.

Much more often, I think, it's because the caregiver has not been willing to ask for help. Don't be afraid to ask for help. You and your friend will be better off for it.

Contact your local AIDS Project to find out about home health care or about AIDS "buddies." Your community may have more resources to help you than you realize. You just have to know how to go after them.

If you can't find community resources, create your own. I know a number of caregivers who have formed their own caregiver network. They organize it so that someone is always with their friend taking care of his needs. They also organize it so that each of them is assured some alone time, some relaxing time.

Even if you are the one who is going to do most of the work, you can still ask someone to spell you for an evening or even a weekend. Be willing to return the favor.

You may be taking care of someone who will resist your taking time off. They may feel as if you are the only one who can do the necessary care. While I can understand their reluctance to let you go, I also know that you must have time for yourself. Do whatever you have to in order to explain this to the one you're taking care of.

First, be sure that the person who is spelling you knows how to do the necessary care. Then lovingly and patiently explain to your friend that you need some time off for yourself. You will take better care of him if you are taking care of yourself.

If he is still resisting your taking time off, realize that you are now being manipulated. This isn't good for you, and it really isn't good for the one trying to manipulate you.

Manipulation will almost always create resentment. Maybe not right away, but eventually you will start to resent the unfair demands on your time.

I know he's scared, and that he may truly believe that you are the only one who knows how to care for him. That doesn't make it so, and you must resist it. If you let him get away with this kind of manipulation, you will set yourself up for even more of it, and have even less time off for yourself.

Once again, you never have to feel guilty for taking time for yourself, even if it is only a few minutes. You owe it to yourself.

Find a support group. There are many support groups for people who are grieving. There are also support groups for people who are caregivers in one way or another. Try them out and see if you feel supported and nurtured by spending time with them.

You don't have to go to this kind of support group, however. You may be like a lot of my clients and friends who really don't want to go to yet another support group.

Find a group of people to play with. Playing can be extremely nurturing.

Joining a gay softball team or bowling league can be fun and provide you with a lot of relief. Going hiking with a group from Great Outdoors or biking with the Spokesmen can be very relaxing. Most larger cities have their own versions of these groups. Check your local lesbian/gay newspapers to find out about them.

You could get involved in politics or in other forms of social service or community activism. You could go to work for your favorite political candidate.

The point is for you to be doing something just for the fun of it. Play however you want, just play.

It's OK if you want to choose an activity that doesn't involve AIDS. You may want a break from AIDS. Please don't feel guilty about that.

There's nothing wrong with going for several hours in your day without thinking about AIDS and about who is ill and who has died. There's nothing wrong with wanting a break from illness and dying.

You don't have to feel guilty if you feel like shouting, "If I hear AIDS one more time I will freak out!" I don't know anyone who doesn't feel that way at least once in a while. It goes with the territory.

Be sure that whatever support group you choose is willing to support you in the way that works for you. Be sure that being with them is empowering for you.

If you leave feeling worse than when you came in, you probably need to talk about that with your group. Then be prepared to leave if it can't be changed.

Deal realistically with demands on your time. If you are experiencing caregiver burnout and still taking care of someone else, you need to explain to him what you are going through. Tell him the truth, lovingly.

Don't try to spare his feelings. If you are stressed and burning out, he is probably already aware of that. He may even think the situation is more serious than it is, and be expecting total abandonment.

Many people who are ill are painfully aware that they are desperately in need of help from their friends in order to survive. That need doesn't make it easy to accept your assistance. They feel like burdens, as if they are imposing on your time. They will be very sensitive to indications of your burning out.

Do them a favor and tell them the truth. Tell them that you have no intention of abandoning them. You want to be there for them, no matter what. At the same time, you do need to find more time for yourself. Most of the people you are caring for will understand that. Others may not be as understanding. They may become demanding and selfish.

First of all, don't get sucked into feeling guilty about getting angry or resentful at such unreasonable demands. Whatever you do, don't just grit your teeth and try to do even more.

You must express yourself to the one you are taking care of, even if he doesn't want to hear you, even if he tries to make you feel guilty for not being a better friend. Brand that behavior sheer manipulation.

Understand that he is probably terrified as he faces a life-and-death situation. Such stakes can create a lot of dysfunctional needs and inappropriate behavior.

You still don't have to let the fact that he is ill and frightened cause you to give in to such manipulation. You can lovingly set limits and boundaries.

Setting limits. All this means is lovingly letting the other person know what you will and what you will not tolerate. It means telling him that you won't tolerate verbal or physical abuse. It could mean telling him that you don't want his guilt trips.

Many will understand this, particularly if you are able to do it in a very calm and loving way. If you do it in an angry, confrontational way, it probably will get more complicated.

If the person has dementia, your job will be a lot tougher, but you can at least try to make yourself heard and understood. You will probably need some professional consultation with his doctor or therapist for ideas about how to handle dementia. It manifests differently with different people.

Express yourself fully at all times. Telling the truth about how you are feeling is one of the most powerful ways to deal with caregiver burnout. This means telling the truth to the person you are caring for, to your friends, to your partner, and to your family.

Dealing with someone who may be dying while you are also grieving for someone who has died can be a wrenching experience. Your emotions will be blaring. You dare not try to stifle them.

You have a right to your feelings. You have the right to express them. You have the need to express them.

Stifling your feelings will only increase the possibility of your burning out. The strong and silent types are sometimes the first to crack under the pressure. They are sometimes the most fragile. You will pay a high price for your desire to keep silent about your feelings.

If you don't like something that someone else is doing, tell them that. If you like something that someone else is doing, it is just as important to say something about that, too.

If you feel like crying, you must allow yourself to cry. If you are feeling angry, it is really important for you to safely express that. If you do it in private or with someone who knows what you are doing, you will create no damage and you will relieve yourself of lots of intense and painful feelings.

If you need something, please learn how to ask for it. You won't have much chance of getting it otherwise. If you don't ask for it, you will set yourself up to feel resentful if you don't get it.

You can't fix it for him. AIDS creates a powerful feeling of helplessness. Until recently there was so little we could do except just be with the person as he was dying.

Even with the recent advances, there are still a lot of reasons to feel helpless. If you are a rescuer, this will cause you immeasurable trouble.

As much as we don't want to hear it, we can only do what we can do: take care of him while he is ill. We can't fix it for him. We can't make him get well. We can't keep him alive by our strength alone.

If we try to take the responsibility for his health, we will vastly increase our burnout potential. Our feelings of helplessness and our feelings of hopelessness will mushroom.

Fortunately, as bad as the situation is, there is still much we can do. We must do those things instead of being victimized by things we have no control over.

Keep hope alive. One of the most important things we can do is to keep our hope up, and his. Hope is one of the most healing of emotions. Hope can empower us to achieve more than we dream, and more than we fear. I am convinced that hope can keep many people alive. The absence of hope has caused people to die.

Don't take your friend's hope away, no matter how dire the predictions and statistics. Help him nourish it.

Hope will also be a potent antidote to caregiver burnout. Nourish your hope.

The human spirit dies when there is no hope. Keep hope alive.

When it's time, be willing to let go. One of the most difficult decisions a caregiver has to make is when it's time to let go. Our refusal to let go can make it very difficult for our dying friend to let go.

There is no way I know that can help you decide when that time is. You must be willing to trust your own instincts and the information you are getting from his physician. You must be willing to respect the wishes of your friend who may be ready to let go.

When that time comes, just quietly and lovingly let go and accept the imminence of death.

If you are experiencing caregiver burnout, love yourself and allow yourself to be loved. Forgive yourself and allow yourself to be forgiven. Love and forgive others.

Take time to play and have fun. Take time for yourself.

Express your feelings safely and freely. Above all, don't hesitate to tell the whole truth. Communicate how you are feeling as completely as you can.

CHAPTER THIRTEEN

when someone you care about is grieving

Unfortunately, due to the numbers of those who are dying, most of us are not only grieving ourselves but also comforting others who are grieving, who are in turn comforting others.

It's very difficult to watch someone in pain, someone who is hurting. If we love that person, we want to do whatever we can to help him or her stop hurting.

Unfortunately, this fear of hurting can cause a lot of damage. It can result in a lot of bad advice.

If, as you read this chapter, you discover that you have given inappropriate or just plain bad advice, don't feel guilty. Just clean up any damage you may have done and forgive yourself. Remind yourself that whatever you did you did with the best of intentions, given what you knew about grieving.

As I have said over and over again, our society doesn't prepare any of us to deal with our own grief, nor does it teach us how to take care of someone who is grieving. Confronting death has been a fearful prospect that is best avoided until it is inevitable.

This attitude leaves us unprepared to face death when it presents itself. We have to fall back on whatever resources we have. We try to comfort the way we would want to be comforted, or we try to comfort the way we have seen someone else do it. This may work sometimes. It will produce disastrous results at other times.

The aim of this book is to encourage people to grieve in the way that works for them, that fits their emotional needs and emotional styles. This idea must be honored by anyone attempting to comfort a friend who is grieving.

The best way for you to comfort your friends is to help them find the way that works best for them. This doesn't mean that you can't share your own experiences. Remember, however, that they are your experiences. They may not work for everyone else.

Hurting is inevitable and shouldn't be short-circuited. This is a tough concept. We don't like to hurt, and we don't want someone we love to hurt. Unfortunately, this belief can lead to our short-circuiting someone else's grief process.

Much of our advice can be about asking him or her to stop hurting, to stop crying, to stop grieving. We want to see the person get through it as soon as possible and begin to live life again. We want to see him or her be happy again.

Our desire to do this can sometimes really get in the way. If we are especially vigorous in our approach we can actually prolong the suffering, and add a lot of other emotions to it, such as resentment and anger.

I know how hard it is to watch someone who is in pain. When we see someone we love being miserable and despairing, we want to fix it. We want to rush him or her through it.

We just can't do that. To do so would not be good for that person in the long run.

Our society doesn't teach us to tolerate pain, physical or emotional. Think about the billions of dollars that are spent each year, by people who don't want to hurt, for pain killers, muscle relaxants, and tranquilizers, not to mention booze and drugs.

Unfortunately, pain is inevitable in life. It can't be avoided, no matter how hard we try, and the harder we try, the more we suffer in the long run.

When someone dies, hurt will follow. It must be experienced or it can never go away.

As hard as it is, allow your friend to have his or her pain. Allow that person to express his or her feelings fully as long as is needed. We'll look later at how you might be able to tell if it really has gone on too long and your friend needs to get professional assistance.

Your friend may grieve differently. Your friend may not grieve the same way you grieve. In fact, your friend may grieve in opposite ways. You may be the "hurry up and get back out there" type, while your friend may need to spend time alone and withdrawn. Your way won't work for him or her.

Your friend may cry longer than you would. He or she may cry more loudly than you would, be angrier than you would be, be more terrified than you think is reasonable.

So be it. That is your friend's style. That is where he or she needs to be.

You may want to have someone with you constantly when you are grieving. Your friend may need just to be left alone.

You may find it helpful to go out and party and forget what is going on for a while. Your friend may not be able to do that.

You may want to start dating as soon as possible as a way of getting through your grief. Your friend may not want to hear about that.

Do what you can to support your friend the way he or she needs and wants to be supported. If you're not sure how to do that, just ask.

Support does not have to mean shoulders to cry on. There are lots of ways to support your friend. One of the ways is to give him or her a shoulder to cry on, and a hand to hold. But that isn't the only way.

He or she may just want someone around to watch TV with or someone to go to a movie with. *Your friend may want distractions, not grief counseling.*

Don't feel as though support has to be long crying sessions. If someone needs that, fine. If he or she just wants to have fun with you, that's OK too.

Be sensitive about holidays and special occasions. Your friend may not be aware that these days may be tougher. Be willing to be available if you're needed and wanted. Just be sure you are needed and wanted. There is nothing wrong with your friend spending the holiday alone if that's what he or she really wants to do.

Just ask. So how do you find the best way to support your friend? You merely have to ask how he or she would like to be supported. Does your friend want a lot of attention and tender loving care, or does he or she prefer to be left alone?

If you are supporting someone who is grieving, I think you must periodically ask that person if you are doing it in a way that works. "I want to be here for you. Am I doing it in a way that works for you, or am I getting in your way?" It's a simple question, and we need to be prepared to hear that maybe we could do it a little differently. Then we should honor that request.

Sometimes your friend may not be able to let you know because he or she doesn't know for sure what would be supportive. This may be a new experience for that person.

• In that case, trial-and-error learning is all that you can do. You give it your best shot, and then sit back and see if it worked. Pay attention not only to what your friend says, but how he or she acts.

For example, if you rush up to your friend and enfold him in a giant bear hug, does he hug you back? Does he stand there stiff and unresponsive? Does he push you away? A hug may work for you. It may feel terrifying to him. It's OK if you don't understand that; just be willing to let your friend have what works for him.

Don't assume that if you like lots of chicken soup that everyone else does too. Others may just need to know that you are there, but not too close.

Bottomless pits for support. Some of those grieving will turn into bottomless pits for more love and sympathy than any of their friends have available. They demand time and maximum attention. No matter how much they get, they need more.

This must be lovingly and supportively confronted. It can't be allowed to go on. The friends will eventually run away, and the one grieving will be left alone.

The one grieving gets to do it his or her own way, but you also get to tell the truth about your reaction to the way your friend wants it. This is especially true if he or she is asking for more than you have to give. It's OK to say no.

Most people who are bottomless pits for love and support will need to seek professional help. It's a difficult and complicated issue that probably has its roots far back in childhood experiences. This kind of problem is tough enough for a professional to deal with. There may not be much you can do.

Whatever you do, don't feel inadequate for not being able to meet impossible needs. That won't help you; in fact, it will hurt you.

What if your friend is a "tough guy"? Remember that people grieve differently. Don't gauge your friend's grief by how you would be reacting to the same situation.

Some people have a difficult time asking for support. They don't want to be a burden. Others have a "tough guy" image to live up to, and asking for help doesn't fit that image.

If your friend isn't asking for your support, don't assume that this means that he or she doesn't need it. Neither should you put it upon yourself to be a mind reader.

Periodically ask your friend if there is anything you can do to help out. Be sure he or she knows that you are willing to do anything if it will help, no matter how insignificant. Helping with grocery shopping or laundry may be greatly appreciated, but your friend may be reluctant to ask for that kind of help. (Don't offer to help if you aren't willing to follow through. Your friend will sense your lack of sincerity.)

Once you ask, be prepared to accept the answer patiently and graciously. Just remember that accepting help may be much more stressful than doing things by him- or herself. Respect your friend's individual needs and wishes.

What if your friend becomes self-destructive? This is a tough call. Even professionals can't always know when someone has crossed the line and is moving in a potentially self-destructive direction.

There are a number of things you can look for in order to determine if your friend is becoming self-destructive and requires more professional help. These are just suggestions. All self-destructive people won't necessarily fall into these behavior patterns.

Your friend may be drinking too much or using too many drugs. He or she may be driving like a maniac, or picking fights with total strangers, or getting hostile and belligerent at work and risking his or her job. Your friend may be holing up and totally ignoring friends, not even willing to see them. He or she may undergo a startlingly apparent personality change.

Your friend may be talking about suicide directly, or setting him- or herself up for suicide in more subtle ways.

Your friend may be obsessing on the idea that life isn't worth living anymore. Nothing is important. Nothing will ever feel good again. No one will ever love him or her again. (It's not uncommon for someone who is grieving to have said any of these things a few times. I am referring here to constantly being stuck in this kind of talking.)

Your friend may seem completely stuck in a victim stance. He or she may feel completely helpless. Life is hopeless. There is nothing to be done about it.

If you observe any of these behaviors, I would suggest that you discuss your observations with your friend. Just having you bring them up and express your concern may be enough to get him or her moving again. If it doesn't, then it is most probable that your friend will need to seek professional assistance.

Gently suggest that he or she make an appointment with someone to talk about grief. Let your friend know that it can really help him or her not to hurt so much.

I have found that it works best if you don't make the appointment. If your friend doesn't have enough motivation to make the call, then he or she likely doesn't have the motivation to get to the first session.

If your friend is willing to make the appointment, you can agree to go to the first appointment. Even though I generally wouldn't prefer having a friend sit in on the first session, I have allowed some to do that since it seemed to make the client more comfortable. After the first session it wasn't usually necessary.

If your friend won't make the appointment, but is willing for you to do that, then go ahead. He or she will probably need a lot of support getting to that first session. Just don't nag. That will usually get the opposite result.

If your friend won't agree to see someone, and you are convinced that he or she has become self-destructive, then you may have to gather together a support network of friends and family, if that's appropriate. Confront your friend as a group with your concern and your desire that he or she find some professional help.

Even this approach may not work. Your friend may abjectly refuse to have anything to do with professional help, and may make it clear that he or she has no intention of trying to change anything that is going on.

As tough as it is, it's now time for you to let go. That doesn't mean that you have to abandon your friend. It does mean that you need to back off from pressuring him or her to seek professional help.

If your friend won't go, maybe you should. I have spent time with a number of clients who came in to discuss how they might better take care of someone who was grieving and seemed self-destructive, but who refused to come in themselves. Most professional therapists will be willing to do this kind of consultation. Besides, you could probably use some support for yourself.

If you are worried about your friend, you must just tell him or her the truth. Whatever you do, don't try to trick your friend into seeing someone. I've had people offer to invite me to a party in order to "accidentally" meet someone whom they felt needed professional help. I won't do that, and neither will the vast majority of professionals. It won't work. It will make it tougher to ever get that person in to see someone.

The bottom line is, you can't help someone who doesn't want to be helped. That's called a "rescue," and it won't work.

I know how painful it can be to watch someone slowly destroying him- or herself. Yet you can't do more than let that person know how much you love him or her, and how willing you are to help him or her.

If your friend won't let you, then there is little that you can do. I wish I could tell you something magical that would work in this situation. I can't.

All you can do is love your friend, and be there for him or her as best you can. The rest really is up to your friend.

The fine line. It must have occurred to some of you that there is a fine line between respecting someone's wishes and giving a needed gentle kick in the butt. I wish I could give you a clear-cut way to determine which is best. I can't.

Just know that sometimes a gentle kick in the butt is necessary. By that, I mean confronting your friend with your concern and strongly urging him or her to get moving. Obviously you wouldn't want to do this too soon. What's too soon? I don't know.

That is a very individual matter. If your friend is grieving in a way that is risking his or her career or the ability to keep a roof over his or her head, you may need to do it sooner rather than later.

If the situation is not that serious, then you may want to wait. I know this is frustratingly vague. There just isn't any easy answer. There is just no way to know with certainty that you are doing the right thing.

You must trust yourself. Check out your ideas with other friends. Then gently do it. Be prepared to back off if your suggestions meet with major resistance or outrage. If you do it gently enough, you will still be able to back off without damaging the relationship.

If you do it too harshly, you may find yourself excluded from your friend's life. Be gentle, and always be sure you are reminding your friend that you care about him or her and are just concerned.

You must always ultimately allow your friend to make his or her own choices. You cannot be responsible for his or her life and decisions. You can only care, and make sure your friend knows that.

What if your friend is drinking too much? It's not uncommon for some people who are grieving to start to drink too much or use drugs. Their feelings are just too scary and painful. The booze helps keep them numbed out.

As understandable as this is, it's not healthy. A serious problem could be developing.

As usual, the only thing you can do is to gently confront your friend with your concerns. Let him or her know that you have noticed the increased drinking and that you're concerned.

Don't do this angrily. There is no reason to blame your friend for drinking. That won't be of much help. Just lovingly let him or her know that you care.

The reaction to any confrontation can range from mild denial to outrage. Your friend may just give you lip service, "I know, and I'll do something about it." Yet weeks later he or she is drinking more than ever.

If you don't get a good response to voicing your concern, you may need to go to an Al-Anon meeting. Al-Anon is an A.A.-related group designed for the family and friends of people who have a drinking problem. The people there can support you in being more effective at confronting your friend.

It may be necessary to bring together all of his or her friends and possibly his family in order to confront the problem. Be sure you have already discussed your perception that he or she is drinking too much. Be sure the problem is indeed serious.

Don't make it easy for your friend to drink by cleaning up the messes caused by the drinking, such as by calling in sick for your friend when he or she is too hung over to go to work. Let your friend live with the consequences of his or her behavior.

Whatever you do, don't ignore the problem. It must be dealt with, or your friend could be in real trouble.

Setting up blind dates for your friend. Don't. (Unless your friend asks you to, of course.)

Socializing. If your friend and your friend's partner were part of a social group that spent a lot of time together, don't be surprised if he or she needs to pull away from the group, particularly if it is a group of couples. Some people feel like fifth wheels when they are out without their partner. No amount of urging can get them to rejoin a group.

Don't take this personally. Your friend isn't angry with you. It may be that he or she just needs more time. Being with the old gang may bring up too many painful memories.

Of course, there are those who will need their social group even more. If you're not sure what's needed, ask.

Taking care of someone who is grieving can be tricky. There are no rules or protocol. There are no sharply defined lines.

The only solution is for you to be willing to ask your friend what he or she needs. Tell your friend the truth about your experience and perception of how he or she is handling it.

If you don't think *you* are handling it, don't hesitate to ask for support from your other friends or from a professional.

saying goodbye

Saying goodbye is one of the most crucial parts of the grieving process. Saying goodbye will be your acknowledgment that it is now time to let go, time to accept the death and its impact on your life.

Saying goodbye can be sad and painful. Once said, however, it can become a liberating act, freeing you to rejoin life.

I don't know of a single society, even the most primitive, that doesn't include rites of passage that allow members of that society to say goodbye when someone they love has died. Funerals, memorial services, wakes, and viewings are all about allowing us to say goodbye.

While it isn't absolutely necessary to attend such an event, it is vital that you find a way to say goodbye. It will be more difficult to grieve well if you do not.

People who request that there be no memorial service are actually doing their friends a disservice. It makes saying goodbye more difficult for them.

Saying goodbye includes a little more than just the word *goodbye*. It includes saying whatever else you need to say to or about the person who has died.

Saying goodbye can certainly include saying "I love you"; "I miss you"; "It feels like the most important part of my life is gone."

It's not too difficult for most of us to be able to say the loving, positive things. It's much harder when it comes to some of the more negative feelings.

Saying goodbye means that you express everything that you are feeling, the sadness as well as the anger, the guilt, the fear, the loneliness, the sense of abandonment.

This is where you allow yourself to say anything that you have not said because it seemed too scary or inappropriate. Nothing is too ugly or too angry for you to say. Nothing is too petty or insignificant for you to say.

It can include saying "I am so angry with you for dying," or "I feel so bad about the way I treated you," or "I feel bad about the way you treated me."

You may need to express guilt or anger over other things. You may need to forgive. You may need to ask for forgiveness.

Whatever you are feeling about the fact that the one you love has died is what you need to express as part of saying goodbye. Don't try to hold anything back.

There are times when this communication is possible before the death. You are fortunate, indeed, if you are able to say everything you need to say while the person is alive, and then are able to hear his response. Unfortunately, that's not always possible.

Some people die before that can be done, and others are not conscious enough to be able to have that conversation. This does not mean that you are stuck with all of your unexpressed feelings and ideas. You can still express them; it is never too late for you to do that.

Expressing what you are feeling is a vital part of your grieving process. You need to express it all, the love and the sadness as well as the anger, guilt, and fear. If you're not willing to do this, you probably won't complete your grief. As always, do this in your own way, when you are ready. Don't force it.

How to say goodbye. Like grieving, saying goodbye is a process rather than a simple act. Just as we all grieve differently, we all need to say goodbye differently.

For some people, saying goodbye can create a very significant sense of completion with the grieving process. Others will have to say goodbye over and over again. Don't assume that just saying good-bye one time will complete your process. It may, and it may not.

Some people have trouble saying goodbye because it feels too strange to be talking to someone who has died. It seems too unreal, maybe even a little crazy.

You don't have to feel ashamed about talking with the one who has died. It may feel a little strange and you may be self-conscious about it, but it isn't crazy. Say whatever you have to say. *The important thing is that you express it, not that he actually hear it.*

If you believe in the concept of an eternal soul that outlives the body, and if you believe that that soul has any awareness of those left behind, then you can say goodbye and feel sure that the one who has died will hear you. Saying goodbye may be a little easier for you.

If you aren't sure of the eternal soul, it's still important for you to say goodbye, express your feelings, and complete your communication. Whether the person who has died hears you or not, you still need the opportunity to express what you are feeling.

There are a number of ways to say goodbye. As usual, there is no Right way to do this.

Some people use prayer as a way of expressing themselves. Others find meditation or guided imagery very powerful and effective.

You can imagine that you are with your friend just having a conversation. You can say everything you need to say, knowing that he will just listen and understand. Remember to say it all. Tell the whole truth, even the stuff that may not seem nice.

Remember to express "I am mad at you" as well as "I love you." You must not sit on any of your negative feelings because the one you're angry with is dead and you don't think you should speak ill of the dead.

You must just tell the truth, even if it's ugly. Once you've expressed it, then you can effectively let go of it, challenge it, and get on with your life.

You can say goodbye by just talking out loud. As we said above, you must say it all. Don't censor or monitor what you are saying.

You can also say goodbye by writing a letter expressing everything you are feeling. The important thing is for you to have expressed what you are feeling, not that you are able to mail the letter.

Some people prefer visiting a special place in order to say good-bye. This can mean a visit to the cemetery, where you can sit beside the grave and just talk.

Since a number of the people who have died of AIDS have requested that they be cremated and their ashes scattered, you may not have a specific location to visit. That's OK. You can either visit a favorite place for the two of you, or just say goodbye in the privacy of your own home.

The location is only as important as you make it. You can accomplish the same thing in any location. Do what feels good to you.

This doesn't mean that once you have said goodbye your grief and sadness are over. That isn't the case. Unhappy feelings will probably continue to come up. It doesn't mean that you have failed at saying goodbye. It's just the way it happens. If the feelings are there, remember that you must express them.

Unexpressed feelings will tend to keep grief alive. This is another of those principles that will hold true for just about everyone who is grieving.

Please notice if you have trouble saying "I love you." If you can't say it, it's probably due to anger that you are hanging on to, and you don't want to do that. Let go of your anger so that you can still find the love that has always been there.

Before reading further, give yourself the opportunity to choose when you will be willing to say goodbye. Make a commitment to do it. If you're not quite ready to do that just yet, that's OK too.

Before life can go on, we must be willing to say goodbye. We must be willing to embrace the awful reality of life without him. As painful as this can be, we must never forget that life has gone on, and that we must rejoin it.

Rejoining life as valiantly as possible is one of the most effective ways for us to honor someone's memory. Living today well is not a betrayal, it is a gift in honor of the memory of the one who has died.

REJOINING LIFE

Living well and grieving well mean recognizing that life does go on. It is essential to the grieving process to get involved in life again.

This is a difficult step for many to face.

Remember, there is no timetable for getting on with your life. You don't have to do it the way someone you know did it. You don't have to take other people's advice about how they would do it.

Just gather information and advice, then make the best decision you can. Do what feels right to you.

If you try to get back into life too soon, it isn't a catastrophe. You can always choose to back off a bit or maybe even hide out for a while. When you feel ready again, get back out there.

You can rejoin life gradually. You don't have to start out with a major leap into the thick of things. Just spending quiet time with old friends can be one way of rejoining life.

VALUES CAN CHANGE, BUT AVOID DRASTIC CHANGES

There is no Right way to rejoin life. Some people find that they can return to life as it was and, except for the absence of the one who has died, it continues forward pretty much the same as before. These people make few changes.

Others may discover that their experience of the death of their loved one has caused them to take a hard look at their values and needs. They may find a major shift has occurred in what they want from life and from their friends.

Things that used to be important just aren't anymore. Things they used to need don't seem appealing. Things they never thought about now seem vital to them. Stuff that used to drive them nuts just doesn't seem worth the effort now.

For some people there is a heightened appreciation for life. Life seems more precious. Loving relationships may take on a powerful aura, becoming more important than ever before.

While this values-clarification process can be magical, remember what we've said about major decisions. You may want to wait for a while before making drastic changes.

Sometimes when we give up our old ideas about how life should be and about which values are important to us, we may go through a period of confusion. Don't let that throw you. There is nothing wrong with being confused, especially if you are dealing with new ideas in the absence of comfortable old ones.

Being confused is not a sign of weakness. You don't have to know the Right way, right now. Give yourself some time. Try out your new ideas, your new values. See how they feel. If they feel good, keep doing them. If they don't feel good, consider trying something else.

IT MAY FEEL STRANGE

As you rejoin life, be prepared for it to feel a bit strange. You may have been taking care of someone for so long that you have forgotten what it was like to have a free evening, or the time to go out for a drink or for coffee with an old friend.

No matter how familiar the setting, it may still feel unusual to you. You may be extra self-conscious. You may feel uncomfortable.

It is important that you don't wait until it feels completely comfortable to get back out there. That will take a much longer time than you need to take.

Feel uncomfortable, self-conscious, maybe even fearful, and do it anyway. As you rejoin life, the discomfort will begin to fade, along with the self-consciousness and fear.

Anything new will always feel a little strange. Life without your loved one will be no exception to that. It will take a while to get used to. Give yourself time, and don't be dismayed if you feel uncomfortable.

Whatever you do, don't get stuck in your grief or fall victim to the disability syndrome.

THE DISABILITY SYNDROME

There are some people who may never feel ready to rejoin life. In fact, they don't even feel ready to get on with daily chores. Going to work seems like an impossible task for them. Some of these people have the luxury of going out on disability for a while in order to heal emotionally.

This means that they will be able to stop working, and will receive disability payments from either the state or from a private disability insurance policy.

I have worked with people on psychiatric disability for the last twenty years, long before AIDS arrived. I am convinced that disability can be a dangerous thing. Going out on disability is something that should be done only after very careful consideration.

If you are truly disabled and absolutely unable to function, then disability may be a *temporary* solution, but it is not an easy solution.

Your position will be seriously challenged by whomever will be paying the bill. Disability insurance companies are highly suspicious of psychiatric or stress-related disabilities. Such disabilities are impossible to prove or disprove. You will be subject to much questioning and challenging before you are approved for disability.

To be on disability, you will need to be evaluated by medical doctors, psychiatrists, and possibly psychologists. You will have mountains of forms to fill out, in some cases over and over again.

Once you're approved for disability, your job isn't over. Payments will frequently be late, and you will need to make many phone calls to try to track them down. You will have to be willing to submit to periodic reevaluations.

I have worked with a number of people who have been on disability. They have consistently reported that being on disability requires as much work and creates as much stress as going back to their regular job. It doesn't pay well, either.

In the meantime, their self-esteem suffers as they become couch potatoes or tube turnips. Even though our self-esteem is not really linked to the things we do, it is hard for someone who has always been identified with his or her career to be without that career.

Most people have their sense of worth tied up with the contributions they make at their job. If they deprive themselves of making that contribution, they can suffer significant self-esteem damage.

It is easy for self-esteem to get shaky, especially since the very act of going on disability is proof that you are not handling things. The people writing the reports about you have to say that you aren't capable of living a normal life.

People on disability will have many more hours free to sit around and think about how awful everything is. They can easily get lost in obsessive thinking about their loss. They can start to drive themselves nuts with mind chatter.

Having too much time on your hands with nothing to do can

increase depression, decrease motivation, increase apathy, and increase a sense of powerlessness.

Going on disability isn't always wrong. I don't want to give the impression that going on disability is to be avoided at all costs. For some people it is absolutely necessary in order to survive. If your survival is at stake, then disability is something you need to think about.

If you are on disability I firmly believe that you also need to be in active psychotherapy. By this I mean regular, weekly, hour-long therapy sessions, not ten-minute checkups by someone who is writing letters to your disability carrier claiming you are indeed disabled. Those letters have to be written, but you need to be in therapy also, working on getting back to work as soon as possible.

In my experience, without exception, the longer a client stays out on disability, the more he or she suffers in the long run. The longer you are out on disability, the harder it will be to get back to work.

If you can't afford to be in therapy, please find some kind of support group. Don't try to do it alone. If you are out on disability, you need to recognize that your self-esteem isn't really connected to those things that you do. You can be off work and still maintain your sense of self-worth. It may be tougher, but you can do it.

If you can, stay at work. Find an effective support group. Ask your friends for support. It will get easier, I promise. It just may take a while.

GETTING INVOLVED AGAIN SOCIALLY

One of the easiest ways to begin rejoining life is to get involved again socially. This will mean rediscovering old friendships and finding new ones.

You may need to aggressively pursue some of the people whom you avoided while your partner or friend or family member was ill. Most of them understand what you were going through and will be anxious to see you again.

If someone gives you a hard time, don't waste a moment of time worrying about it. That degree of pettiness is not something you need to put up with.

Dating again is a very important part of rejoining life. We discussed that thoroughly in the chapter for partners, so I won't repeat that information here, except to say do it when you are ready.

If you don't want to be fixed up by your friends, tell them so and refuse to cooperate. If you want to be fixed up, ask your friends to do that.

Use trial and error. Try something, and if it doesn't work try something else. You may not know if it will be OK to go out to dinner with several other people who were close to you and your partner, family member, or friend.

Being with them could be wonderfully enriching, or it could just bring up painful memories that you're not ready for. Try it and, if it doesn't work, hang out for a while and try again later.

The more you get out socially, the easier it will be to start living life again. That's hard to do when you are hibernating or hiding out.

GETTING INVOLVED BY HELPING YOUR COMMUNITY

This theme runs throughout this book. As I have watched so many people moving through their grief, I have seen a distinct difference in the experience of those who continued to hide out and those who got involved in their community.

Those who hide out tend to take longer to grieve and tend to experience more negative feelings and more pain. Conversely, those who get involved tend to get happier faster, and tend to spend much less time in their pain and sadness.

Of course, getting involved won't mean that you will totally avoid any more pain or the other emotions of grief. Getting involved is not a cure-all, but it will help you avoid becoming a victim.

Being involved in making a contribution to the quality of someone else's life is healing and energizing. It will definitely help you through the grieving process.

Getting involved produces a win-win situation. No one loses. Your own life and health will be enhanced. You will work through your grief more quickly. The people whose lives you are affecting will be much better off for it. The entire community will thrive on the time and energy you put into making it a better place.

You will be enhancing your sense of personal power as you begin to make your contribution. You won't have to deal with feeling like a burden to your friends and loved ones. It will be much harder to get involved in relationships on the victim triangle.

The potential for involvement is practically unlimited. In most major cities there are dozens of organizations that were founded to help take care of the needs of people who are affected by AIDS.

Of course, you don't necessarily have to choose to work for an AIDS organization. You may need a break from AIDS. Working for the homeless, for the environment, for social issues such as reproductive choice, human rights, or world peace can help you gain a sense of personal strength and value.

I would like to suggest that gay men consider getting involved with the lesbian community and their struggle to see that their health care needs are better met. Lesbians have been working with us in our fight against AIDS since the beginning of the crisis. They need and deserve our help now. Your local Gay and Lesbian Community Services Center will be able to put you in touch with the lesbian community and tell you how you can help out.

If you do choose to get involved with the fight against AIDS, most cities will have either an AIDS Project or a Gay and Lesbian Community Services Center. These organizations will offer a wide range of services to a cross-section of the community. They utilize the services of tens of thousands of volunteers. They need your help. All you have to do is find them.

As I've said before, finding the local gay and lesbian newspaper or newsmagazine will give you a pretty good idea of who is doing what in your area. Calling the regional resource numbers at the back of this book is also a way of finding out what's available in your area.

There are organizations to take care of virtually any need experienced by a person with AIDS. You can match your interests and skills.

Organizations such as Project Angelfood in Los Angeles utilize the services of hundreds of volunteers who cook hot meals and deliver them to people who are no longer able to cook for themselves. Many of the cooks and deliverers have AIDS themselves, but are doing whatever they can to ease their brothers' suffering. Without Project

Angelfood, there are many people with AIDS who would go without a hot meal, or perhaps without eating at all.

There are also organizations such as PAWS: Pets Are Wonderful Support. PAWS volunteers help take care of the pets of someone who is too ill to see that they are walked and fed, or that the cat box is cleaned out.

PAWS people will also make sure that in the event of a death, the pet finds a new home. As a pet lover—my partner John and I have two dogs and two cats—I am well aware of the critical importance of such an organization.

A person who has a much-loved pet will find it excruciatingly painful to have to part with that pet because he can no longer take care of it. Worse is the thought that his pet could be destroyed after his death. PAWS will ensure that such a thing doesn't happen.

Being Alive is an organization of people who are affected by HIV. It provides emotional support as well as the most up-to-date information about AIDS treatment protocols. It is a powerful organization of people living with AIDS. It can be a wonderful source of support for you. They could also use your help for their various educational and support programs.

Shanti is another organization that offers counseling, support groups, educational programs, and safer-sex programs to persons who are HIV-affected as well as HIV-infected. They utilize the efforts of many volunteers and can always use new energy.

The AIDS Coalition to Unleash Power (ACT UP) is an energetic coalition of gay men and lesbians who have chosen to express their outrage at government inaction where AIDS is concerned by committing acts of civil disobedience. They demonstrate in the streets, drawing public attention to the needs of the AIDS community.

There are those in the community who find ACT UP's tactics offensive. They are concerned about a heterosexual backlash in response to ACT UP's kiss-ins, die-ins, or other demonstrations.

Unfortunately, civil rights movements for any minority group have been based on civil disobedience. Someone has had to get upset enough to threaten the majority in some way. It is essential to get the attention of the white heterosexual male establishment in order to make the powers-that-be realize they have a job to do.

The African-American community needed Malcolm X as much

as it needed Martin Luther King. The AIDS community needs ACT UP and Queer Nation as well as other more mainstream groups such as the political action committees (PACs), lobbies, and political clubs.

There are PACs such as the Human Rights Campaign Fund (HRCF); The Municipal Elections Committee of Los Angeles (MECLA); and the Elections Committee of the County of Orange (ECCO). They raise money and make campaign contributions to sympathetic office-seekers. They register voters and try to "get out the vote" on election day.

There are lobbying organizations such as the LIFE lobby in California. There also are political clubs for both Democrats and Republicans.

PACs, lobbies, and clubs all spend time and energy trying to educate our elected officials about the needs of the lesbian and gay community as well as people with AIDS. These organizations can take much of the credit for the pro-AIDS legislation that has been passed. They have also been able in some cases to stave off bad legislation that punishes people with AIDS.

Unfortunately, there is still a whole lot more work to do with our elected officials. People with AIDS in states that don't have large and powerful gay and lesbian organizations face Neanderthal legislation that punishes instead of helps, that offers discrimination instead of compassion. Those of us in large cities dare not forget our friends out there.

All of these organizations need your help. Whether you lick and stuff envelopes, answer phones, make speeches, raise money, or just sit and listen, your efforts will support these organizations that in turn support your community. You will be strengthened and your community will be strengthened. Everyone wins.

AFTER YOU SAY GOODBYE

Before, during, and after you say goodbye, life goes on. It will be very difficult for a while. It will be full of sadness and grief. It may even be ugly and painful. But life does go on.

Always remember that no matter how bad you are feeling today, you won't always feel this bad. It will get better, no matter how unlikely that may look right now. Hang in there.

As you face life without the one you love, ask yourself what he would want from you now. Would he want you to suffer, or would he want you to get on with your life as best you can?

I think the answer is clear. He would want you to go on as valiantly and courageously as you can. He would want you to enjoy life once again. He would want you to love again.

Be willing to feel your pain, and be willing to move through your pain. I know it hurts. I also know it will hurt less with time, especially if you are concentrating on telling the whole truth about how you are feeling, if you are grieving your own way, and if you are committed to making a difference in a world in desperate need of change.

Before, during, and after you say goodbye, be willing to love. Be willing to be loved. Be willing to live today well.

APPENDICES

Federation of Parents and Friends of Lesbians and Gays, Inc. (PFLAG)
202-638-4200, P.O. Box 27605, Washington, D.C. 20038-7605

PFLAG by region:
Pacific Northwest	503-233-5415
Pacific Southwest and	213-472-8952
Metropolitan Los Angeles	
Mountain	303-333-0286
Great Plains	402-435-4688
Central	502-454-5635
Southern	318-984-2216
Metropolitan New York	212-752-4220
Northeast	413-532-4883
Mid Atlantic	703-768-0411
South Atlantic	704-922-9273

Mothers of AIDS Patients (MAP)
For information on the chapter in your region   213-542-3019

AIDS HOTLINES

National AIDS Hotline	1-800-342-AIDS
Spanish AIDS Hotline	1-800-344-SIDA
Hearing Impaired AIDS Hotline	1-800-243-7889
National AIDS Information Clearinghouse	1-800-458-5231
AIDS Clinical Trials Information Center	1-800-TRIALS-A
Project Inform (AIDS Experimental	
Drug Information)	1-800-822-7422
Drug Abuse Hotline	1-800-662-HELP
National Gay/Lesbian Crisis Line	1-800-767-4297

Recorded information from the Centers for Disease Control:
Current number of AIDS cases and deaths   1-404-330-3020

AIDS HOTLINES STATE BY STATE

Alabama	1-800-228-0469	Missouri	1-800-533-AIDS
Alaska	1-800-478-AIDS	Montana	1-800-233-6668
Arizona	1-800-334-1540	Nebraska	1-800-782-AIDS
Arkansas	1-800-445-7720	Nevada	1-702-687-4804
California (N)	1-800-367-AIDS	New Hampshire	1-800-342-AIDS
California (S)	1-800-922-AIDS	New Jersey	1-800-624-2377
Colorado	1-800-252-AIDS	New Mexico	1-800-545-AIDS
Denver	1-303-333-4336	New York	1-800-541-AIDS
other cities	1-303-331-8310	Albany	1-800-962-5065
Connecticut	1-800-342-AIDS	New York City	1-212-340-4432
Delaware	1-800-422-0429	North Carolina	1-800-342-AIDS
D.C.	1-202-332-AIDS	North Dakota	1-800-472-2180
Florida	1-800-352-AIDS	Ohio	1-800-332-AIDS
Georgia	1-800-551-2728	Oklahoma	1-800-522-9054
Atlanta	1-404-876-9944	Oregon	1-800-777-AIDS
Hawaii	1-800-922-1313	Portland	1-503-223-AIDS
Idaho	1-208-345-2277	Pennsylvania	1-800-662-6080
Illinois	1-800-243-AIDS	Puerto Rico	1-809-765-1010
Indiana	1-800-848-AIDS	Rhode Island	1-800-726-3010
Iowa	1-800-445-AIDS	South Carolina	1-800-322-AIDS
Kansas	1-800-232-0040	South Dakota	1-800-592-1861
Kentucky	1-800-654-AIDS	Tennessee	1-800-525-AIDS
Louisiana	1-800-992-4379	Texas	1-800-255-1090
Maine	1-800-851-AIDS	Utah	1-800-537-1046
Maryland	1-800-638-6262	Salt Lake City	1-801-538-6094
Baltimore	1-301-333-AIDS	Vermont	1-800-882-AIDS
Massachusetts	1-800-235-2331	Virginia	1-800-533-4148
Boston	1-617-522-4090	Washington	1-800-272-AIDS
Michigan	1-800-872-AIDS	West Virginia	1-800-642-8244
Minnesota	1-800-752-4281	Wisconsin	1-800-334-AIDS
Mississippi	1-800-826-2961	Wyoming	1-800-327-3577

Information provided by the American Association for World Health (AAWH), *Action Kit for World AIDS Day,* December 1, 1990.

AAWH, 2001 S Street, Suite 530, Washington, D.C. 20009, 202-265-0286.

suggested reading

The following is a list of books that you may want to take a look at after reading *After You Say Goodbye*. They are not all about AIDS or about death and dying. Many of them deal with the problems of self-esteem, self-empowerment, and relationships, which can be intensified following an AIDS death.

Berzon, Betty. *Permanent Partners*. Dutton: New York, 1988.

Bloomfield, Harold, and Robert B. Kory. *Inner Joy*. Playboy Paperbacks: New York, 1980.

Callen, Michael. *Surviving AIDS*. HarperCollins: New York, 1990.

Colgrove, Melba, Harold Bloomfield, and Peter McWilliams. *How to Survive the Loss of a Love*. Bantam Books: Los Angeles, 1976.

Cousins, Norman. *Head First: The Biology of Hope*. Dutton: New York, 1989.

Dyer, Wayne W.
> *Your Erroneous Zones*. Funk & Wagnalls: New York 1976.
> *Pulling Your Own Strings*. Simon and Schuster: New York, 1978.
> *The Sky's the Limit*. T. Y. Crowell: New York, 1980.
> *You'll See It When You Believe It*. William Morrow: New York, 1990.

Ellis, Albert A. *A New Guide to Rational Living*. Prentice-Hall: Englewood Cliffs, New Jersey, 1975.

Fairchild, Betty, and Nancy Hayward. *Now That You Know: What Every Parent Should Know about Homosexuality*. Harcourt Brace Jovanovich: New York, 1979, 1989.

Froman, Paul Kent. *Pathways to Wellness: Strategies for Self-Empowerment in the Age of AIDS*. Plume: New York, 1990.

Jampolsky, Gerald. *Teach Only Love*. Bantam Books: New York, 1983.

Kübler-Ross, Elisabeth. *On Death and Dying*. Macmillan: New York, 1969, 1970.

Monette, Paul. *Borrowed Time: An AIDS Memoir*. Harcourt Brace Jovanovich: New York, 1988.

Satir, Virginia. *Meditations & Inspirations*. Celestial Arts: Berkeley, California, 1985.

Shilts, Randy. *And the Band Played On.* St. Martin's Press: New York, 1987.

Silverstein, Charles. *Man to Man: Gay Couples in America.* Morrow: New York, 1981.